NORTHERN IRELAND
SOLDIERS TALKING

NORTHERN IRELAND
Soldiers Talking

Max Arthur

SIDGWICK & JACKSON
LONDON

*First published by Sidgwick & Jackson Limited
in Great Britain in 1987*

Maps drawn by Neil Hyslop

ISBN 0-283-99375-8

*Photoset by Rowland Phototypesetting Limited
Bury St Edmunds, Suffolk*

*Printed in Great Britain by
St Edmundsbury Press Limited
Bury St Edmunds, Suffolk
for Sidgwick & Jackson Limited
1 Tavistock Chambers, Bloomsbury Way
London WC1A 2SG*

This book is dedicated to the memory of
Hilarian Roberts

Acknowledgements

I would like to thank the Ministry of Defence for allowing me to interview serving members of the British Army, Royal Navy, and Royal Marines.

Members of the following regiments and corps told me of their experiences in Northern Ireland: Army Air Corps; The Coldstream Guards; The King's Own Royal Border Regiment; The King's Own Scottish Borderers; The Parachute Regiment; The Prince of Wales's Own Regiment of Yorkshire; The Royal Anglian Regiment; Royal Army Medical Corps; Royal Army Ordnance Corps; The Royal Green Jackets; Royal Horse Artillery; Royal Military Police; Royal Regiment of Wales; Scots Guards; Ulster Defence Regiment; Welsh Guards; Women's Royal Army Corps Provost. I thank them all. I would also like to thank members of 40, 42, and, in particular, 45 Commando Royal Marines.

My thanks go to Carey Smith at Sidgwick and Jackson for her encouragement throughout. The idea of this book came from Nigel Newton, and I thank him.

Finally, I am indebted to two people who from the beginning were vital to the organisation of the book and worked with me in the closest of co-operation: Maureen Davenport who with great care and diligence transcribed the bulk of the taped interviews and typed the whole book, and Robert Allen who listened to all the taped interviews, skilfully researched and orchestrated the historical aspect of the book, and continually gave sound advice which I was glad to follow.

M.A.

Contents

Acknowledgements	vi
Preface	viii
Chronology: 1969–May 1987	xvi
Prologue	xxviii
Belfast	1
Winning Hearts and Minds: 1969	6
Bricks and Gas: 1970	18
The Shooting Starts: 1971	40
Internment: August 1971	56
'Bloody Sunday': 30 January 1972	70
'A War Situation': 1972	78
The Changing Role of the Army: 1973–9	94
Warrenpoint and the Death of Earl Mountbatten: 27 August 1979	133
The Eighties	139
South Armagh	173
Bombs and Bomb Disposal	203
Ulster Defence Regiment	222
Conclusions	241
Appendix I: Army Force Levels 1969–May 1987	255
Appendix II: Deaths, Wounded/Injured, Bombs, Shootings 1969–May 1987	257
Glossary	259
Index	263

Preface

The British Army has been part of the community in Northern Ireland for 300 years. The Province, like the rest of the United Kingdom, has its old garrison towns, its war memorials and its famous old regiments – which still draw recruits from both sides of the Irish border.

Yet for nearly twenty years, Northern Ireland has been synonymous with terrorism and, within the British Army, with one of the longest military campaigns in its history. Soldiers were ordered onto the streets of Londonderry and Belfast in 1969 when the exhausted police force was overwhelmed by the scale of inter-community violence. Soldiers endured and contained the appalling violence of the early 1970s. They protected Loyalists and Nationalists and they were attacked and killed by terrorists from both communities. The Army handed back prime responsibility for security duties to a re-modelled Royal Ulster Constabulary in 1977 and throughout the 1980s the Army has soldiered on in support of the police.

Internal security within its own country can never be a welcome role for an army. For there can be no glorious milestones or victories to add new titles to the colours of its famous regiments. Only the cold statistics of reduced terrorist activity demonstrate any achievement and progress.

Soldiers' experiences changed with the years. Certainly in the 1970s most soliders serving in combat units of the infantry, armour, artillery or engineers could expect to serve gruelling four-month emergency tours in the Province as infantrymen. Meanwhile tanks and artillery stood idle during NATO exercises because their crews were in Northern Ireland. Wives and families, left behind in Britain or West Germany, had to put up with repeated separation from husbands. However, in the 1980s by far the majority of soldiers in Northern Ireland serve two-year tours and are accompanied by wives and families, and their children are educated locally. Most of those soldiers are from infantry regiments (including Royal Marines). No longer do artillerymen, engineers, armoured corps soldiers expect routine duties as stand-in infantrymen, for Northern Ireland has ceased to be an emergency for the Army.

Preface

In the early 1970s, some units serving in notoriously volatile areas could suffer spates of shootings, bombings and mob violence during a four-month tour. In 1972, 129 soldiers were killed and 566 were wounded. Yet in the 1980s in most areas of Northern Ireland soldiers do not hear an angry shot, let alone use their rifle in a two-year tour. In 1986, twelve soldiers were killed and fifty-five wounded.

The last year in which soldiers withstood direct confrontation with major, prolonged street rioting was in 1981 when the IRA hunger strikers died. That year the Army fired 9,952 baton rounds during street riots. Since then the RUC have rarely called on Army assistance in riot control. In 1986 soldiers fired 325 baton rounds and these mostly by small foot patrols to keep petrol-bombers at a distance.

One regiment which features in these pages is a product of the 'troubles'. The Ulster Defence Regiment who serve throughout the Province was raised in 1970 when the police reserve – the B Specials – was disbanded. Some UDR soldiers are still serving who enrolled in 1970 – longer than any other British infantry have served on operations since the Napoleonic wars. The full-time UDR soldiers are equivalent to any other infantry in Northern Ireland, but the backbone of the Regiment is the part-time soldiers who serve at nights and weekends, sparing time from ordinary civilian lives. UDR soldiers never serve outside the Province, they live in their own homes and accept the risk of intimidation and death without respite. Of the 163 UDR soldiers (including four women) killed by terrorists, 133 were attacked while off duty.

The Ulster Defence Regiment's nine battalions now provide first-line military support for the police as required in eighty per cent of Northern Ireland. The UDR often take regular Army units under operational control and in turn UDR battalions are commanded by the two Army brigade headquarters.

In 1987, six regular Army infantry battalions serve in Northern Ireland on two-year tours of duty accompanied by wives and families. They operate from permanent bases and live in purpose-built married quarters and barracks. Only two battalions at any time serve on *roulement* tours or what used to be called emergency tours – one each in the residual hard-line Nationalist areas of West Belfast and South Armagh. (But since 1986 two extra battalions have served four-month stints to meet particular new operational requirements identified by the police. Yet these are not expected to become permanent deployments.)

Army Headquarters is at Lisburn, County Antrim – Thiepval Barracks, named after the Ulster Division victory on the Somme. Command devolves through two brigade headquarters – 39 Brigade, also in Lisburn, for the east and 8 Brigade in Londonderry for the west of the Province. The Army's task remains to support the police but in vast areas of the Province normal policing goes on with minimal need for Army support and regular soldiers are rarely seen. But in the hard Nationalist enclaves of West Belfast, Londonderry and some border areas the RUC still require substantial Army support to sustain routine police work without undue risk.

The scale of terrorist violence has been ground down and in many ways has been hemmed into quite localised areas by security forces' operations. But soldiers know that they still face an increasingly cunning and resourceful enemy. There is no complacency about the abilities of the IRA, in particular, to kill. Real dangers still exist for the soldier on patrol. In the 1970s, there were more than one hundred IRA operations for each soldier or policeman killed or seriously injured. In 1987, the ratio is fewer than twenty IRA operations for each injury or death caused to the security forces. But the frequency of IRA attacks has been drastically reduced compared with the seventies.

The Army's strength and its style of operations have evolved with changing perceptions of the campaign. Massive house searches are a thing of the past. CS gas has not been used for many years by troops and the big, heavily armoured Saracens were all sent back to Britain years ago. Covert operations by specialist troops operating on RUC Special Branch intelligence now account for almost all the rare occasions when soldiers fight gun battles with terrorists. Major attrition of terrorist groups comes from police work leading to suspects facing charges in court, not from battles on the streets.

Having troops on the streets of the United Kingdom is not normal or desirable. But until some alternative is found, it will be necessary in the foreseeable future for several thousand British soldiers to 'stag on' as many have done before.

I felt those soldiers who had served in Northern Ireland had never really been given an opportunity to express their thoughts and feelings about their experiences in the Province. When I approached them, the Army had serious reservations about helping with this book. It was not that they were unduly worried about what soldiers or ex-soldiers, speaking privately, might say about

Northern Ireland, because after eighteen years in the campaign, the Army was confident enough about the level-headedness of its ordinary soldiers. And Queen's Regulations prevented any soldier's political opinions being offered for publication.

The Army's concern was that a book recounting soldier's experiences could not give a faithful picture of what Northern Ireland is, or was, like. Each individual's account would be true of course, but would the sum total of the book be representative of Northern Ireland or the Army's long experience there? The concern was that soldiers would recall the incidents and the tragedies which are only a part of the Northern Ireland experience. The book might become a catalogue of death on death, bombing on bombing, riot on riot, sustaining the cruel caricature of all of Northern Ireland being lost in strife and mayhem. This, however, was not my intention, for I was aware of the range of experience soldiers gain from Northern Ireland.

Apart from the UDR, all the soldiers were interviewed outside the Province. They were selected by me from regiments and corps which have served in the Province. The infantry predominates but I was mindful that similar experiences could have been culled from the thousands of armoured corps soldiers, sappers and gunners who served on the streets. The work of the RUC was outside the scope of this book, as was the work of those soldiers engaged in covert operations.

It is because the infantry predominates that many accounts, perhaps inevitably, describe experiences in the hard-line Republican areas of West Belfast and West Londonderry. These are the 'hardest' operational areas but they are local, very small and not typical of the soldier's experience across the whole of Northern Ireland.

It has to be said that most soldiers, even at the height of the 'troubles', did not personally encounter armed terrorists or fire their rifles in anger. But equally, most soldiers in operational units have experienced the tensions of successive patrols even when they proved uneventful. And very many soldiers have experienced the aftermath of terrorist actions and the corrosive bitterness within some sections of both communities in Northern Ireland.

Wherever possible I interviewed a broad cross-section of ranks within each regiment, from the private soldier to the commanding officer, in the hope that I could create a tapestry of voices. Many of those who had served in the Province on a number of tours had difficulty recalling even what year they had been there; others had remarkable recall. Some of those interviewed took on a reflective tone, others spoke with an immediacy, a gut feeling. Many were articulate, certain and forthright, others not so sure of their thoughts or feelings. There are many extremely frank portrayals and a few of the stories had been well honed before being recounted to me, but they lost nothing in the retelling. Wherever possible, I have removed accounts which I felt had been embellished; some, however, may still have got through.

The memory of a soldier or anyone else asked to cast his mind across eighteen years could throw up a distorted picture. There may be some accounts where details like street names or months etc. may be incorrect, but the depth of feeling or thought within is more important than such detail. However, where soldiers have erred on a historical point, I have endeavoured wherever possible to correct this.

I adopted a neutral and non-political approach to these interviews and hope that this is reflected in these accounts. During the time I spent on these interviews I found many soldiers had little perspective on the 'troubles', either politically or historically. To most it was a task, a job to be done as professionally as possible.

In the first part of the book I have arranged the memories of the soldiers in a chronology of experience from 1969 to 1986. Some events that occurred during this span are not covered in these accounts, because the soldiers I interviewed did not witness them. I have made it a faithful tapestry of experience rather than a comprehensive history.

South Armagh, bombs and bomb disposal, and the UDR have been treated separately. Much of the historical narrative is inevitably centred on Belfast and Londonderry where, by the nature of the urban environments, soldiering is very different from operations in the rural landscape of South Armagh. To have interwoven South Armagh into such a history, so intensely urban, could have been distracting. I have therefore kept it as separate chapter with its own particular colours intact.

'Bombs and Bomb Disposal' spans both rural and urban landscapes and I felt the nature of the work of the RAOC needed to be concentrated in order to show how they handle various situations.

The UDR, the youngest regiment in the British Army, is unique in its structure. It is in many ways a citizens' army and clearly needed a chapter of its own to show the reality of many of the lives of its soldiers, especially those who are part time.

Preface

For reasons of security I have not named the soldiers I interviewed, and where names are mentioned they have been changed. The rank given at the beginning of each account is that held at the time concerned; on occasion the rank has been changed to protect the individual from recognition. Names of regiments, battalions and corps are either given in full or in their widely used abbreviations. The commanding officers of each were sent a draft copy of his soldiers' accounts and given the opportunity to question any material and make changes. Only two did so: one in order to prevent further grief to the parents of a soldier killed; the other for reasons of security.

In the chronology I have adumbrated the overall political background to the past two decades, focusing especially on those events critical to the soldiers' experience: the politics of Northern Ireland have been described in many other works.

In this book I have tried to provide a glimpse of the many aspects of the soldiers' lot during the last eighteen years. I will let others decide whether their accounts fairly reflect the situation in Northern Ireland, or could ever do so. I hope their experiences will give readers an understanding of the soldier: their words must speak for themselves.

Max Arthur
London
June 1987

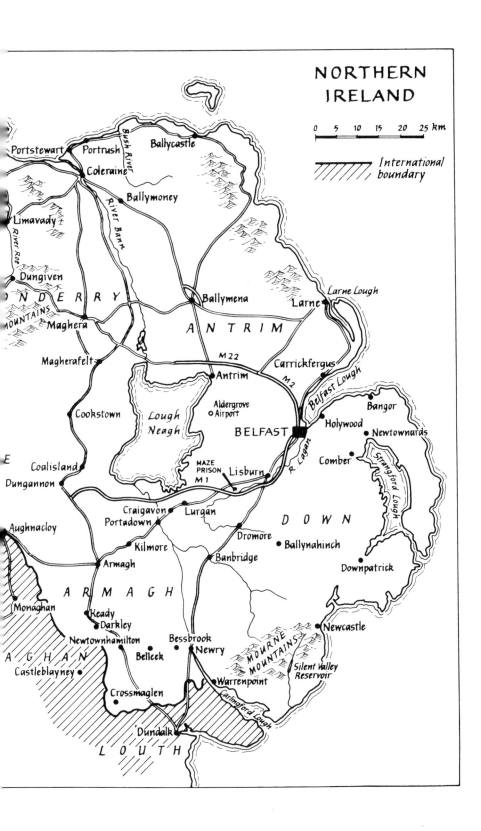

NORTHERN IRELAND

0 5 10 15 20 25 km

International boundary

Portstewart • Portrush • Coleraine • Ballycastle

Bush River

Ballymoney •

River Bann

Limavady •

River Roe

Dungiven •

LONDONDERRY

MOUNTAINS

Maghera •

Magherafelt •

Ballymena •

ANTRIM

Larne • *Larne Lough*

M 22

Antrim • Carrickfergus

M 2 *Belfast Lough*

Cookstown •

Lough Neagh

Aldergrove o Airport

BELFAST

Holywood • Bangor •

Newtownards •

Comber •

Strangford Lough

Coalisland •

Dungannon •

MAZE PRISON M 1

Lisburn •

R. Lagan

Aughnacloy •

Craigavon • Lurgan •

Portadown •

Dromore •

Ballynahinch •

DOWN

Kilmore •

Banbridge •

Downpatrick •

Monaghan •

ARMAGH

Armagh •

Keady • Darkley •

Newtownhamilton •

Belleek •

Bessbrook •

Newry •

MOURNE MOUNTAINS

Newcastle •

MONAGHAN

Castleblayney •

Crossmaglen •

Silent Valley Reservoir

Warrenpoint •

Carlingford Lough

Dundalk •

LOUTH

Chronology
1969–May 1987

1967

Northern Ireland Civil Rights Association (NICRA) formed to promote one man, one vote in council elections, the prevention of discrimination against Catholics by local authorities, the ending of 'gerrymandered' electoral boundaries, and fair housing allocation.

1968

5 Oct

Civil rights marches begin, with violence in Co. Londonderry.

1969

4 Jan

Civil rights march from Belfast to Londonderry attacked by Loyalists at Burntollet Bridge, Co. Londonderry.

30 Mar–
24 Apr

8 explosions at electricity and water installations in Co. Down and Co. Armagh, almost certainly inspired by Protestant paramilitary group Ulster Volunteer Force (UVF).

28 Apr

Terence O'Neill, Prime Minister of Northern Ireland, resigns and is replaced by James Chichester-Clark.

July

Some 2,500 British troops stationed in Northern Ireland, about half guarding public utilities.

12–14 Aug

Prolonged rioting in Londonderry following annual Orange Order march past the Catholic Bogside estate. British Army deployed on 14 Aug to assist exhausted Royal Ulster Constabulary (RUC) and Ulster Special Constabulary (B Specials).

14/15 Aug

Severe rioting between Catholics and Protestants in West Belfast; Army deployed on late afternoon of 15th.

Sept

'Peace Line' established between Falls and Shankill Roads in West Belfast; Catholic barricades dismantled. Army strength in Province rises to 6,000 men.

16 Oct

Following recommendations of Hunt Report, decision taken to reform RUC and disband B Specials. Serious riots ensue in Protestant Shankill Road against Army; Constable Arbuckle (RUC) and 2 Protestant gunmen shot dead.

Dec	Irish Republican Army (IRA) splits into two factions, the Official IRA (OIRA) and Provisional IRA (PIRA), the latter formally established in Jan 1970 with the aim of prosecuting a military campaign in Northern Ireland.
31 Dec	In 1969 1 policeman and 12 civilians were killed. There were 9 bomb explosions and 73 shooting incidents.

1970

1 Jan	Ulster Defence Regiment (UDR) officially born, raised on 1 April to replace B Specials, disbanded 31 Mar.
1 Apr	Riots between Catholics and Protestants in the Ballymurphy estate, West Belfast.
26–27 June	Severe riots around Butler Street on the Ardoyne/Shankill interface in West Belfast, stimulated by annual Orange Order marches; PIRA in overnight gun battle with Protestants in Ballymacarrett, East Belfast.
2 July	Arms find in Balkan Street, West Belfast, leads to severe riots against Army and consequent curfew of Falls area 3–5 July. Troop level in Province rises to 9,000.
31 July	Petrol-bomber shot dead by Army in New Lodge area, North Belfast; 5 nights of riots ensue.
31 Dec	In 1970 2 RUC and 23 civilians were killed, 620 Army and 47 police injured, and 60 civilians wounded. There were 170 bombs, of which 17 were rendered safe by the Army, and 213 shooting incidents.

1971

11–18 Jan	Severe riots against Army in Ballymurphy.
3–4 Feb	Severe riots in the Clonard and Ardoyne areas of West Belfast. PIRA launch military offensive against Army in Catholic areas of city.
6 Feb	Gunner Curtis, 94 Locating Regiment, Royal Artillery, shot dead in New Lodge, Belfast, the first soldier to be killed on duty during current troubles. Army shoot dead James Saunders, staff officer, PIRA Belfast Brigade.
11 Mar	3 Scottish soldiers found shot dead at Ligoniel, North Belfast.
20 Mar	Chichester-Clark resigns, replaced by Brian Faulkner.
Apr–Aug	Escalating violence: 37 bomb explosions in Apr rising to 47 in May, 50 in June; during this period a further 10 soldiers and 13 civilians die.
9 Aug	Internment without trial introduced under Special Powers Act, 1922; 342 Catholics suspected of terrorist activities or

	sympathies arrested. Widespread riots and gun battles throughout Belfast and elsewhere.
Aug	NICRA organise civil disobedience campaign, including a rent and rates strike, in protest against internment.
27–28 Sept	Widespread violence: PIRA apparently growing in strength.
Oct	Troop level increases to 13,600. Attacks by PIRA on UDR personnel start.
4 Dec	15 die in UVF blast explosion at McGurk's bar, North Belfast.
Dec	Car bomb introduced.
31 Dec	In 1971 48 soldiers, including 5 UDR, 11 RUC, and 115 civilians were killed; 390 soldiers, including 9 UDR, 105 RUC, and 1,880 civilians were injured or wounded. There were 1,022 explosions, another 493 explosive devices were made safe; 1,756 shooting incidents were recorded.

1972

30 Jan	13 shot dead by Army following civil rights march in Londonderry ('Bloody Sunday').
24 Mar	Stormont Parliament prorogued when Faulkner government refuses to accept reduction in law and order powers, and is replaced by direct rule from Westminster. William Whitelaw appointed first Secretary of State for Northern Ireland; subsequent Secretaries of State have been Francis Pym (1973–4), Merlyn Rees (1974–6), Roy Mason (1976–9), Sir Humphrey Atkins (1979–81), James Prior (1981–5), Tom King (1985–).
10 Apr	Widgery Report on 'Bloody Sunday' published; it rules that 'there is no reason to suppose that the soldiers would have opened fire if they had not been fired upon first', and finds 'no general breakdown in discipline' although 'some firing bordered on the reckless'.
April	No-go areas established by Catholic communities in Belfast and Londonderry.
29 May	In a situation of growing violence, OIRA calls a ceasefire, which by and large has prevailed ever since.
20 June	Special category status established for convicted terrorists.
24 June	100th British soldier killed.
26 June	PIRA begins 'bi-lateral truce'.
1 July	Loyalist paramilitary group Ulster Defence Association

	(UDA) sets up no-go areas in Protestant Belfast in protest against perceived Army reluctance to combat Catholic no-go areas.
7 July	Secret talks in London between PIRA and British government.
9 July	PIRA calls off truce following confrontation with Army and Loyalists over housing rights in Lenadoon area of West Belfast.
21 July	9 killed, 130 injured in 22 PIRA explosions in Belfast ('Bloody Friday').
31 July	Operation 'Motorman': Army enters no-go areas in Belfast and Londonderry. Troop level in Province highest during period under review, 21,266 men.
11–12 Oct	Gun battles between UDA and Army throughout Belfast.
31 Dec	In 1972, the height of the bloodshed, 129 soldiers, including 26 UDR, 17 RUC, and 321 civilians were killed; 578 soldiers, including 34 UDR, 94 RUC, and 3,902 civilians were injured or wounded. Of 1,853 bombs, 471 were made safe, and shooting incidents numbered 10,630, a sixfold increase on 1971.

1973

8 Mar	Referendum on border issue: results show 98 per cent of votes cast in favour of UK link, but 42 per cent of electorate, including the Catholic Social Democratic and Labour Party and most Republicans boycott the poll.
20 July	Northern Ireland Assembly elections, by proportional representation.
8–9 Dec	Sunningdale Conference discusses power-sharing in Assembly.
31 Dec	1973 saw a reduction by approximately half relative to 1972 in the number of deaths (66 Army, including 8 UDR, 13 RUC, 171 civilians), civilians wounded (1,765), and shootings (5,018).

1974

1 Jan	Power-sharing Executive with Faulkner as Chief Executive formally takes office.
4 Jan	Ulster Unionist Council rejects Council of Ireland proposed in Sunningdale Agreement.
7 Jan	Faulkner resigns as Unionist Party leader.
14 May	Power-sharing Executive wins Assembly vote on the Sunningdale Agreement.

15 May	The Loyalist Ulster Workers' Council (UWC) power cuts and strikes begin in protest against power-sharing and the proposed Council of Ireland.
20 May	UDA sets up 172 road blocks around Belfast.
28 May	In the face of UWC strike, Unionist members of Executive resign and Assembly collapses. Direct rule resumes.
29 May	UWC calls off strike.
June	PIRA increases activities on border and opens campaign in England.
2 Sept	Expansion of RUC and UDR announced.
6 Nov	33 Republican prisoners escape from Maze prison; 32 captured by same evening.
9 Nov	Ministry of Defence rules that since Northern Ireland is not a war, names of soldiers killed will not be added to war memorials.
21 Nov	19 killed, 182 injured in Birmingham pub bombings. PIRA denies responsibility.
25 Nov	PIRA declared illegal in Great Britain, and Prevention of Terrorism Act introduced on 29 Nov.
20 Dec	Following talks with Protestant churchmen at Feakle, Irish Republic, PIRA announces ceasefire from 22 Dec to 2 Jan 1975.

1975

16 Jan	PIRA calls off ceasefire, extended from 2 Jan.
9 Feb	PIRA announces indefinite suspension of military activities, new ceasefire to be monitored by Provisional Sinn Fein and government officials. This results in a marked reduction in Army casualties but increasing sectarian killings.
5 April	7 killed and 75 injured in two pub bombings in Belfast.
24 July	Phasing out of internment without trial begins.
2 Oct	In a series of UVF attacks, 12 killed, including 3 women and 4 UVF men.
3 Oct	UVF declared illegal.
5 Dec	Last detainees released.
31 Dec	A year of greatly reduced terrorist activity, reflected in 20 Army dead and 167 injured, compared with 35 and 483 respectively in 1974, but an increase in sectarian violence, 216 civilians killed relative to 166 in 1974. Bombs and bomb explosions fell to 635 from 1,113 in 1974, and shooting incidents to 1,803 from 3,206.

1976

7 Jan	SAS unit moves into South Armagh.
21 Jan	Government says 25,000 houses in NI damaged in current troubles.
1 Mar	Special category status for convicted terrorists abolished. PIRA initiates attacks on prison staff, killing 3 in the year, and organises blanket protest.
9 Mar	Constitutional Convention dissolved after British government refuses majority report rejecting power-sharing.
30 Mar	NICRA calls off rent and rate strike originally started in August 1971.
22 May	UVF announces three-month ceasefire.
2 July	Expansion of UDR and RUC announced; UDR strength 7,960.
3 Aug	6 PIRA bombs explode in Portrush, Co. Antrim.
10 Aug	2 children of the Maguire family killed in Andersonstown, West Belfast, by a car whose driver had been shot dead by troops. Third child dies from injuries the next day.
12 Aug	Women demonstrate for peace in Andersonstown and women's peace movement (later Peace People) founded.
1 Dec	Fair Employment Act making it an offence to discriminate in employment on religious or political grounds becomes effective.
9 Dec	PIRA fire-bombs cause more than £1m damage to Londonderry shops. SAS allowed to operate throughout Province.
25–26 Dec	PIRA Christmas ceasefire.

In 1976 Army deaths numbered 29, including 15 members of the UDR. The RUC sustained their highest number of deaths since the troubles started (23) and civilian deaths rose to 245.

1977

Jan	Secretary of State launches 'Way Ahead' policy to re-establish the primacy of RUC. The Army's priority would be the elimination of terrorism with the aim of restoring RUC to their normal policing role.
11 Mar	26 UVF men sentenced to a total of 700 years' imprisonment.
3 May	Short-lived Loyalist strike demanding restoration of majority government; 730 barricades removed by security forces.
20 May–4 June	UVF ceasefire.

21 June	Unemployment in Northern Ireland reaches 60,000, highest June total for 37 years.
27 June	4 killed and 18 injured in Belfast feud between OIRA and PIRA.
10 Oct	Betty Williams and Mairead Corrigan, founders of Peace People, awarded Nobel Peace Prize.
22 Dec	PIRA says there will be no Christmas ceasefire.

In 1977 figures were similar to 1976: the Army lost 15, while the UDR and the RUC both lost 14. Civilian deaths, however, fell dramatically to 69. Shooting incidents continued to decline (366) and explosions numbered 1081.

1978

17 Feb	PIRA fire-bomb at La Mon restaurant, Co. Down, kills 12, injures 23.
Mar	Speakers at PIRA celebrations of Easter Rising say their campaign will be stepped up.
13 Mar	Republican prisoners at Maze launch 'no wash, no toilet' campaign in protest against conditions in the prison.
30 Nov	PIRA warns it is 'preparing for a long war' and admits setting off explosives and fire-bombs in 14 towns and villages.

In 1978 Army deaths numbered 14, the same figure as the RUC. UDR deaths fell to 7 and civilian deaths to 50. Although there was an increase in explosions (455) compared with 1977, there was a marked decline in shootings (755).

1979

30 Mar	Airey Neave, Conservative spokesman on Northern Ireland, killed by Irish National Liberation Army bomb outside House of Commons.
2 July	INLA declared illegal throughout UK.
27 Aug	Two PIRA bombs kill 18 soldiers near Warrenpoint, Co. Down, the highest death toll in 10 years of violence. Earl Mountbatten killed by PIRA at Mullaghmore, Co. Sligo, when his boat is destroyed in radio-triggered explosion; 14-year-old grandson Nicholas and 14-year-old crew member Paul Maxwell also die. Dowager Lady Brabourne dies later of her injuries.
29 Sept	The Pope, on a visit to Irish Republic, appeals 'on my bended knees' for an end to the violence.
2 Oct	PIRA rejects Pope's plea and declares it has widespread

	support, and only force can remove British presence.
16 Dec	5 soldiers killed by PIRA landmine.
31 Dec	Mainly because of the Warrenpoint ambush, Army deaths in 1979 rose to 48, from 29 in 1977 and 21 in 1978. The total number of people wounded or injured showed a steady decline from 1,425 in 1976 to 575, as did shooting incidents, 728 compared to 1,908 in 1976.

1980

6 Jan	3 UDR die in culvert bomb blast at Castlewellan, Co. Down, bringing death toll since 1969 to 2,001.
7 Jan	Constitutional Conference to discuss political settlement opens.
9 July	Internment without trial law dropped (not been used since 1975).
8 Aug	3 killed in widespread violence on ninth anniversary of internment.
27 Oct	7 H-Block prisoners at the Maze begin hunger strike in support of demand for right to wear their own clothes, among other things.
18 Dec	H-Block hunger strike called off with one PIRA prisoner critically ill.
	In 1980 there was a very marked decline in losses: the Army sustained 8, the UDR 9 and the RUC 9, while civilian killings were down to 50. There were 280 explosions and the lowest number of shootings since 1970 (642).

1981

1 Mar	New H-Block hunger strike in support of political status for convicted terrorists begins when PIRA prisoner Bobby Sands refuses food.
9 Apr	Bobby Sands elected MP in Fermanagh and South Tyrone by-election.
15–21 Apr	Prolonged rioting in Belfast and especially Londonderry.
5 May	Sands dies on 66th day of his fast. Widespread rioting in Londonderry, Belfast and Dublin.
6 May	600 extra troops sent to Northern Ireland as sporadic violence continues, bringing troop strength to 11,550 men.
19 May	5 soldiers killed when their Saracen armoured car blown up by landmine near Bessbrook, Co. Armagh.

4 July	H-Block hunger strikers agree that any concessions granted to them should apply to all prisoners.
5 Aug	PIRA car bomb and incendiary attacks in 7 centres, including Belfast, Londonderry and Lisburn.
8 Aug	2 people die during violence in Belfast – more than 1,000 petrol bombs thrown at security forces.
4 Sept	INLA announces no further volunteers will join hunger strike.
3 Oct	H-Block hunger strike, which has led to the death of 10 Republican prisoners, called off.
6 Oct	Secretary of State announces all prisoners will be allowed to wear their own clothes.
10 Oct	PIRA sets off remotely controlled nail-bomb outside Chelsea Barracks, London; 1 woman killed, 23 soldiers and 17 civilians injured.
Oct–Nov	PIRA bombing campaign in London.
16 Nov	Anglo-Irish summit.
23 Nov	Loyalist 'Day of Action' in protest against security policy.
14 Dec	Belfast city centre opens at night for private cars – first time for 7 years.
31 Dec	The total number of deaths in 1981, including 10 hunger strikers, increased from 76 in 1980 to 111, and of wounded or injured from 479 to 792. The total of shooting incidents also rose, from 642 to 1,142.

1982

25 Mar	3 soldiers killed in PIRA ambush in Crocus Street, West Belfast. British Cabinet approves 'rolling devolution' plan.
20 July	8 soldiers killed and 51 injured by two PIRA bombs in London – one near the Household Cavalry barracks in Knightsbridge, the other at the Regent's Park bandstand when an Army band was playing. 3 more people die later.
23 July	Northern Ireland Assembly Bill receives royal assent.
3 Oct	Last recorded case of tarring and feathering.
20 Oct	Polling day in Assembly election.
6 Dec	17 people, including 11 soldiers, die in INLA bombing of Droppin' Well pub disco in Ballykelly, Co. Londonderry. This brought the year's loss for the Army to 21, the UDR 7 and the RUC 12. Civilian losses were 57. Explosions continued to decline (220) and shootings again fell to 547.

1983

5 Jan	INLA declared illegal in Irish Republic.
11 Apr	14 UVF men jailed, 2 for life, on evidence of supergrass Joseph Bennett.
10–11 May	Assembly has all-night sitting on devolution but fails to agree on any approach.
24 May	1,000-lb PIRA bomb outside Andersonstown police station in West Belfast causes £1m damage.
12–17 July	Serious riots in Londonderry.
13 July	4 UDR soldiers killed by PIRA landmine in Co. Tyrone.
5 Aug	120-day trial of 38 people implicated in terrorism by PIRA supergrass Christopher Black ends: 22 jailed with sentences totalling 4,000 years; 4 acquitted; the rest mainly receive suspended sentences.
25 Sept	38 Republican prisoners escape from Maze.
17 Dec	5 people, including 2 policemen, killed and 92 injured at bombing of Harrods in London by PIRA.

1984

6 Mar	William McConnel, Assistant Governor of Maze, is shot dead.
Apr–May	Attacks on RUC and UDR intensify.
12 Oct	Bombing of Grand Hotel at Brighton during Conservative Party conference; 4 killed, 32 injured.
19–23 Oct	Vehicle hijacked on 15 Oct at Crossmaglen, Co. Armagh, takes 4 days to clear: longest time on Improvised Explosive Device.
31 Dec	A total of 19 soldiers, including 10 UDR, 8 RUC, and 37 civilians were killed in 1984. The figures for wounded or injured were 86 soldiers, including 22 UDR, 189 RUC, and 252 civilians. Shooting incidents reached a new low level at 334.
	In 1983 there were 5 deaths sustained by the Army, 10 by the UDR and 18 by the RUC. Civilian deaths were 44. The number of explosions rose slightly from the previous year to 266, but shootings were lower (424).

1985

8 Feb	9 RUC killed in PIRA mortar attack on Newry RUC station.
25 Apr	Largest find of explosives by security forces near Dungannon: 1,000 kg of homemade explosives.

15 Nov	Anglo-Irish Agreement signed.
23 Nov	Loyalists stage rally in Belfast to oppose Anglo-Irish Agreement.

In 1985 the Army had only 2 deaths, and the UDR 4, but with the Newry explosion the RUC figures rose to 23. There were 226 shootings and 176 explosions, again showing a decrease on the previous year. Civilian deaths numbered 24.

1986

3 Jan	Following widespread attacks by PIRA on RUC, troop level increases to 9,550.
3 Mar	Loyalist day of action in protest against Anglo-Irish Agreement.
July	Increasing attacks by PIRA on RUC.
9–10 Aug	15th anniversary of internment; rioting in Downpatrick, Belfast and Armagh.
27 Aug	Renewed PIRA threat to serving security forces personnel.
25 Sept	Announcement that the Divis Flats, West Belfast, are to be demolished.
Oct–Nov	PIRA and INLA mortar bomb attacks on RUC stations in Belfast, Carrickmore, Middletown and Newry.
10–16 Nov	Violence as new paramilitary style group Ulster Resistance Force leads demonstrations against Anglo-Irish Agreement throughout Province.
22 Dec	INLA feud; 10 people shot in following 3 months.

1987

Jan–Feb	Further widespread mortar bomb and grenade attacks on security forces bases.
27 Mar	Ceasefire in INLA feud.
25 Apr	Against background of mounting attacks on UDR and RUC personnel, Lord Justice Sir Maurice Gibson and his wife killed by PIRA car bomb explosion on the border near Killeen, Co. Down.
8 May	8 PIRA activists and a passing motorist killed in SAS ambush during an attack in Loughgall RUC station, Co. Armagh; the highest number of terrorists to die in a single incident during the period under review. Riots ensue on 10 and 12 May.

A monthly average of 10,170 troops is currently stationed in Northern Ireland.

Chronology

In 1986 the Army lost 4 soldiers, the UDR 8 and the RUC 12. Civilian losses were 38. There were 218 shootings and 120 explosions, the lowest figures recorded since 1969.

This chronology, up to 1984, could not have been compiled without the invaluable assistance provided by *The British Army in Northern Ireland* by Lieutenant-Colonel Michael Dewar, RGJ (Arms and Armour Press, 1985) and *Northern Ireland: A Political Directory* by W. D. Flackes (Ariel Books, British Broadcasting Corporation, 1983).

Prologue

Lieutenant-Colonel, 1 King's Own Scottish Borderers

It is difficult to be detached about Northern Ireland because inevitably, in the nature of having been personally involved, having seen friends who suffered, one has an emotional involvement and immediately ceases to be objective, to be able to look at it from a different viewpoint. Perhaps we are still too close to the tragedy of the whole business. When we look at the First World War we see small fragments of the whole, but we all know so much about Ireland, its good and its bad and its horrible aspects.

Lieutenant-Colonel, 1 Para

A private soldier will have a view, and it will be his view, valid in so far as he sees it. His sergeant will have a broader perspective, his company commander will have yet a broader picture, and on it goes.

Lieutenant-Colonel, Army Air Corps

There were three types of soldiers we used to fly in Northern Ireland. There were young lads who were scared to death, couldn't wait for their tour to be over; there were the big brave guys who treated the whole thing as a joke, like being at home but different, and thoroughly enjoyed it all; and then there were the quiet, professional chaps who thought about their jobs, got a bit involved in what Northern Ireland was all about – they were few and far between.

Captain, 2 Royal Anglian

There's nothing the guys like more than telling war stories. When I joined the battalion in 1975 if you hadn't been on the '72 tour you really were nobody. And, of course, by the time the '81 tour came round, if you hadn't been on the '75 tour . . . The difficulty is finding people who will listen: you can spend hours trying to find someone to listen to you.

Sergeant, 45 Commando

Northern Ireland's like everything else: if you discuss it in a good mood you pick out the good points, if you discuss it in a bad mood then you pick out the bad points.

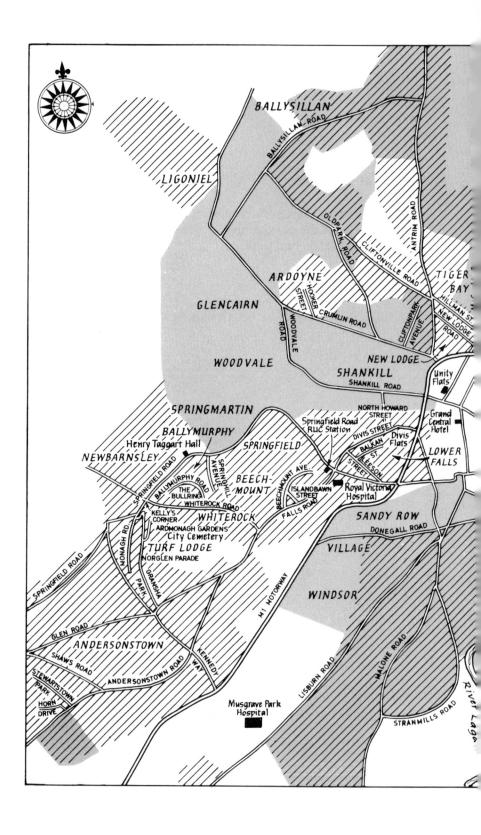

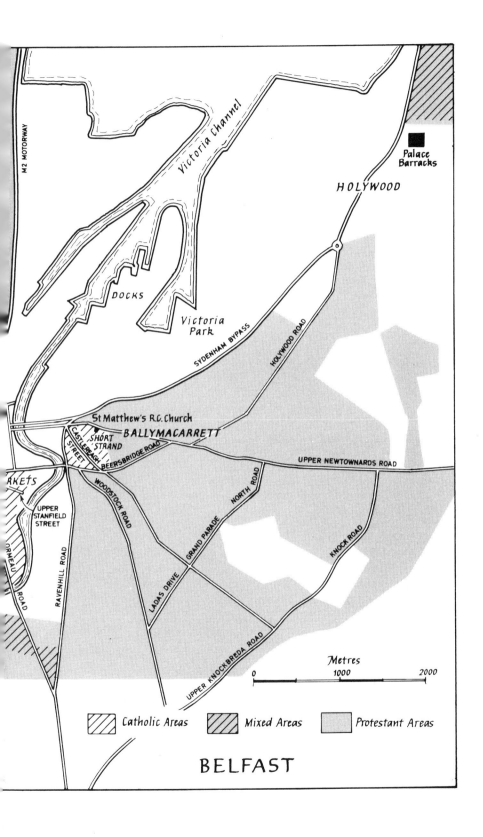

M2 MOTORWAY

Victoria Channel

Palace Barracks

HOLYWOOD

DOCKS

Victoria Park

SYDENHAM BYPASS

HOLYWOOD ROAD

St Matthew's R.C. Church

BALLYMACARRETT

CASTLEREAGH STREET

SHORT STRAND

BEERSBRIDGE ROAD

UPPER NEWTOWNARDS ROAD

RKETS

UPPER STANFIELD STREET

WOODSTOCK ROAD

NORTH ROAD

KNOCK ROAD

ORMEAU ROAD

RAVENHILL ROAD

LADAS DRIVE

GRAND PARADE

UPPER KNOCKBREDA ROAD

Metres

0   1000   2000

Catholic Areas   Mixed Areas   Protestant Areas

BELFAST

Belfast

Senior Officer, Ulster Defence Regiment

The frontier mentality that we have lived with in Northern Ireland is rooted so deep. It's a different way of life, a completely different approach that one could never have dreamed up, and yet it has come naturally to people here. As a youngster, as a teenager coming home from school in England, I don't remember when I didn't carry a pistol, a licensed weapon, in the school holidays. We always had either a pistol or a shotgun. I would have slept with a shotgun beside my bed or a pistol on my pillow. And that would have applied to many, many people, certainly during the 1940s. In our family's factories, the cashiers going for wages would be sent round to the bank to pick up, say, twenty thousand pounds, and those cashiers would carry pistols in their pockets. And they weren't soldiers or policemen.

Sergeant, Royal Military Police

I was kicked out of school at fifteen. I didn't like it, I didn't go. In them days in Belfast there was always something better to do. People my age, who went through the late sixties, usually joined an organisation: it just depended which one you joined. My particular hero was Gusty Spence, leader of the Ulster Volunteer Force, and I supported the UVF along certain lines, as did most of my family. It was like the bloody Secret Service, that was the attraction. You felt like a James Bond character, running around secret houses and all that. I'd leave home at night and I was secret agent 00 bloody 7. You've got to bear in mind I was only a young lad then, fifteen or sixteen. We'd all pile into buses, into Belfast, and wait outside the pubs for the boys. There was a pub in the Shankill Road called the Brown Bear – it's gone now, blown up ages ago – and the boys would come in, shoulder holsters and all. In the old days they never carried guns to kill people, just to shoot them in the arm, things like that. They weren't allowed to take their guns into the actual bar so there was a table in the entrance hall, and halfway through the night this table would be packed

1

with pistols of all bloody sorts. They'd be inside getting pissed and we'd be outside making sure no one stole their guns. Then once they'd got tanked up, out they'd come and away they'd go. There was one guy – in fact he's one of the hardest men in Belfast, even nowadays – he would start at one end of the Shankill Road with a shotgun, blow a street lamp out, run across, blow another light out, load up, and work his way up the Shankill until he'd blown all the lights out. That was his job. And as things progressed, the IRA – this is the old IRA – used to fire down the Shankill Road. I don't think they wanted to kill anybody. In those days it was just a bit of aggro, nobody was ever killed.

Sergeant, 2 Para

When I was a kid, Belfast was divided up into ghettos. Belfast was actually a lot of little Belfasts. They all had their own names, like Shankill or Tiger Bay. My personal one was Sailortown, which consisted of about eight streets divided by one street, Nelson Street. All the streets running off one side were Catholic and all the streets running off the other were Protestant, and you'd have found that people would've gone down Nelson Street on their side to walk round the district on the other. They kept on the outskirts, they'd never walk through. I'm sure there were Protestants born on the Protestant side of Nelson Street who had never been into our town. We used to go to dances and pubs and the pictures, and we used to meet people, and they could tell where you came from. Those little communities were so tight-knit they could tell where you came from just by your accent, in the same city. It was fear that dominated, fear: keep together.

Of course, when they started the civil rights movement it brought it all home to the Catholics. Actually, I was quite happy. I mean, I didn't know I was an underdog. People were telling me I was an underdog but I didn't realise it, 'cos I was a merchant seaman, the same as everybody else. The employment situation wasn't all that good but there were always jobs somewhere if you wanted them. But with the civil rights thing, Catholic people were watching telly and asking 'What are these civil rights?' You see, before 1968 a lot of things were not reported, like the B Specials. Why they had B Specials in the towns I could never understand. B Specials used to carry Sten guns and .38 Webleys, big old-fashioned pistols, and it wasn't unknown for them just to take out

2

their pistols and shoot at people. I remember one time when I was twelve I was at a big dance hall above Bellevue Zoo. Something had happened, I think there'd been a fight, and for some reason the B Specials did a raid and locked everybody in. When they were letting us out they asked me: 'What religion are you?' If you were a Protestant you'd get a smack on the lug and be sent home, but if you were a Catholic you'd get a ride in a Black Maria. You know, those were the type of things that happened then.

Sergeant, 1 Para

The civil rights movement was quite right about Northern Ireland in those days: housing, the electoral system and everything else was appalling, absolutely appalling. Although the civil rights thing was definitely exploited, they were quite right, and on both sides. The Protestants admitted it themselves at the time. Their housing was just as bad as the Catholics', and it was only the higher-up Protestants and the higher-up Catholics who had the right to vote: if you owned your own property you had a vote; if you didn't, well, you had no vote. Ninety per cent of the Catholics didn't own any property, nor did many Protestants. Now, the Shankill Road is the Protestant road, and the Falls Road the Catholic road, but if you just forgot the two names, Falls Road and Shankill Road, the standard of housing on each was exactly the same. In effect the Falls Road housing had been improved a bit with the building of the Divis Flats, but the Shankill was evil. It was terrible housing there, all those terraced houses. It was terrible, the conditions they lived in, on both sides.

Major, 1 King's Own Scottish Borderers

Belfast felt like a large provincial town which was out of date, in terms of the mainland, in terms of the stores and everything else. It had a feeling of being a town rather than of a city. The biggest shop was a large general store, there wasn't much in the way of C&A, and things like that. Even very close to the city centre it was more a collection of corner shops strung together, and that feeling of everybody knowing everybody else made it tight like a town, or a village.

Many of the pieces making up Belfast seemed to be the same as in Glasgow, but they were put together so differently that the overall picture was quite different. Although in Glasgow you could pick out elements, strong elements, of similarity, somehow they were juggled so as to produce a pleasant picture, whereas in Belfast the impression was corrupt in some way.

The only money in Belfast that I saw was traditional money, the same as in Britain fifty or a hundred years ago. Family businesses were being run in a Victorian hangover: there were a lot of rich youngsters, but the population was so busy fighting each other that they never got round to proper trade unionism and fighting the people who were employing them. They were living in dreadful conditions and putting up with it because they had something else to complain about, which was the other side.

Lieutenant, 1 Prince of Wales's Own Regiment of Yorkshire

We flew into Aldergrove and moved down to Ballykinler weekend training camp in County Down. It was grim, like hutted camps down on the Nile. Nobody did four-month tours in those days – this was early 1969 – it was 'as required'. We could see ourselves being there for a year: our experience in Aden had been a year, and that was the order of the day then. We'd read in the newspapers that there'd been the odd pipeline blown up and some other trouble, but we really didn't think there was too much of a problem, not at grassroots level anyway. As a lieutenant I didn't really feel I had a job; I'd hardly been briefed at all.

We spread the soldiers out in the countryside throughout the Province doing Vehicle Check Points, particularly in the Sperrin Mountains and on the Black Mountain above Belfast. The soldiers were still dressed in their Aden gear: shiny helmets with no camouflage on them, banners saying, '"Whack off, whack off" or we fire.' It was that sort of rushed, primitive approach: we'd done it in Aden, we'd done it in Crater, so we'd do it in Belfast.

We flew the helicopters a lot, which was brilliant: we'd go up into the Mountains of Mourne, see lovely valleys and reservoirs; fly over to Rathlin Island and pick up lobsters and bring 'em back for supper; look down at the beautiful north coast, the Giant's Causeway, all that area. And a lot of Irish people, a lot of the staff that worked the messes, were great characters, very patriotic – smashing people. So it became a bit of a holiday. At one stage

4

we were going to take the helicopter down to Dublin for the weekend, to see the horse show. We rang up the Irish Army and they said: 'Yeah, Jesus, no problem.' That was the attitude.

Lieutenant, 1 Royal Regiment of Wales

In July '69 there was a certain amount of precaution in the air and we'd revved up our Internal Security drills before going to Northern Ireland. The main things one was aware of were Bernadette Devlin, civil rights, demonstrations and a feeling for change in the Province, without really having any idea what the appeals for change were all about, or what they were based on. But one wasn't shocked or worried at all because the late sixties was a time of protest, whether it was a university campus in America or Vanessa Redgrave in Grosvenor Square. I think the world then was very keen on mass numbers on the streets, marches and demonstrations, some of which spilled into violence which at the end was often contained by troops. So I think one thought that it was just another demonstration. It was the world as a village: protest and demonstration, really. I don't think that we were aware of the voting systems in Northern Ireland, or how the Province had been maintained.

Sergeant, 1 Para

That August (1969) my father was working at Mackies, and so was my brother, working the night shift, and they went off to their work without realising anything was going to happen. My mother was downstairs and a woman came to the door and she says: 'Oh Sally, come on quick. There's a crowd coming up the street waving a tricolour, a crowd of about two hundred coming to burn us out of our homes.' My mother ran out, and there was about six women there, with this crowd coming up, and two B Specials, one about nineteen and one about forty-five. And my mother says to one of them, 'I'm going to get the men out of the pubs,' and as the men came out of the pubs the fighting started. And they fought all the way down Percy Street, all the way up the Falls Road to the Royal Victoria Hospital, and it was the following night the soldiers come in.

Winning Hearts and Minds
1969

Lieutenant, 1 Royal Regiment of Wales

On the Friday afternoon we were moved up to Belfast, to Gird-wood Park. The decision had been made to try and drive a wedge down the Falls Road between the two communities, and my company commander gave us a briefing on what we as a company were going to do. He said: 'I'm afraid I can't give you much information on what to expect. We've just to be ready for the worst. We know that there are quite a lot of weapons on the street, we know they're being actively used, and we have information that the place is burning quite badly. That's why it's been decided that we get in there tonight before anything worse happens.' I remember that my hands started to shake as I was taking down notes. The company sergeant major was sitting next to me, a hardbitten old bugger who'd been in Korea, and I can actually remember stopping writing and tapping his hand to stop mine shaking. I looked at him from time to time and I could see he was thinking the same – we were all slightly glassy-faced. I think the fear of the unknown is always the worst, and the information was so limited that we had to be prepared for everything.

So in we drove, and I remember the commuter traffic of Belfast going home that evening, all aware of what had been happening in the city for the past couple of days, all sticking their thumbs up in the air as if to say, 'Right. Long overdue. The Army's going in to sort this problem out.' I led my company along the Shankill and then down to the Falls, and the dear old Protestant ladies came out of their houses thinking we were going to sort out the troublesome Catholics. There were lots of shouts of encourage-ment: 'Get in there and smash the bastards.' We went down in box formation, as though we were putting down a riot in some banana republic, complete with our furled banner – I saw a film of it recently, and it certainly looks more than twenty years ago.

I halted my platoon because a doubledecker bus was blocking

6

the street and dashed forward to see what was happening. Beyond in the Falls Road was a burning garage and a shirt factory on fire, all six or seven storeys absolutely alight. The streets were strewn with stones and pebbles and cars on fire. The whole place was a nightmare. The houses on either side of the Falls Road probably going six houses deep into the side streets had all been burnt out, from petrol bombs through the front windows. There was the odd crack in the background, but one couldn't be sure whether it was from the fires or whether some actual shooting was going on. I think all our faces just showed disbelief.

The boys knew where they were supposed to go in terms of sealing off streets, so it was then a question of getting men down to the corners and road junctions and giving them cover in case there was shooting. We hadn't a clue what was going on really, but the feeling I got within half an hour was one of relief, on both sides. The Irish are terribly curious and they came out of all sorts of corners, and I think both Protestants and Catholics were relieved that there might be some stability, because when you live through that sort of thing as a civilian you're dreading another night. I think there was particular relief on the Catholic side because they were under tremendous pressure, and I think the first cups of tea we were given were Catholic tea.

As darkness came down it was mostly the Protestants trying to get down at the Catholics and do some stoning, and so we fired tear gas, maybe six canisters in all. The other impression that comes back strongly is small boys, who have been one of the perpetual problems of Northern Ireland ever since: you know, the hooligans that emerge from nowhere just to cause trouble. I think that night we had more problems from them than from anything else. The company sergeant major gave a couple of these lads the biggest bollocking of all time. Normally he would have frightened anybody, but they just went off down the road whistling. I don't think he could believe it himself.

Having worked out some sort of guard system for the night, my platoon sergeant and I unrolled our sleeping bags on a bit of grass in somebody's garden on the Falls Road. It was August, and we were both lying there looking up at the stars with this shirt factory still smouldering away, and I said to him: 'Do you think if that lot fell down in the night it'd reach us?' And with that I remember him standing up, rolling up his sleeping bag and going to the garden edge.

Apart from the odd incursion in the night, in most cases people trying to throw stones, and the occasional crack of gunfire, nothing more came our way.

The following day was interesting. All the boys had offers of breakfast from the Catholics, to go into their homes. It was the quietest night they'd known for a long time. And then the most amazing sight: the regimental sergeant major came down the Falls Road, pace stick under arm, followed by the regimental police with wheelbarrows and brushes, and yelled at my platoon sergeant: 'Come on, let's get this place cleaned up, get it sorted out.' The whole of the road was littered with broken glass and bottles and smashed-up paving stones, and within half an hour the lads had all got brushes and were sweeping the pavement, tidying the place up. The irony was that there was a general feeling, which I remember so vividly, of: 'Let's get this place cleaned up and hand it back to them and then we'll be back off home.' And of course the other irony is the subsequent feeling that the whole problem might have been removed if the Army hadn't gone in until the following Monday: expensive on lives and property, but perhaps that might have been the end of it all, because at that stage a number of Catholics were quite prepared to cross the border.

Not having had a clue what to expect – which is not the first time the Army's been in that position – I think we all found it rather more difficult to accept because here were people who actually spoke English. They were obviously different, but you only have to travel a hundred miles in England and people are different, aren't they? So we had no real understanding of why on earth all this had happened, and it was only in the next three days or so that we actually started to learn of the problems of the Catholic community, how the two religions had managed to co-exist, and how matters had been handled in the past. So one started to get a certain sense of what Bernadette Devlin was all about.

There was probably an early perception of something wrong, that these sorts of things didn't just happen for nothing, and I think that when the soldiers discovered a little more about how votes were allocated in the Province, heard about job restrictions at Harland and Wolff, and learned that, basically, if you were a Catholic your chances weren't quite so good, then probably their sympathy lay with the Catholic people. But within ten days or so we'd started to get information on both sides and there was a quick realisation among the lads who hadn't met too many Ulstermen before that everything should be taken with a pinch of salt. They were very much in the middle getting both stories, and I think they just made up their own minds about what the truth was. They probably thought, 'What a mad bunch this lot is,' and I think within quite a short space of time they'd rather lost patience: reason and good sense and fair play and the idea of co-existence didn't seem to apply.

The other strong feeling was that the IRA had found the pressure too much for them at that stage. IRA was daubed everywhere, of course, but it stood for I Ran Away. The potential terrorists were, I think, completely discredited at that stage because under Protestant pressure they'd just found it too much and they had no standing in the Catholic community whatsoever. The Catholic community felt very let down, which in retrospect is such a pity, because the Army having come in and restored a physical situation, the only long-term solution had to be of a political nature. If only the political wheels had moved a bit faster: that couldn't have happened in weeks, but when you think that the first shot fired in anger at a British soldier was something like a year later, there was some time.

Subaltern, 1 Royal Regiment of Wales

We looked after the Springfield Road/Cupar Street area in Belfast, which of course had been the heart of the rioting with the Protestants on the Shankill and a small enclave of Catholics coming up from the Falls Road. All the buildings down Cupar Street had been completely gutted. The only way to describe it is that it was just like the photographs of Dresden, like the devastation in Germany in the Second World War. There were just skeletons of houses and factories, the whole lot had been burned out.

For the first week I slept underneath an awning by a baker's shop. I'd chosen the baker's shop because I knew we'd get fresh bread and buns each day. This was the period of complete daze, immediately after the initial rioting. No one knew what was going on, so we had to start talking to the people to find out what might happen. We felt we were terribly welcome, particularly by the Protestants, but they kept on saying: 'Why have you got your rifles pointing at us, and your backs to the Catholics, when they're the ones who started it?' So immediately we came up against the

9

sectarian problem: which way do you face? Who do you defend? Which side do you protect?

The soldiers were very, very good. We insisted that every morning everybody would parade outside the platoon locations and we held inspections to make sure that people were smartly dressed, that boots had been polished and trousers were clean, everyone washed and shaved. That kind of thing caused amusement. We'd started off with bayonets fixed – we were still talking about the same principles of warfare as the British Army had taken up in Aden – but then we realised that this was very aggressive, so the bayonets came off. We were in full webbing, which was dangerous because people could grab your equipment, and we had the old-fashioned A41 radio sets on our backs: in a street environment they didn't necessarily work, so we had to position ourselves where we could have good communications, which probably weren't the best locations strategically.

We soon began to realise that people wanted to get back to work, but barricades had been built on every single street coming off Cupar Street and they wouldn't remove them. So what we tried to do – a typical British Army response – was make them look a little nicer: 'Look, this is a bit ramshackle. Why don't you tidy it up a bit?' I remember that just down the bottom of Cupar Street on the corner was a factory which employed mainly blind and disabled people weaving baskets. An enormous number of the blind wanted to get to work, and of course they couldn't. So every morning the soldiers used to take these people down, and every evening bring them home. That was the very first bit of community relations that went on, and the soldiers were very good at it, so we immediately became popular, we immediately became liked. And of course we were fed cakes, buns, tea in unlimited quantities.

Rifleman, 1 Royal Green Jackets

My first five days in Belfast were spent on the junction of Grosvenor Road and Leeson Street in the Falls. Leeson Street became, in 1971, two years later, one of the worst streets in the Province, but it was fine then. We were protecting the Catholics from the Protestants and the Catholics brought out coffee and dinners to us. They were very good to us, excellent. They were really glad we were there: it was, 'Thank you for saving us.' We had our backs to them and our fronts to the Protestants over the other side of the road. There was some taunting from the Protestants but it was all fairly friendly, apart from one night when somebody over the Protestant side came across with what appeared to be a submachine gun and just sprayed the houses on the other side with machine-gun fire, a burst of about twenty rounds. We all got down and tried to crawl in between the cracks in the pavement. I'd cocked my weapon but I was told by my section commander not to open fire. I think he was Irish as well.

Then '69 was basically trying to win hearts and minds. There was no problem at all. There used to be three-man patrols in those days, and we'd walk and just carry on walking for twelve hours, just around the Falls, the Catholic area. We made our head-quarters in a paper mill in Northumberland Street, and we used to go to a school every evening where the locals used to come and play games with us.

Corporal, 2 Para

We didn't know what to expect at that time. We hadn't really got a clue why we were there. The first night, I remember we were all in a little Portakabin and the corporal, he says, 'Right, who's going to go out and get the fish and chips?' I mean you could just walk out. So a couple of us went into this fish and chip shop, just chatted to everybody, got us fish and chips and went back. Next day we moved into the company location which was Sugarfield Street, at the top end of the Shankill Road. We spent four very happy months there with nothing happening. We had, I think, one demonstration outside the little bakery where we were, and our OC just went outside and politely told the people that if they didn't clear off he would let his blokes loose on them. So they cleared off and came back next day and apologised.

Senior Officer, 1 Para

We went to Belfast in the October of '69. I was taken onto the Shankill the night Constable Arbuckle was shot. There was a pool of blood on the road and I remember going and walking round it with a bunch of flowers.

When we arrived, there were so-called no-go areas. Even British

11

troops weren't allowed in. I thought this was absolute nonsense. We were there to try and protect them, and that's what we were going to do. But we had to disobey all the logical military principles because of the political forces and because it was the United Kingdom. It was a frightening thing I found to watch in the Shankill Road at night people in Territorial Army uniforms, people carrying Union Jacks, singing God Save the Queen, and slinging petrol bombs at us. We'd be standing there with the police in front of us, because we were still sticking to the principles of Internal Security: police in the front line standing there, no shields, torches, truncheons, we behind with the wire, the armoured vehicles, the guns and everything. But as soon as they started to throw the bottles and things, the police would break up and there'd be blood and we would then have to move in.

Private, 1 Para

The only Internal Security drill we ever knew, or were ever taught, was the square. The front rank faced forward, the side ranks faced inwards and outwards to cover rooftops, and the back rank faced outwards. There was a banner man holding up the banner, saying, 'Halt. This is an illegal gathering.' That's what we used to do. We should have had a Justice of the Peace, but we used to have a policeman with us as the local authority instead. That was our IS drill. Only one man in the front rank had ammunition, the rest of us had blanks. We were meant to shoot the local ringleader. The platoon commander would identify the target, like: 'Man in red jumper, weapon in his hands, controlling. One round – fire.' We all used to fire; but only one man had the live round so they could never identify him. We had no batons, no shields, no baton guns, just CS gas. We did the square just to make a show, a fright. It looked ferocious, it was all show business, especially with the bayonets, before they took them off us. It worked in India, it probably worked in Saudi Arabia, or Kenya and Africa, but it would never have worked in the UK homeland.

Senior Officer, 1 Para

We started to develop street-fighting tactics to try and deal with the Shankill mobs. These were the Protestant mobs, and although the Protestant members of the Shankill suggested there were foreigners coming in and stirring it up, usually you could predict when the trouble would happen. After turning-out time and after the fish shops closed they'd all stand on the streets, some drunk would have a go and it would all build up. It usually wasn't necessary to do much. I found that by going over the wire, taking the padre or the RSM (regimental sergeant major) in a small group, you could go in amongst them, break up the groups and explain what was going on. You'd find they'd say, 'Ah, all right sir. I'll be going home now.' And they would disappear and go off, and there'd be no problems.

What we had to learn was how to communicate with people and to give them a feeling of security and confidence. So I said to everybody in the battalion, 'Whatever you do, no matter what the situation, smile. Disarm everybody with a smile. Greet them and laugh.' Because there's so much laughter in Northern Ireland and it seemed to me that if we could do that, then we would begin to get their confidence, providing we maintained the steel of the military presence. Combined with humour, we could perhaps then get some communication. Every Sunday, I detailed everybody in my headquarters to go to church. Everybody had to go to church. It was all part of the community relations game. The only way to get their confidence was to do what they wanted us to do: tea parties, helping with the chores, playing football with the kids – you name it, we did it. It was part of the integration.

When we went into such things we didn't have the kit, so I had to go down to a local factory and say: 'Look, there's my beret, I wonder if you can make me a number of sweaters that colour. Maroon. They've got to be under two pounds each.' They did it, and we had some lovely sweaters made. All the officers and warrant officers were given one each so they could go on these community relations larks looking reasonably tidy, not like bohemian authors.

The soldiers warmed to the idea. It was a challenge and they thought they were cracking it. But it took a long time to get the locals' confidence. They were trying desperately to convince us of the philosophy of the Protestant community: we are the people with the right; we look to the Queen; these people are infesting our country from the South; we don't want trouble but there are those who do; their birth rate is higher than ours and they're going to take us over. We slowly began to disillusion them about some of these things.

13

Corporal, 1 Para

I knew what was going on in Belfast, or I thought I did, but the bigotry and the hatred there was quite new to me. It threw me quite a bit, did it ever. I didn't believe that people could be that spitting type of bigotry, I didn't believe it existed, because I hadn't ever lived in the North. I knew Protestants in the South and went to school with them. We had a Protestant neighbour in Dublin: it didn't mean much. My father had been in the British Army. In fact, I'm the eighty-first member of my family to be in the British Army, on both sides of the family. I grew up with pictures of Michael Collins all over the house – we were totally against de Valera.

We used to patrol the Shankill and the Falls Road, the peace line was being created then, and people said to me when they heard my accent: 'Are you a Taig, a Fenian?' A Taig is a Catholic and I'd never heard that before I went to Northern Ireland as a soldier. I was actually advised, and I did it for a while, to tell people on the streets I came from Manchester. But people knew. People picked up my accent, especially on the Falls. Being Irish cost me sore ears, mostly from the Protestant side. A funny thing was said to me one night. I decided I wasn't going to masquerade as an Englishman any more, it seemed stupid once I got to know the situation. We were stood round and they were going on about Fenians. There'd been a lot of houses burned on both sides, and all these people were saying 'Fenians this, Fenians that', and all the rest of it. I turned round and I said, 'Well, I'm a Fenian.' They replied, 'But English Fenians are different to Irish Fenians.' That was said to me in 1969, and I couldn't believe it. I started to realise then what it was all about.

It was a confusing time, a very confusing time: but there again, a hell of a lot of Protestants took to me, more so than they did to the English blokes, for whatever reason I don't know.

Private, 1 Para

The civilians weren't too sure of us. We did have some trouble in the Shank, but on the Catholic side it was open arms. We couldn't go wrong there. These were early days. The Protestants were upset, because they were stopped doing what they wanted by the government abolishing the B Specials, which they did in October.

We were slowly filtered into locations up and down the peace line, and I ended up in Boundary Street where the local Corporation kept their dustbin wagons, and we had three-floor accommodation, which was quite good, actually. We were told we'd be there for a few months, so we did the best we could, painted it up and had ourselves a bath put in. We got on very well with the local Guinness people down the road, and got on very well with the females. Some of us got on very, very well with the females!

Not a lot really happened then. There were no problems about going out at all. We used to do observations from the top of the Divis Flats – always tea and coffee from the Catholics. We had a position down on the peace line, and every morning at 6.30 this little old lady used to travel across with a fully cooked breakfast for two of us, every morning – we used to fight to get that one. At Christmas we were invited out for dinners and on every step there was a bottle of whiskey to take back to the boys. It was brilliant. We felt like knights in shining armour, like Sir Galahad. We were the do-gooders: Her Majesty's Government had sent us there to put things right. At that stage I had no fear. Things were good.

Senior Officer, 1 Para

At that time we were not allowed to talk about either the UVF or the IRA. We were told that there was a sectarian problem, we were not to get involved, all we were to do was keep the peace. Our task was to maintain a balance between the Catholic community and the Protestant community and to indulge ourselves in community relations while keeping the lid on the violence. We were not in any way to infringe the basic principles that we had been given. The trouble was we were being drawn into the political level because we did not have any intelligence, and the police seemed even more desperate for knowledge. There was absolutely no information at all about people we wanted to know about. So we decided we had to do it ourselves and set about systematically building up a map of where people lived. We had about twenty patrols out every night, and more during the day and we were able, by talking around, to find out who lived in every house, how many people, where they worked. Slowly we built up a pattern, and as a result we were then able to pick up who was shacking up with who, whose husband wasn't actually quite as good to his wife

15

as he should be, and so on. We were then able to use those details as levers to get further information later. Because once a chap was found out by his wife, she'd give him the Belfast kiss, a bottle round his face and all the flesh hanging off. Rather nasty, but slowly we built up a massive dossier.

We also got drawn into the political bit through the Shankill Defence Association, which was allegedly the representative voice of the Shankill. I got on to a number of platforms with them and was invited to take military questions. It was incredible: you had instant politicians at any meeting you went to. I remember a great meeting of ex-servicemen at the school hall in Tennent Street. They were a very, very aggressive audience. The first question I got was, 'Sir, would you shoot a Protestant?' I was being invited to jump to my feet and counter by saying, 'I'm a good chap.' But you were really on your mettle on those occasions, the adrenalin was pumping, and I can remember saying to this bloke, 'If I see your face again I'll shoot you, you bugger.' It was the only way. You had to counter by attacking them, by amusing them slightly and returning the humour. If you got that right you'd get the response you needed, and by the end of the meeting we had a considerable amount of support. The ex-servicemen there were enormously helpful once they realised we were trying to do a job of work.

In addition to this street business, there was an awful lot of social activity. We got to know a large number of people. We went to a lot of parties and met people who we liked and they invited us back. In the early days we were living in school halls, pretty primeval conditions. There wasn't any water around, no means of laundering or washing, so they'd invite one out for a bath – and thereby hangs one or two tales. It was all fairly warm, fairly carefree, almost as if the people had suddenly found a wartime atmosphere and were genial and friendly. Underneath, there was still the basic bigotry, the ignorance, but there was always that hope, a certain amount of confidence between us and the people on the ground. We thought, naively, we had some solutions to the problems.

When we came back seven months later we'd lost that link. Once you get that warmth between people, in any community, in any walk of life, and you put somebody else in, it's all got to start again. It's impossible, that passing on of trust. You can't do it. I think the biggest mistake that was made in the beginning, and it's easy to say this now, was that we had the four-month tour. The battalion changed over after four months with all this knowledge, with all this confidence, and you put in another battalion which had a completely different view. So immediately in this Internal Security situation the thread of confidence was lost and the troubles began again. If we could have kept those battalions there a little longer whilst there was a little more political activity I believe we wouldn't have developed so drastically into the next phase of the operational situation. We could have perhaps avoided some of the bloodshed. But it just wasn't possible.

Private, 1 Para

When the boys left in February it was like the Wailing Wall of Jerusalem. All the girls were there crying and what-have-you. It had been a good adventure, a good experience. We did the job, and got on very well. Things certainly were different when we went back again, and that was within about six months.

Bricks and Gas
1970

Private, 2 Para

We'd heard about the initial troubles in '69 from the newspapers when we were in Anguilla. I'd always imagined Northern Ireland being like a Welsh mining area, and it showed a street map of Belfast: it could have been anywhere. We got on the ferry at Liverpool in February 1970 and, really, if you'd gone to sleep when you'd got on the ferry and woken up when it had docked, you'd still think you were in Liverpool. That amazed me – it was just like Liverpool.

When we arrived there wasn't any proper terrorist threat that we knew of, though the Intelligence people may have known there was going to be a phoenix rising from the ashes. So it felt strange: you could have been at home until the people opened their mouths. At first I found walking along carrying a rifle very embarrassing – embarrassing's not the word, more self-conscious – I wasn't embarrassed to think the Army was there, but self-conscious about walking about the High Street with a gun. We were restrained, but there was no need for restraint. What we were looking for was – in fact, it's hard to say what we were looking for in the first place, because during the day we patrolled round, stopped off for cups of tea, and in the evenings most of the work we did was with drunks, yobbos, stolen cars and the dancehalls turning out. They'd wait for each others' dancehalls to turn out and then go and battle each other, which was fists, bottles and glass: nothing really severe, more of a gang warfare, which you get in any big city, except that I suppose it was categorised Protestant versus Catholic. I arrested a drunk; that was probably the hardest thing on that tour. I can't remember any shots being fired against us. It was quite monotonous.

Corporal, 2 Para

We used to just wander around in pairs like policemen. You'd go out for a two-hour patrol and in two hours you drank twenty cups of tea because everybody wanted to give you a cup of tea and a sandwich. We called it the honeymoon tour. We had a disco every night and the girls used to come in, all the girls used to come in. That's where a lot of the lads met their wives. Because we were in a predominantly Protestant area we had all Protestants, but down at TAC HQ on Hastings Street, right on the peace line between the Falls and Shankill Roads, they had a big massive disco and used to get women from both sides. Everybody used to mix together. There was no trouble at all.

Private, 2 Para

Round at Albert Street Mill they had a fantastic discothèque. They'd done up the dance floor all black and psychedelic, murals, nude women on the walls, ultra-violet paintings. They had a really good disco, as good as any professional disco anywhere. Most of the girls that used to come in were in fact Catholic girls; one or two Protestant girls, but there wasn't that much tension there. They were a little bit shy, they didn't mix initially, but us, we weren't bothered. I mean, religion didn't come into it.

The women liked the soldiers because they had more to offer than football and motorbikes. Girls come and go, and obviously a lot of us soldiers did marry Irish girls. Not all of them happy, successful marriages: in fact a lot of them in the early days ended in divorce, separation. There's very few whose wives are still with them. A lot of the marriages have not worked out: whether it was the soldier, or that they were young and hero-worshipping – they jumped in with both feet.

Officer, Ulster Defence Regiment

I'd held a senior post in the B Specials, and when the Ulster Defence Regiment was mooted to replace the B Specials I said to my platoon, 'Gentlemen, this is the answer. I'm joining as a private soldier.' In April 1970 my company performed the very first UDR patrol in County Fermanagh.

Major, Ulster Defence Regiment

The UDR's job at first was very different from what we do today. Mine was one of the first operational companies deployed in Belfast. Our nightly tasks involved guarding some ten or twelve key installations in and around Belfast: the gasworks, the ship-yard, electricity stations, police stations, waterworks, all the places which were vital to the maintenance of normal life. Each night the men did their duties, slept through the hours, finished at 5 a.m., were relieved and stood down. They'd go back to base, put their weapons away, and have to find some way of getting home, because in those days not everybody had a car. If someone had a car they'd share, but then there were those who put their uniform in a suitcase and caught the first bus home to change to go to work.

That was the general pattern of soldiering for the following four years. People were flooding in. When we weren't going out on duty we were busy training or recruiting, testing people, getting them in, dealing with all the normal day-to-day activities of any formal unit of the Army. In the early days I used to drive the Land Rover, in uniform, because all the men would be deployed and I'd visit each of the men on the installations twice a night. As the company commander, I came in at seven o'clock, and didn't get home until everybody else had gone. I was probably doing that two or three nights a week.

Captain, 1 King's Own Scottish Borderers

We flew from Germany to Belfast in April 1970 wondering how the men would react to dealing with problems in the UK. We'd been in Aden and Borneo, and as far as the soldiers were concerned that was easy because they were dealing with a person of a different colour, which at that time, during the decline of the colonial era, was significant. When suddenly asked to deal with an operation within the United Kingdom, certainly I thought: 'How is the soldier going to react to these people, apparently his own kith and kin?' I remember my fears were dispelled on the first riot. We had a rock slung at us, so there was the enemy: no problem at all. In fact, it was probably much easier to deal with the situation because we had come from being in Germany, from being part of the NATO shield. What does the NATO shield mean to privates? Very little. Standing in the streets of Belfast in a riot, the task was tangible. I think we all found it very clear: we were there to stop rioting and if we could react quick enough, then we could stop a riot.

Subaltern, 1 King's Own Scottish Borderers

'Mrs Murphy's murderers', the King's Own Scottish Borderers were known as. Mrs Murphy had been killed by a ricochet in 1920 in what is now the South, and in Belfast there were still people who called us that fifty years later. I hadn't come across the Irish before then and had no particular feelings in any political way about the situation. I really didn't know very much about the IRA. I thought it was no more than a historical anomaly. I didn't feel for a moment that they were the threat. I felt that we were going simply to help the police out because they were having a hard time. There was no view that we were going to tackle the IRA because they weren't significant. It was really civil disturbance on both sides and I probably was not even very clear as to the shades of influence between the Catholics and the Protestants. I had some idea of the background but that really didn't concern me. I was there just to calm things down: you know, whichever crowd I was told to go and stand in the way of, I would go and stand there.

Accommodation was very basic indeed, but no different from going on field-training procedure. Although there were great photographs of soldiers sleeping in the streets, that really was no irritation whatsoever; if anything, it contributed to the fun, the feeling that you were there to do a short job, and do it as well as you could.

We once spent two weeks sleeping in a public lavatory on the Catholic/Protestant interface at the top of the Shankill Road. If you were within, literally, seconds of those flashpoints, if you could get there in seconds, you could stop a riot. But if you took ten minutes to get there, it was too late.

Marine, 45 Commando

We got sent over to cover the Orange marches in West Belfast. We never saw them, we were too busy keeping the crowds back.

21

In late June there'd been some shooting from the Ardoyne into a Protestant area, they'd hit a young girl and the Protestants were coming in to burn the place out. We were there to protect the Catholics, because they were having a rough deal, everybody agreed.

We were dropped off at Butler Street, on the edge of the Ardoyne. I said: 'Right. Nobody gets through.' And this crowd came round the corner and just kept coming and coming. And that was the most frightening thing – I mean, riots these days ain't riots – there were thousands of them and eighteen of us. We were all looking at each other waiting for the first one to run. I'd have been the second, but there ain't no way I was going to be the first.

We just stood our ground. We had a single span of Dannert wire across the street and we started firing CS gas, because we didn't have rubber bullets in those days. We had the old-style steel helmets with visors, the metal shields with which you could cover either your face or your bollocks – it was up to you – and the old green combat trousers and combat gear. That was one of the first big riots so we hadn't switched then, but after that we used to shove paperback books inside our socks. You didn't really notice when you were getting hit, but when you'd come out of it you'd be black and blue. And you couldn't get derigged because at that stage we were on immediate reserve, ten minutes for anywhere in Belfast and thirty minutes' notice for the rest of the Province.

That day every soldier in Belfast was deployed. There were no reserves. The only people left in the camp were the cooks and clerks. We were sixty-eight hours in that one street, and there was a thing in the *Mirror*, which doesn't normally like troops. Some civvie car firm was going on strike for extra money and a thirty-five-hour week, and somehow they'd photographed our lads as we came back in at the end of the riot, and there on the centre pages was a photograph of a corporal in a stripped-down Land Rover: he was sitting on the tailgate and had been unfastening his puttees while he was talking to his mates, and he'd fallen asleep with his puttee in his hand, with the rain coming down. The comment was: 'On strike for a thirty-five-hour week already earning twice the money these lads earn – and they've just come back after sixty-eight hours on the streets and they'll be back out again in twenty-four hours.'

Bricks and Gas

Captain, 1 King's Own Scottish Borderers

I remember those riots in Ardoyne as being particularly vicious.
When you looked up, the air was full of rocks, literally full of
rocks. They very quickly ripped up all the paving stones, just
dug them up and broke them, and that was the ammunition. I
remember writing home and saying, 'Go to a sports shop and send
me a box.' Quite a lot of us had shin pads and cricket boxes sent
out.

In the early days they were very fond of seizing buses and
burning them. I remember watching them prepare a big barricade
and hijack a bus. I suddenly saw, through the barricade, a couple
of bus inspectors racing down the road to talk to the rioters. We
subsequently discovered that what they'd said was, 'Look, please,
that's a brand new Leyland Atlantean. We'll get you an old bus
out of the depot if we can have our new one back.' But the rioters
set fire to it all the same.

Subaltern, 1 King's Own Scottish Borderers

The streets were the settings for the riot, but once the riot had
finished the ghettos went back to being villages again. I never felt
after a riot that I couldn't walk out and go to the local shops. And
the rioting seemed to be enjoyed by both sides, by the soldiers as
much as the rioters. It was a bit of a game really, until the shooting
started. And I never felt that I was being taken advantage of by
the government or the system, being told to stand there and take
the hail of bottles and bricks. The outrage in the papers about
how our soldiers shouldn't have to put up with it, I never really
felt that at all. I just felt I was doing a job, and it was a bit more
interesting than some of the other things I might have been doing.

Private, 1 King's Own Scottish Borderers

In the Ardoyne, off the Crumlin Road, there was a massive big
factory called Flax Street Mill and we were just about a hundred
metres away from it. There was a big threat to this mill because
it was Protestant-owned and right in the middle of the Ardoyne,
a Catholic stronghold, and we had to guard it. They had a citizens'
thing going at the time, and one of their vigilantes spotted this

chap climbing over the fence of the main gate, which was all padlocked, and breaking into the mill. We went down, grabbed the guy, up against the gates and asked him what the hell he was on about. He was saying: 'I own the mill, I own the mill.' And he was American, this guy, and he was swearing away. Well, we were quite happy about this, we'd been guarding the place for a week and nothing had happened, and all of a sudden we had a capture, an excuse to get down to the company HQ in Leopold Street and have a cup of tea. So, this guy was a wee bit sore around the crotch area and everything, but we managed to take him on down. The police came, got him, took him round to Tennent Street, just round the corner, and the word came back and we were sent for. The guy *was* the mill owner, he'd forgot his key. We had to go and apologise. No way were we going to. I said, 'You should be chuffed that we arrested you, you should be quite pleased.' He said, 'Well, I see the funny side of it now, Jock, but I did think at the time there was no need to put your knee in my balls.'

Corporal, 1 King's Own Scottish Borderers

It was just before the Falls Road curfew and we were doing an outer perimeter patrol in Unity Flats near the Shankill Road. We were coming across some waste ground, open scrubby parkland with derelicts, when we got opened up on by Protestant gunmen, definitely by Protestant gunmen. The Protestants were firing into the Divis Flats, and as far as they were concerned we were tarred and classed as the same, we were the baddies too, because we were protecting the Catholics in the Divis and Unity Flats. We were crossing in single file, very exposed, when we come under fire. The bullets were hitting the ground, and we were shocked, we couldn't believe it was for real. It was the first time they'd actually opened fire on us. Up till then they'd only been just rioting and throwing bricks. Well, we just hit the deck, crawled round the bushes. Nobody returned fire: we thought we'd better not because we couldn't see a real target, only the gun flashes coming at us. I got on the radio and gave a contact report. I asked permission to put on the steel helmets instead of our Glengarries. 'No' was the answer I got for that.

Bricks and Gas

Corporal, 1 King's Own Scottish Borderers

When the curfew was imposed on 3 July we were split up into small detachments of three men and put out at various road junctions. We were told to stay there and keep the curfew. The rules were given that if anybody was out, we were not, obviously, to open fire indiscriminately but to challenge them and find out why they were on the street. If they were unaware of the curfew, we were to make them aware of the situation and then urge them to go indoors under cover and stay there until such time as they were allowed out. There was a helicopter going round at various intervals giving Tannoy messages.

The curfew area was the Falls, lower Shankill, Unity Flats, Turf Lodge, Ardoyne, all that part. The actual city centre didn't have a curfew. You could draw a line right along Royal Avenue and dog-leg it down Churchill Street, and anything above that line was in the curfew. If I remember right, there wasn't much movement in the city centre at all. I was at the Unity Flats junction, and the only traffic I remember was a milk lorry and some bread vans, which were allowed to travel around. The streets were dead, very dead, deserted, in a major city. The traffic lights were still going as if there were people there, still going in sequence, but no traffic. That's what struck me: watching those traffic lights working and nothing going through them, still continuing to function. It was as if there'd been a nuclear war and I was the only one left. The shops were all shut, everything was shut. I tell you what else struck me: the newspapers blowing about the streets, and nothing. It was just like one of those things you see in a movie. Deserted. The place was just deserted.

When the curfew ended, it started off very, very slowly. You got the odd person coming out, mainly the older people first, and it wasn't for about an hour after that that the rest came out in any great volume. Things started to bustle slowly. I think the end of the curfew was put over radio and television, but we bought a paper to find out what was happening, because we were on the ground all the time. We did it for five days, and we were fed on the ground: we got fed where we got fed. I mean, we slept where we could sleep, so to speak, we slept in the streets. We had a blanket and a sleeping bag between three of us. There was only one down at a time and two was up. So you worked it between yourselves. Soldiers sleep anywhere, I mean, you can actually sleep anywhere. In fact, it's not that uncomfortable.

After the curfew it was mainly a lot of searching being done. I think the politics – looking back and understanding what I understand now – I think what the commanders were probably told was not to antagonise the situation, to try and keep the calm and have as much low profile as possible, to go in but not stir things up unnecessarily. Because the place was like a tinderbox.

Private, 1 Para

The curfew stemmed from the time the Scottish regiment did those searches, and that was probably when the real trouble started – not from '69, with all the civil rights and the focus of attention on the plight of the Catholics, but 1970. That's when the IRA first emerged. They'd say, 'Look what the soldiers are doing to you. Look how they treat you. We want to protect you.' And the people would think, 'Ah, we need some protection here.' That way the IRA got support for their cause, and still does. The IRA could have laid dormant for years, but they were looking for an excuse and they found it then, during that time when that Scotch regiment did those searches.

Corporal, 1 King's Own Scottish Borderers

We were the first unit to be issued with rubber bullets. It was 1970, June or July. I've got photographs from the paper of us in the Crumlin Road Jail doing trials with the new Macralon shields, the Macralon helmet – which actually saved my life from a petrol bomb – and the rubber bullet guns, the FRGs. We were the first troops on the ground to actually be issued with them because we were in the Falls, New Lodge, Shankill, Unity Flats, all the hard areas. I thought the new guns were marvellous; before, what we had was a gun that you put into an aircraft to fire a cartridge in to start the engine, and all they'd done was extend a barrel on it. The FRG was the same gun, same action, which we use today, with a barrel on it and a shell. There's a wee button on the side, you'd push that, break the gun in half, put the bullet in, shut it up, push the button again, which took off the safety catch, and it was ready to fire. The bullet was rubber; it wasn't PVC till later on.

26

Bricks and Gas

Subaltern, 1 King's Own Scottish Borderers

The FRG guns were very inaccurate. We were meant to bounce the rubber bullets off the ground but that was hopeless, so we ended up firing them directly at people's feet but, frankly, it really didn't stop anybody. The main effect was the noise: it produced this 'crack-crack', and that created a fear on both sides and actually made people run away. I think the noise was more effective than the bullets themselves, and in the same way the Saracens, the six-wheeled armoured vehicles we used, whined terrifically excitingly compared with the Pigs, which just made a nice hum. We would sometimes quite consciously decide it was worth putting in the Saracens because they had this scream from the gearbox. If you wanted to stop a crowd coming down a road the whining and screaming really was most intimidating, and in some cases we could actually sort out the problem before we even got out of the vehicles.

The crack and bang of firing CS gas canisters similarly helped prevent the riots becoming a form that was acceptable. Nothing would change the direction of a riot unless something happened on one side or the other to destabilise it, and firing rubber bullets or gas altered the circumstances and thus made a riot more likely to come to a conclusion sooner rather than later. Generally the conclusion reached was the one we wanted, but occasionally the riot escalated and we were landed with far more trouble than we'd started with. Then we really were responsible for the escalation, but mostly the methods we employed in changing the circumstances worked.

We didn't often have problems from CS gas because we mostly fired away from ourselves. But sometimes the wind wasn't all that obliging or the respirators didn't work very well, and then you became aware that it was thoroughly nasty. It smelt like being too close to a newly struck match: that inhibiting aroma stuck in the nose and throat. You felt that you were about to cave in, that if you stayed there a moment longer life would be just impossible. But it caused panic rather than any real symptoms, and if you were strong enough you could breathe it perfectly properly. It was never likely to produce serious ill effects, and nor was it designed to, and in fact many of the rioters got used to it and could cope with just simple handkerchiefs over their mouths. It didn't cause the panic in them that it would have caused in our soldiers if they'd unmasked, and it became counterproductive if it crept, as of course it did, into buildings and affected people in their homes who were quite uninvolved. So we found it was not really a precise enough aid to catching people and putting them in jail.

Sergeant, 1 King's Own Scottish Borderers

In our area, the New Lodge, they tended to be fairly set-piece riots at that time. One side would come out and air their grievances, then there'd be a lull of about ten days to two weeks, and then the other side would do the same. I think only once was there intercommunal rioting and strife. There was a lot of burning out by the Protestants of Catholic-owned bars and bookie shops, those sort of places, but there wasn't any great response from the Catholic community on the interface to cross the line, come over and burn up the Protestants. We had to be there to make sure there was no trouble between the two, but it wasn't that we were actually keeping the two communities apart physically. It tended to be one side rioting against the security forces, then there'd be a calm, and then the other side would riot against the security forces. So we ended up very much the German sandwich.

There was always a sort of deadline for the riot. It would normally go on for about eighteen hours and then whichever side you were facing would call a halt for tea and everybody would go home satisfied. Rather like I imagine wars in the sixteenth/seventeeth century: you know, the wives would turn up and battle would end. Both sides were fairly naive, and had a sort of mutual respect – much more than there is today.

The concentration of troops and civilians in a small area like the New Lodge was tremendous: the rioters numbered thousands, and one particular night I saw eleven companies from different regiments in there. And of course, when you had troops in that sort of strength, inevitably there was damage across the board, doors getting kicked in, innocent people being dragged out. The whole thing sort of fuelled itself after a while.

Staff-Sergeant, Royal Army Ordnance Corps

You were always conscious of the theatrical side of life. I think the best comment I ever heard about the Irish was by an Irishman.

He said: 'The Irish don't know what they really want, but they'll fight like hell to get it.' And at the same time they will turn the emotion on and off.

Once I went down the New Lodge Road, which is the heart of the Catholic area, and dealt with this parcel outside a shop. A boy came up and said: 'Me mother says would you all like a cup of tea?' Now this was a surprise. 'Yeah, lovely.' So while I was carrying on he wandered off, then came back, and was speaking to a member of the cordon. 'Me mother wants to know if you English bastards want sugar?' And they would see our Land Rovers – our vehicles were very identifiable, red wings on the sides – going down New Lodge to deal with something, and you'd be a hero: 'Grand lad. Doing a great job.' Two hours later you'd be going down the same road to somewhere else and they'd be bricking you as you went through.

There were two RAOC staff sergeants in Belfast then and we were stationed with an infantry battalion in Girdwood Park. We were working twenty-four hours on and twenty-four off, and since we'd got nowhere much to go on our day off, one of our favourite habits was to wander into court to watch the excuses of the previous night's riots, and not least watch the reactions of the soldiers. The squaddie humour never ceased to amaze me. I well remember one incident where Paddy'd been in a riot down the New Lodge Road and he'd got picked up by an Army snatch squad. Now, the snatch squad was a bundle of about five men, the big heavies, who'd run out and grab the ringleader or whoever. They were lightly armed, obviously they didn't carry personal weapons, so they'd rely on the nightstick. Well, this Irishman came into court, his head swathed in bandages, and his lawyer made a big thing of this, bringing out the Army brutality bit, and Jock was standing there like Neanderthal man, a Kosbie (King's Own Scottish Borderers), four-square and squat and slow. The lawyer said, 'You struck my client on the head?' 'Aye.' 'But why did you hit him?' 'He would nae stop.' 'Yes, but why did you hit him with that stick?' 'I had nae got my rifle with me.' The court came to a grinding halt.

Subaltern, 1 King's Own Scottish Borderers

In late July the riots had been going on for two or three days around the New Lodge. They had been burning out cinemas, and the rioters were moving up and down the New Lodge Road while we blocked the side streets with men rather than any barriers, just to prevent them coming through. We were faced with petrol-bombing and stoning and bottles. The bottles proved most ineffective, most unalarming once they actually hit you. They looked good but they really did not hurt. Stones only hurt if they hit you in the shins, but on the body or the head, again almost irrelevant.

The petrol bombs were more alarming. By that time petrol-bombing was considered to be illegal to the extent that people could be shot for it. In one particular incident we were really being attacked and the platoon commander decided that it had to stop because his platoon was actually threatened, which could be the case if petrol bombs were thrown in sufficient quantity. The platoon commander decided to shoot one of the petrol-bombers, which was done, and he was dragged away before we could get to the body. There was outrage and everything else expressed by the politicians on various sides, but I wasn't aware of any increased animosity from the people that we were trying to cope with. Nor do I remember anyone saying, 'Well done, you plugged him' or anything like that. At that stage we were trying to get our PR right and I don't think we made too much fuss about the fact that we had shot him.

Corporal, 1 King's Own Scottish Borderers

The most serious rioting we could see that night came from the bottom of the New Lodge. It was still pitch dark, and as we were heading down the New Lodge Road, two Pigs up and one Pig back, I saw a fluttering of light up front. The next moment the whole sky just lit up. A petrol bomb hit the top of the Pig, bounced off a stretcher, hit the top of my helmet, exploded and went over the top of the man next to me. In fact, I've got a press cutting of that. We'd just been issued the new helmets with the visors and the photograph says: 'SPACE-AGE HELMET SAVES YOUNG SOLDIER'. Our boots and everything were on fire, we started jumping about to put them out, and then another one hit the Pig ahead, another two came over the top and exploded beside us, then another one hit the front of the Pig behind and then another hit the middle Pig. By this time about eight petrol bombs had been thrown at us. We stopped and, as the NCOs, gave the warning that if anyone threw any more we'd open fire. More came across and we saw this guy on the corner lighting another one. So I gave the word to open fire, and three other people simultaneously, unbeknown to me, were telling others to open fire, and one of the petrol-bombers was hit twice. He went down. As they dragged him away we rushed forward in a baton charge to try and recover the body, but we couldn't see anything. They then petrol-bombed us again as we got caught in some Dannert wire laid across the road, so we had to withdraw a bit and recover ourselves. Things started to calm down then and a couple of civilians came forward and asked if we could get an ambulance because someone had been injured or shot. An ambulance arrived and we then withdrew out of there, just in order not to push the situation any further.

In fact, we reckoned – you'll probably not be able to print this – we reckoned there were two people shot that night, because two separate targets were picked out. Three lots of petrol bombs were coming from different directions, and to this day we swear we hit two of them. Two were seen to go down, but only one was actually claimed by them. His body was taken away to the Mater Hospital. We were right new, green at the game. It wouldn't happen nowadays. The first thing you do is secure the body, because you've got to keep the forensic evidence. In those days we were just completely green, so the body was off.

After that we regrouped and stayed on the street until about half-six in the morning when tea and sandwiches were brought out to us by the Protestants. They knew there'd been shooting, it went round the place like wildfire. They knew we'd opened fire, and they thought that was the first time troops had ever opened fire on a petrol-bomber. The rioters started to come back out again in force when the milk lorry came round, at first light. They started collecting crates of bottles off the milk lorry as ammunition, and the tricolours were up in force. The company commander and the sergeant major were standing at the back of the Land Rover. When they moved forward to try and talk to one of the leaders, they were just lost in a hail of bottles.

Then followed five nights of continuous rioting, non-stop. It was fierce, very tiring. We used to have a bell in the camp which we used to stand to. Platoons were relieved in line as you went back: regroup, wash, shave, dress, have something to eat and a quick cup. This bell was used to get you up, get you back out again. You were lucky if you were getting about two hours' sleep a day. You used to sleep with your boots and your flak jacket on and your CS grenades in your jacket, which were leaking half the time. That whole tour was literally like that. Non-stop for the whole four and a half months. We were busy. It was one of the hardest tours I've ever done in fact, that very first one. Physically and mentally it was the hardest.

Corporal, 1 King's Own Scottish Borderers

We'd been involved for two months in Unity Flats, which is Catholic. We knew everybody by name, and they knew us by name, it was quite intimate. The policy was: get to know the people, help them as much as you can, so we were building community swing parks, trying to build trust. People in the Protestant areas were doing the same.

One Saturday in August we got brought back because six, seven thousand Protestants were outside Unity Flats, co-ordinated to invade and burn the place down. It was a nice day and they'd all come back from the football. The Catholics came out to antagonise this lot and remarks were being passed and returned. So our platoon marched down the front of the Catholics, halted, and they all thought we were going to turn outwards to take on the Protestants. So did we. But we got turned inwards to face the Catholics and were told, 'Right, get that lot back in through that door there.' It was just an ordinary door and three hundred of them. So the platoon commander got onto the Tannoy and told them, 'Women and children, please move back.' Got no response. Next thing we knew we were being hit with sinks, you name it, from the roof above us. We then got: 'Go. Remove them.' So we moved them back through. We had to use hand-to-hand fighting and CS gas to get them back through the door. The guy standing next to me, his girlfriend was in the crowd, and she actually hit him on the head and tried to stick a bottle inside his throat. That was his girlfriend and he'd been going out with her for the last two months! We'd been there for two months and we'd got to know them. Just shows how quick they turned on you.

At one stage in that battle there, myself and another man stopped six youths who had broken into the back of a butcher's shop to steal our weapons. There were magazines stacked up in there, and the weapons weren't even padlocked. The signalman was the only guy left inside that little shop and he had the headset on and didn't hear a thing when they battered the back door down. When we went in they were starting to pass the weapons out, so I picked up the nearest thing, a juice bottle, and hit this guy with it. They then all started going into reaction, held the door and began pushing beds in front of it.

They were being inspired by someone who was far more advanced about the situation than we could predict. They'd obviously cased the joint, it was a come-on: while we were all being engaged out the front, there they were stealing the weapons at the back of the shop.

That was our first encounter with hand-to-hand fighting. I mean, people were actually gripping you by the throat, and you were trying to hit them with the baton at the same time. There was kicking and kneeing, my shoulder got dislocated by a cobble, guys were getting hit in the head with bricks, there was people going down left, right and centre. It was really vicious. They were giving more than we were giving. I mean we were a bit restrained, a bit more analytic, so to speak.

The situation quietened when we secured the butcher's shop. Once we'd got that back door closed they started to go away. We were really green. I mean, we were using IS tactics, playing cricket. But they weren't playing cricket at all: they were out to win, first chance they got.

Private, 1 Para

We went back again to Belfast in September 1970, to Palace Barracks, at Holywood. When we arrived, the commanding officer said that as reserve battalion we would never go on the streets unless the place was running with blood. I remember putting my suitcase down, sorting my locker out, getting an issue of flak jackets – not that I asked, we had flak jackets given to us anyway – and being called out. We'd just arrived, and we were on the Shankill! The King's Regiment were having a few problems, they'd been turned off the bottom of the Shankill, and it was chaos. They fired the gas and they missed the crowds, and it landed amongst us. Our respirators were still packed, we stood behind the Pigs and got gassed quite severely. Gas is not nice, no – you can be in pain. We were out there in an IS situation getting gassed by friendly forces. When we got there they were saying, 'Take your helmets off, put your berets on', so the people could remember who we were from our previous tour. We took our helmets off and put our berets on, and we got bricked even more. We got bricked and gassed, so I was disillusioned with it. The change from when we were last there seven months before was very saddening, disturbing. I must admit I was getting frightened. This shouldn't have been happening. You couldn't put your finger on what had gone wrong: there were lorries burning on the streets, paving stones ripped up – it was different.

I was shocked at the changes. We were expecting the same as when we left in February. We went to visit people who we'd seen earlier in the year, but they weren't the same. They did speak, but they were not like they were. They never told us why, that was for their own community: you had to be part of their community before they'd tell you what was going on, like anywhere else. I popped up to see the old lady, the one who'd brought us breakfast every morning. Before I'd seen her every day for four months, and she'd got to like me. But this time she didn't want to know. It had gone from open arms to, not so much hostility at this time, but wariness of the armed forces, the security forces. Before, the door had always been open, the doors were closed this time, a great change, and that was within a period of a few months. They would look at you and try to be friendly, but . . . like, before there was a little shop just off Crimea Street, and the man and his wife were terrific. As we had nowhere else to go they always got baps in for us to make our sandwiches – we would pay for them! Then the shop was burnt down because they'd been friendly with us. It was getting to that stage now. I saw them, and they weren't nice. Fear had caused that reaction.

Senior Officer, 1 Para

There was an incredible change in the attitude during the course of 1970, and I think it stemmed to a large extent from disillusionment. The first time we went in there, October '69 to February 1970, there had been this feeling of hope, but by September that year the frustrations had set in on the streets and of course that was another fillip to the rioting. They couldn't get out, they couldn't get what they wanted, and they realised that the situation didn't have any solution. At that time the IRA were beginning to flex their muscles, although it wasn't until way into 1971 that Tony Farrar-Hockley said, 'The IRA are behind this.' Nobody was talking about it before. You were not permitted to talk about it, you couldn't declare the IRA as the culprits. It was all political sectarian violence, one of those things which occurred because

34

the Prods had been so beastly to the Catholics for so many years, and it was historical, and so forth.

Subaltern, 1 Royal Regiment of Wales

We went out to Belfast and immediately got involved in those Protestant riots up and down the Shankill, the every-Saturday-afternoon riot of the football supporters coming back up from the football ground and past the Unity Flats. The rioting was vicious. It was vicious, it was nasty, it was frightening. I still have the chisel that stuck in the door behind me, rather like some arrow from a Western. I never discovered where it came from, but it's a very nice chisel, I assure you. I recall the RSM walking up and down in the front rank with his pacing stick, declaiming: 'Well, boys, no need to worry, only just a little bit of stone-throwing. Steady boys, steady boys. No need to panic.' A large brick hit him on the head, and he was carried off shouting: 'Bugger me, I'm going to get that sod!'

Corporal, 2 Para

We'd gone to a riot in Flax Street. Everybody went. If you was on fatigues, you'd leave the fatigues and get out just to go to the riot. There'd be about seventeen inside the back of the Pig. You can only get about ten in a Pig but everybody would just try and get in to get to the riot. We were expecting a small riot and as we drove up the corporal was holding the doors, saying, 'When we get out, we'll rush, charge, and beat the hell out of 'em.' As we got there he opened the back doors and we thought, 'Bloody hell!' There was millions of them. And as the Pig stopped, we jumped out the back, banged into each other and fell on the street, and the rest fell out on top of us in a big heap. All the Paddys started laughing at us. We had our rifles tagged to our wrists and of course there was a sling round somebody's neck and you was trying to get your rifle out and they started throwing bricks at us. They couldn't throw straight for laughing at us.

Private, 1 Para

The way we lived was fantastic. You'd walk into a warehouse, it was always dry, the food was always fantastic, everything was very good. I don't think anybody had any complaints at all about conditions, it was marvellous. It was a very glamorous job. I mean that. If you were in Belfast I think it was very glamorous. It was very strange because it's paradoxical to call Northern Ireland glamorous. But it was. I think if you were walking down the city centre you were like King Dick. In London the Met Police think it's a very glamorous job, you see them strutting around – same in Ireland with the troops: power. This is the point: if you are in your own environment then you are in control of the situation. You are King Dick. It's a crazy thing to say, but you were, you were in command of the situation, because you had your gun, you had your radio and you had command over all the things you were trained for. In a city environment it was down to you.

Belfast then was tremendous. You'd come off the streets from a riot in the Falls and for 2p you could say hello to your wife. You'd have glass in your hair and your beret, and she'd say: 'Everyone's sitting here, we've been watching the television this afternoon.' You might have seen it too, and I thought that was amazing. Whereas before, in Aden and Borneo, you'd be waiting for that letter. It was absolutely amazing: you could actually leave a scene, an incident, and you could be talking to your wife in her front room. The MOD, the generals, the civil servants could visit there as well, take the shuttle, go across and see for themselves. But most important of all was the glamour. You could watch yourself on telly that evening. You could see the incidents: that's communication, but it also brought home to people what conditions were like for the soldiers. The gap was much closer, and so things got done.

Subaltern, 1 Royal Regiment of Wales

It was peaks and troughs. Our particular company tried to live life to the fullest, and we were the envy of everybody. We were five officers and we used to hold a black-tie evening every week. Just a couple of glasses of wine and a glass of port, that was all, but we dressed up and we made an issue of it, partly because it was our night off and partly because it was relief. I'm actually probably one of the few people who's faced a riot in a black tie and a black jacket and a steel helmet, with a glass of port in one hand and a baton in the other. And for that I got two bricks in my knees one after the other, and I ruined the dinner jacket.

And of course that was the beginning of the great disco era, when there were discos in every single location – biggest knocking shops in Belfast, weren't they? I lived next door to one in an old church hall in Percy Street: I mean, the name says it all.

Private, 1 Para

I thought the nicest thing about Ireland, the most pleasant memory, was the women. I don't think there's another place like it. 2 Para had gone to Belfast for their first tour and I'd heard stories about these discos. But imagine, you come to a location with three platoons, one on the streets, one on sentry duty and one on stand-by, so there's thirty guys on stand-by sitting around this disco, music fantastic and all these fifteen upwards incredibly attractive ladies, and all of a sudden the bleeper goes and there's our little group left because the stand-by platoon was called out. It was absolutely amazing. I mean, I remember the stories about the Americans during the war and all that, but this was true and it was fantastic. I think the only thing that spoiled the girls was the accents because some of those Belfast accents were terrible, but I think the women were absolutely fantastic, different attitude altogether. In fact it's a shame there's trouble over there because if there was more toing and froing I don't think Brits would go to Spain for their holidays, I think they'd go to Belfast and Ireland because of the crumpet.

Sergeant, 2 Para

If World War III broke out and you were off duty, you'd have nothing to do. So I decided to show blue movies – not for my own profit, but because I always had that entrepreneurial skill. I'm good at procuring, negotiating, and I used to go round bases all over Northern Ireland, to the Air Corps at Long Kesh, everywhere. I'd take six films from a pool of forty, eight millimetre, all silent, because I wasn't that sophisticated. It was absolutely fantastic, like a spiral ride. We weren't ripping people off; we used to have collections after the shows to cover the wear and tear on the films. It was very good. But because I was so successful the old jealousy started creeping in, so I decided to go into clothing, because they make shirts in Ireland. I rang up some manufacturers, went round the camps with the old suitcase and took orders for shirts and jeans. I did very well. I fitted the colonel up with a black shirt and an incredible pair of tartan golfing trousers, which cost me an arm and a leg. That was a good tour.

Sergeant, 1 Para

I used to fill in Freepost ads out of the newspapers: double glazing, encyclopedias, hair transplants – everything. I picked on one of the guys who kept on about not getting any mail from home. I filled in all the coupons in this corporal's name and he got bags and bags of mail for months after: bullworkers, 'Learn to speak Japanese' records, anything I could find for him. He got one letter apologising that 'because of the present troubles in Northern Ireland we are unable to send you a greenhouse'! I mean, that corporal was going daft.

Captain, 1 Para

You see, there was Northern Ireland and Northern Ireland. There were the streets of Belfast, the well-known battlefields of Belfast: the Republican areas, the Shankill Road, the Ballymacarrett and the Newtownards Road. But outside, in the country, from Palace Barracks going east, you'd come to the northern County Down coast which is full of pleasant little villages along the south side of Belfast Lough. Bangor was a nice seaside town, like many British resorts. The boys would go there in the evening: discos, pubs and all the rest of it. So in some sense you were living in a normal community: the keen fishermen would join the local fishing club, for example.

So you had this slightly schizophrenic existence. I always used to think of the parallel with the fighter or bomber pilot of the Second War. He lived a schizophrenic existence: he would kiss his wife goodbye, cycle or drive or walk to his airfield, get on board his bomber, have twelve hours of merry hell and, if he survived, land his bomber, go back, kiss his wife hello and attempt to live a normal domestic life until he went again, Well, that to some extent was the way we, as a resident battalion on an eighteen-month tour, lived there, unlike the four-month *roulement* battalions who were living in the middle of it and for whom it was unrelenting. But for us it was fighting, fucking and fishing, basically. For that eighteen-month tour we brought back seventy Irish wives: something like ten per cent of the battalion married Northern Irish girls.

Chaplain, 2 Para

Marriages were an awful problem. In the early days, the soldier would do a four-month tour, get his leave at the end of it, go back to Ireland, marry a girl and bring her out to Germany. For her it was a passport out of Ireland, and the romance of the soldier: the Irish are very conscious of the military and romance. And of course, she'd find herself in a hiring in Germany where nobody spoke English and the husband away for six months of the year. Such marriages often fell flat very quickly, so we tried to discourage them; but it was not easy.

Lieutenant, 1 Coldstream Guards

The first time we were actively deployed in Londonderry was at seven o'clock on New Year's Eve 1970. Ours was the first company onto the streets from the Waterloo car park. Our helmets weren't actually polished, but they were brightly painted, and all we had were the small square metal shields. Everyone was intent that the Guardsmen kept the step, by the right, as we marched out. The first thing that hit us was a piano from the fifth floor of the Embassy Ballroom where there was a New Year's Eve party going on, and the CSM was shouting at the Guardsmen to keep the dressing. The piano was just hurled out on top of us, followed by chairs and goodness knows what. Eventually we got the message and rapidly disappeared into doorways. We didn't get back till four in the morning, and I suppose we realised then that it wasn't going to be a quick thing. The bitterness in the young people in the Bogside was there to be seen and I think it came home to us all very quickly that it was going to go on for some time.

The Shooting Starts
1971

Private, 1 Para

It was New Year 1971. The Ballymurphy had really blown up and I was sent up there to help the Royal Anglians out, driving a Saracen ambulance. I ended up there for about three weeks, and it just kept blowing up. One night I brought the Saracen down to the Bullring in the Ballymurphy and there was a lot of shooting going on, petrol-bombing, and they came up and attacked me. I was on my own in the Saracen, but all I did was just haul down, pull all the battle hatches in, and I was all right. They hit it with five or six petrol bombs, the whole thing looked ablaze, but it didn't matter because the flames didn't get in. You're quite safe inside. They knew that once you'd hauled down you were driving on periscopes and that if they threw paint at you, you couldn't see, but what they didn't realise was that you carried a spare set and you changed them from the inside. It took about two seconds, so all you did was pull the periscope down and shove another one in.

Lieutenant, 2 Royal Anglian

The Ballymurphy was the hub of the trouble in Belfast. They would come out and riot every night, on the nose, and it went on day and night. We heard shooting, mainly 'overs', Protestants and Catholics shooting each other. Certainly the Ballymurphy had a siege mentality: you very rarely went out into the estate, you probably did about one patrol a day because if you did more you'd just get cut off, and we weren't in the business of shooting them then. It was very heavy stoning and huge crowds drummed up. The IRA were consolidating, building up their support, getting their structure right, moving the weapons in, and fuelling the crowds. There was nothing they wanted more than to be hit with baton sticks, for the British Army to be seen as repressive. That

40

was the phase we were going through, but we didn't realise it, and certainly if you'd asked me then I really wouldn't have thought we'd still be there two years later. It seemed rather like going into Birmingham after some bad rioting just to help the police. That's all we thought it was. We never dreamed, I never realised at the time what was happening behind the crowds, why the crowds were there, and why the IRA puppet-masters were pulling those certain strings.

Corporal, 1 Para

It seemed very, very strange in the early days. You'd be in the Falls Road on a cordon waiting for something to happen, an ambush or an incident, you'd be sitting there in the dark and the camera team from BBC or ITV would arrive. They'd put up this incredible light, and you'd have to say, 'If you don't put that fucking light out . . .' I broke one camera team's light, I just smashed it, 'cos the guy ignored me, and I got a hell of a rocket for that. You'd be very wet, cold, you'd be on the streets for a few hours, and an English voice would say, 'What do you think of the situation here . . .?' When you are on operations, you get this vision, your senses – your sight and your listening – are heightened: you'd see someone coming, maybe from where the commander was, and he'd walk across and his voice would say, 'What do you think about these waterproofs? I'm from the *Daily Mail*,' and I'd say, 'If you don't fuck off . . . We are trying to do a job.' With all due respect we never had very good press briefings, and I don't think we do now. If they'd briefed us, if they'd trained us on press and communication, we could have done much, much better PR. A squaddie is a good PR guy, but we didn't know how to talk to the press, we didn't know how to treat them.

Captain, 1 Para

I remember the first time I came under fire very well. It was in early February, the same night that Gunner Curtis, the first British soldier to be killed, was shot in the New Lodge. I was accompanying a TV crew in the Ardoyne, which was a strong Republican area at the top end of the Crumlin Road. There'd been a lot of shooting, and petrol bombs were flying around, and

41

then came the crack and thump, which to the soldier is an unmistakable sound.

Private, 1 Para

In the Ardoyne that night, 6 February, D Company had had their Pig blown up by a petrol bomb and then a grenade ruptured its fuel tank. They all got out, including the driver, and we were sent in to deal with it. We tried to come in the deep end and snake along the stream. The people in the houses must have been watching us, because after we'd been lying in the stream in our riot gear for about an hour the old busy bomb – gelignite wrapped with nails, detonator and a fuse – came over a wall, as if in slow motion: in the dark it looked like a sparkler. It landed right in front of us, detonated, and I felt a hot flash. Nobody was hurt; we were very, very lucky. Later another guy tried to throw one. We saw him lighting it with a match, and he was immediately despatched to his maker. We didn't mess about, it was either them or us. They didn't like it when they started losing their colours. They got a bit upset.

Private, 1 Para

My reaction the day Gunner Curtis was killed was, 'It wasn't me.' I think that's how we all felt. We realised things were getting worse, and I think what hit us harder was when those three young Jocks got murdered in March. They were in a pub, got picked up and were shot in the back of the head. One was only seventeen and a half. That hurt a lot of us. We saw the old rules jumping: you go out for a drink, get offered a good time, you get in a car and you get topped – it was the dirty tricks starting. That saddened us a lot. It was tragic, a waste of life. It still hurts me now. That could have been me drinking with my mates down the town.

Corporal, 2 Para

Any weekend that I had off I used to go down to the pub for a couple of pints with my fiancée's father. He was a great friend of mine. We'd go in the bookies and he used to get really annoyed because I was always winning and he was always losing. After a while the son used to come down on Sundays with us for a pint. We'd be sat, me, him and his father. The son didn't say a great deal. I got a bit sick of this and one night I went into the house and said, 'Are you coming for a drink? We ought to have a few words.' I was chatting away, something on the lines of, 'Come on, I'm going to be your brother-in-law. Let's get things out in the open, 'cos you've never really spoken to me. What's the score?' He countered by asking me a question: 'You're a soldier. If you're up on the Shankill tomorrow night and I'm in a crowd of rioters and you see me with a petrol bomb, what will you do?' We used to shoot petrol-bombers in those days, and I replied, 'Blow your fucking head off.' And he said, 'Would you? Would you really do it?' I said, 'Yeah, I would.' We became very, very good friends after that.

Private, 2 Para

During R and R (rest and recuperation) we went to Bangor – an apt name for that time. The Army used to pay your ration money straight to the hotel and you'd get bed and breakfast. Me and my mate had been hitting the beer all night, away from the troubles for a little bit, all peaceful, and two quite elderly ladies came in. Being pissed, we got chatting to them, had a few more beers, and I sang a song called 'The Wild Colonial Boy'. A Paddy came over and says, 'There you are, sir. Good luck to you.' He thought I was a rebel and bought me a whiskey.

Private, 1 Coldstream Guards

The third Army bloke to be killed, the MP (military policeman), I'll remember that till the day I die. In those days there was concern about explosions coming up under vehicles but they never thought about the top, so we had canvas trucks, and the Military Police did as well. The MPs were in the Bogside in Londonderry – I think it was a come-on, but we didn't know in them days – and somebody hoiked a sugar-and-petrol bomb at them. One MP was killed. The bomb hit the front – it was all battened down, the front flaps were open – and all the sugar and petrol went inside and burnt up all the oxygen in the Land Rover. He died, basically, of asphyxiation.

We got there about twenty minutes after. The ambulance had already taken him, and there was a very deathly hush. An old woman from the Bogside came up in tears. She said to me, 'Oh, I feel sorry for that poor little lad. What's his mother going to say?' In them days MPs went around with ties on, and she said, 'Here's his tie. I saved it.' And I just thought, 'What are we doing here?' She was an old Catholic woman: it wasn't like later on, when they were really anti. They were still under the theory that the Army was there to protect the Catholics, so you still got the 'We remember the old days with the B Specials'. They weren't for the IRA as much as they are now.

Captain, 2 Royal Green Jackets

We arrived at Ballykelly, County Londonderry, in the beginning of May. We spent most of our time going into Londonderry where an awful lot of the rioting was going on. Being in Battalion Headquarters I had to calculate the statistics for nights in bed and in the first five and a half months we were there, the average number of nights in bed undisturbed for a soldier in a rifle company was five – in five and a half months. On all other nights they'd been deployed in Londonderry or been called out in an emergency to reinforce, or had come to camp and waited or been made to sleep in camp or even sleep at home with all their kit on, ready to go. We'd allow the married men, if the situation was okay, to go back to their quarters in the barracks, but they had to be ready to go at the drop of a hat. So it worked out as five undisturbed nights when an individual could say, 'I went home and I wasn't called out till the next morning.' Which was staggering.

Rifleman, 2 Royal Green Jackets

Summer 1971 was very hectic, very busy. It was a standard pattern: three o'clock every afternoon every soldier put on his flak jacket, put on his helmet and got into the vehicle. You knew as soon as the schools finished at half past three you'd be on the streets in Londonderry at four o'clock for the riots, and that's where you'd stay until midnight or one o'clock in the morning. It was like that all through the summer, every single day. You didn't have to be told to get ready, you just went: you were always deployed. You were working something like a nineteen- or twenty-hour day. If you were getting four hours' sleep you were very, very lucky.

I don't think we'd learned our lessons then, certainly not in '71 and the beginning of '72. We hadn't learned to go into a riot from different angles and put up control points in different places. They were winning then on the rioting side. Nine times out of ten they pushed you back. You couldn't stand there and take the bombardment, the bricks and bottles and all that. If they found a section on its own it was two hundred people against four. I was isolated twice, and it was bloody terrifying. Twice I learned my lesson. Once I got blown up, the second time there was four of us, and luckily enough the sergeant came round the corner with the rest of the platoon, because we were on the verge of opening fire. I think we would have all been prepared to take the consequences whatever the Yellow Card said about your life being in danger. It was really coming to that situation. That's the time I've been the most scared in my life – we were shit scared.

I think the most intimidating thing about a crowd is that you can't get at them. You can take the abuse, I don't think they can overwhelm you as long as you've got the safety of the platoon around you and a back-up force behind, but if you get isolated, then you do get intimidated, and they can do it either physically with bricks and bottles, or with the actual noise. As the crowd comes closer the chanting and howling gets deafening. That was the era of the old dustbin lids the women would bang on the ground. To speak to the platoon on the other side of the road, nine times out of ten the poor rifleman, which I was at the time, would have to run across to pass the orders because they couldn't hear. And that's when they'd get at you.

They were good: they could lob a fair-sized brick a hundred metres and hit what they were aiming at. They were bloody good, they'd had so much practice. I mean, you'd stand there with your shield and they would get it onto the shield almost every time. We started with the four-foot shield but it wasn't very good at all, because if you lifted it up they took your ankles, if you put it down they took your head off. So we went to the six-foots. You'd stand with a six-foot shield and half of it would be full of bricks and mortar: you could let the shield go and it would stand up on its own, wedged there: the bricks would hit, drop down, and build up around the base.

Then we didn't mind the riots so much because there were no gunmen. Bricks we could stop. But we knew that if they got hold of you, they would tear you to pieces. I think that if they'd known in '71 how scared we were, they would have achieved a hell of a lot more. I saw one guy grabbed. They only had him for seconds, no more than ten seconds, before his back-up team got there, but they kicked seven tons of shit out of him. I shouldn't think it'll ever leave him.

Lieutenant, 2 Royal Green Jackets

The maps in those days were awful. We had photocopies of 1:25,000 maps that were last surveyed in, well, if not in 1900, certainly in 1870. They were black and white and so it was very difficult to distinguish features. We were used to very detailed maps from Germany and BAOR, and we knew that scale, but with those photocopies you could easily overshoot your mark and get yourself lost. And of course, because the maps were so old, in a lot of cases the information was quite inaccurate. In mid-1971 there had been numerous border incursions, and for days on end we'd had a patrol in the vicinity of a customs post above Londonderry. We'd report on the radio to the battalion Ops Room, and one evening the duty officer asked: 'Are you quite sure everything's all right with this customs post?' They often used to knock off early, so I said, 'Yes, yes, the lights are on, the doors are locked.' He said, 'That's funny, because I'm sure the particular customs post you're looking at has been closed since six months ago.' Every night for five nights running we had been religiously inspecting the Southern Irish customs post, about half a mile inside Ireland. Nobody knew the difference, and there wasn't anybody there to tell you.

Private, 1 Para

We learned not to get dragged into riots. The best idea was to make an initial line, let them stone and petrol bomb, and gradually draw them back to where you had the advantage. We were in Belfast and got sent down to Springfield Crescent, which is just on the edge of the Ballymurphy Estate. We knew this riot was going to come off, it was a weekend thing, it always happened: they'd give us a spatter of nail bombs, we'd have to withdraw and they'd surge up, the women banging their dustbin lids and shouting abuse. But we'd sussed out that they never looked left or right, they always charged up towards where the Pigs were. The OC said, 'I want you to go through the wood yard alongside the Crescent and get down behind the wall. We'll draw 'em up and as soon as they're in line you fire the FRG rounds and we'll swamp the guys you hit.' It was a great idea, magic. So we crept all over the timber in the yard, hid with our baton guns and laid on the ambush.

It worked a dream. We really outwitted them. They came up, we waited until we could really give them the maximum, and let rip with these six FRG guns. We hit about three or four people, the rubber bullets were bouncing about, and then the lads scooped them up, and took 'em away. Meanwhile this woman came out of her house shouting an absolute mouthful, screaming that her old man was dead. 'Which one's your old man?' we asked, since there were about three or four laying about the pavement. She said, 'He's in the living room.' Her front window was caved in, and we goes in and the old man's slumped in his armchair – one of the rounds had missed, bounced through the window and laid this bloke out. There was a great big skid mark on the wall, and it had hit him on the side of the temple. But he was all right, I mean he wasn't dead or anything. So there we were, trying to pacify her and at the same time hold the mob at bay. All we could do was carry this guy into an ambulance but we were actually in hysterics. We felt sorry, but the funny side of it was, the riot had nothing to do with him, he was sat there watching telly.

Corporal, 2 Para

Things had escalated: there was no more discos. It was getting serious. We moved down into North Howard Street which is on the Falls, predominantly Catholic. On the tour before, we'd been in a Protestant area, and now we saw the other side. We had two companies in the one location. C Company's colours were green and they used to fly their flag outside the base, but our company colour was orange, and we had a deputation from the Falls saying please take your flag down because it's orange. They didn't put it like that, they said we were biased. So, just to keep everybody happy, we took the flag down.

Corporal, 3 Para

It was rioting, non-stop rioting all the time. No sooner had one part of our area, which was the Lower Falls, quietened down, then down the other end they would be rioting again. You'd never go a day without being stoned. And there were the women, always the women: they were the worst of the lot. You'd get the brave ones at the front: 'Come on, you fucking bastards, come on. Come and get us.' You wouldn't, you couldn't. I mean, you would never ever task yourself to go forward and try and get them because they would close in on you. The instigators would stay right at the back, and special snatch squads, teams of heavies under specific NCOs, would go in fast and furious when required and get the guy they wanted and come straight out again. They were extremely good: quick, in and out. No shields, I think one man had a rifle, and the rest would have either coshes or clubs and beat everybody out of the way. The only ones they went for were the one or two people who were the actual culprits, the instigators of the riot.

Private, 1 Para

Most of the trouble we got involved in was when we actually had to go in and physically rip people out. A lot of it was caused by women. Irish women were foul-mouthed and the hardest women you'll ever meet on this earth. They were all Amazons, they really were hard, far harder than the blokes. They were very loyal, for all the wrong reasons. They were passionate, vicious. I mean, I'd never seen women fight, I'd never seen women fight men. You'd come back scratched to blazes, black-eyed, your ears bit. It woke you up, you started looking at the equality of the sexes. You treated them as a different species altogether out there, not a domesticated animal that you keep at home. They were vicious, and if you got attacked or you had to move in amongst them you obviously had to physically baton them on the ground. They'd cling on until you'd knocked them senseless whereas the blokes would run, the blokes would always run away. It was all part of the strategy of moving the women and kids up front.

Marine, 45 Commando

One of the things I remember from 1971 was we had some Kosbies working with us. They'd been involved in a riot and, throughout, this bloke had been singled out by the women. One had been giving him a right earhole for about half an hour, swearing worse than you'll ever hear anywhere. He turned round in the end and cracked. He said, 'Why don't you fuck off?' She reported him for swearing at her, and he got fined about thirty-five quid by his CO. It was in all the papers that this character had got fined for swearing. We were talking to him and his mates and saying he must've been a bit pissed off, but he said, 'No. It's the best thing that's ever happened to me' – because it got in the papers everybody was writing in, saying, 'Here you are, son, here's a quid.' He ended up with enough money to buy himself out and buy a house. I thought, 'Good on you, squire.'

Corporal, 1 Para

We were parked doing riot control. All the rioting was calmed down and we were just waiting to go back to camp. Then this woman came up to the company commander. She spoke very nice and she said, 'Mister, mister, one of your soldiers swore at me.' He turned round, quite concerned because she was nice-spoken, and he said, 'Which one did it? Point him out to me.' And she says, 'That fucking bastard over there.' And you know what he said? 'Go away, madam, go away.'

Corporal, 2 Para

I think the saddest moment of the summer of '71 was when Sergeant Mick Willets got killed down at Springfield Road cop shop in May. Someone threw a suitcase with a bomb into the hallway, and the blast killed him as he stood in a doorway allowing a Catholic family to get to safety. He got the George Cross for that. We were driving around and heard this great big explosion, huge by those days' standards because normally it was just little nail bombs. It was like the last war, we'd never seen pubs and that blown up then. When it went off, there was a great big cheer

49

from the Paddys surrounding the police station. It was a big score for them, that place going up. There was a hit song at the time called 'Where's Your Money Gone?' and all the women and kids were singing 'Where's your barracks gone? Where's your barracks gone?', laughing, joking, dancing, and he was dead on the ground, bubbling, bits of him all over the place. He died saving a kiddie. He should have thought of his own kids rather than that kid, but I know how the bloke felt: he was a father, and you don't want anybody hurt that's not hurting you. I remember the CO telling the sergeant major who was in charge there: 'Get rid of them, those despicable people.' Mick Willets was the first Parachute Regiment soldier to be killed. When a soldier died then, it was headline news. A lot of soldiers were very bitter, including a lot of Irishmen and Southern Irishmen in the battalion.

Sergeant, 2 Royal Green Jackets

It's very hard to quantify these things. A lot of us had a lot of sympathy with the Catholics, even the non-Catholics amongst us. But it's always the same when someone starts shooting at you: you're tired and you're bitter, then you see someone killed who you particularly admire. Everyone's got their own tribe, their own group identity, and that's the strongest thing we all cling to at times of stress.

Private, 2 Para

The first time I came under fire was in the Clonard, from a Thompson machine gun on the Falls Road. As a Catholic I thought I might have had a conflict of opinion, but I didn't – I've never had any conflict within myself. By that time I'd made a new life in England, and I wasn't a young soldier, I was twenty-four, twenty-five years old. And if you looked at it fairly, there is right and there is wrong, and what was happening out there, what they were doing, was wrong. People immediately picked up my accent all the time. That made me a bit more thick-skinned. They used to call me 'traitor'. But we'd been shot at and blown up: well, a chap gets a bit angry about that sort of thing, I took a very dim view of it myself. So I wasn't too bothered about what they thought.

I had the experience of meeting friends quite a few times, which was quite embarrassing for them. They didn't say very much to me, they were avoiding the soldiers then. A young officer, knowing I was from there, put me in the middle of the Falls Road to direct traffic. Obviously he didn't understand the situation at that time, and I was out there a good half an hour before somebody told him. It was daft: make a personality of yourself in Belfast and you make yourself a big target. I'd got family in the area, but I didn't go and see them, it wouldn't have been a good thing to have visited them. I could have gone then, but I was looking to the future, and to actually have gone there would have been very difficult for them in the end. They're ruthless bastards, the IRA.

Private, 2 Para

We were doing a mobile patrol in the Ballymurphy on a road leading up to the Bullring. It was just after dark and a lighted object was thrown at us from behind a garden wall, which we later found to be a nail bomb. Nothing happened, but at the same time, fire was put down on us from the bottom of the Ballymurphy Road near the bend where it curved away from us. The first thing we did was dismount but we couldn't return fire because of women and children at the bottom. We did a quick run, we sort of pepper-footed down the road, but by the time we got to the bend they had gone. But by the light of early dawn we did a thorough search of the area, which was cordoned off, and on the other side of the garden wall, where the nail bomb had been thrown from, we found a pistol and a Thompson machine gun and a rubber glove, a gossamer-type like they use in hospitals, hanging on a hedge where the gunman had obviously made his escape. Their plan had been for the nail bomb to go off and at the same time fire upon us in the open Land Rover. The Thompson machine gun had a drum magazine, something like seventy rounds, and if that nail bomb had gone off, we would have been taken out.

Captain, 1 Para

I remember going to Northern Ireland thinking, perhaps rather idealistically looking back, that it was a situation which could be sorted out by the intelligent use of force, that it was only a matter of getting that right and everything would fall into place. Something of the idealism, if you like, of youth. Which, sadly, didn't last all that long. One grew to realise only too quickly that it wasn't like that, it wasn't that simple. And it became quite hard to justify to the soldiers – no, justify would be the wrong word – to produce the right context whereby the boys would realise that although at times it got pretty warry and people were being killed and hurt on both sides, that it was not battle in the conventional sense of the word, and that restraint was always necessary. It was a difficult concept to grasp because at times on the streets there was no restraint that you could see. In '71, and around internment in particular, it became almost – not completely, but almost – open warfare. And the judgement required of the amount of force which was appropriate and right for any particular set of circumstances was always a very difficult thing, not only to put across to soldiers but, indeed, to work out for oneself.

Private, 1 King's Own Scottish Borderers

That was a terrifying time for me, because I'd seen nothing in my life like that before. In fact, I didn't even know about Northern Ireland when I joined the Army. It hadn't quite got into its full fling: you'd get flashes of it on the TV, but of course being sixteen, seventeen years old I just didn't listen to the news. The only trouble spots that I'd heard of were Aden and places like that from a few years before, and knowing that Aden was finished, I thought, great, I'll go off and see the world, no wars anywhere. The next year I was in Ballymurphy. I mean, it was just a shock to the system. Everyone didn't like you. It was absolutely everyone: old grannies in the street would spit at you and young children would spit at you. Everyone was a problem. Even old men with walking sticks or crutches had nothing nice to say about you. The environment, the atmosphere, was more frightening than the gunmen themselves.

Corporal, 2 Royal Green Jackets

You could almost guarantee that something would happen when you went on patrol then. We didn't used to go out in four-man teams, in bricks, as now, we used to go out in twelves, six on each side, and the contacts we used to have! We were going down Cyprus Street one evening and we suddenly heard a couple of shots, fairly low velocity. Then all hell let loose. I was third in line on the right-hand side and somebody on my left went down. The major, who was two in front of me, opened fire with his pistols and within seconds I had fired something like thirty rounds. I'd changed magazines without even realising it. We followed up and started searching some houses and found weapons. One of the guys who was very, very friendly to us in 1969 was taken away. Apparently in '69 and '70 they'd been bringing arms in, and I must admit I don't think we'd done our job properly then: early on, as soon as you knew them you just waved them through instead of searching their cars, which in any case would have been cursory.

Sergeant, 1 King's Own Scottish Borderers

At that time Intelligence was just being born, and it started to come out that the same guys were turning up all over Belfast, they were being seen in Ballymurphy or the Springfield Road or down the Clonard. So the general thing was that you went out onto the streets and you had Fred, the local informer. He would go into the back of a vehicle, one of the slots would be opened up and you'd travel about, say, the Ballymurphy. You'd watch people walking along the road and he'd say, 'Okay, there's the QM, there's the 21C and there's the OC. Their names are . . .' There'd be another vehicle following behind and they'd be hackled into that and taken back to base. At that time you had no background on these people, nobody knew who was who. Okay, I'm sure that there were people who did know, like the local bobby, but we didn't. We had internment because of that, really. It was old Fred who was instrumental in internment.

Corporal, 1 Para

On the Thursday night before internment they started burning Ardoyne; about four hundred houses got burnt out. I was driving around with the 21C. We'd been out to Stormont, we'd been all over the place, and I remember we were zipping past Palace Barracks when he said, 'How do you view the situation at the moment?' We'd been down to watch these houses burning, and I was feeling very hurt and very disgusted. So I turned round and said, 'It makes me ashamed to be an Irishman to see this carry-on.' And his comeback to me was, 'Don't feel that ashamed. There are lots of things Englishmen do that I'm ashamed of as well. Don't let that bother you.' Then he asked me, 'How do you view the situation?' I said, 'Something's got to give. Something's got to happen.' We kept chatting, and I happened to say just before we got to Helen's Bay, where he lived, 'I think it's now time for some form of internment.' And he said, 'Your wish might be granted.' And of course that was top secret at the time.

Corporal, 2 Para

On the Sunday night we were sent to a street off the Springfield Road. Nearly every other house was blazing, and families were being evacuated by means of a couple of vans and a flat-bed lorry. Confusion reigned: where were the police? Where were the fire brigade? I cornered an old guy who was standing somewhat aloof on the corner and asked him the score. He spat and said that 'the Taigs' were being burned out. I asked him who had started the fires. He just said, 'the boyos', and walked away. I stared down the street at these pathetic figures. A man was trying to stamp out a smouldering mattress before throwing it on the truck; another ran towards our lads yelling, 'Ye bastards ye, ye bastards ye!', then broke down and was pulled towards the vans by his mate; a woman who I took to be his wife ran over with her small toddler. 'Do youse bastards want to throw him in there as well?' she raged, pointing to a house that had flames roaring out of the top windows.

Private, 1 Para

Things were getting very tense then. All that period you came back off patrol, took your jacket off and you were covered in sweat. You didn't realise until you got in. It was all tension: you were really keyed up.

There was talk of internment. Stormont was saying they wanted it, the British were saying they wouldn't allow it. It seemed as if the politicians were throwing out hints that it was coming, but without committing themselves. I'd never heard of internment before, and I thought it was a bloody good idea. Okay, it was against the whole basis of justice, of being innocent until proven guilty, but my attitude was that if it saved lives, then let's get some bastards and put them in jail.

Internment

August 1971

Captain, 2 Royal Green Jackets

The only people in the battalion who knew we were going to lift people that Monday morning, 9 August, were the commanding officer and myself. I personally thought it was a necessary move, but the commanding officer, who was a Catholic, was a very sad man that night. He said, 'This is disaster.'

Corporal, 1 Royal Green Jackets

I was woken up at about two by someone whispering: 'Internment. Go to the Ops Room.' I was given a name and walked down Leeson Street with my team. Our man was in, and came along without any fuss. I tied him with a couple of pieces of string to two riflemen and we set off back. The dustbin lids were cracking away by then, and we were spat at by the women, stoned as we went round corners, kids were out, the dogs barking and going for us. I was afraid we might get cut off, but there were so many soldiers about: in Leeson Street alone there must have been fifty of us.

Corporal, 2 Para

It was around 0400 and pitch dark. Our faces were totally blacked, the only thing we could really distinguish on each other was the eyes and the parachute wings on the arms of our Denison smocks. Each team had one target house and a target person: usually the father or son in that house. One man would position himself round the back of the house leaving the main group at the front. The door would be hammered and as a last resort a four-inch metal picket would be used to gain entry.

We positioned ourselves in the hedge by our target house and waited for the few minutes to zero hour. My adrenalin was up, I felt excited and very impatient to get on with it. We started stealthily approaching the house – six minutes to go. Suddenly there was banging in the next street: the bastards had started too early, so we all broke into a run. I ordered one man round the back through the alley, and then banged loudly with the rifle on the front door – nothing. One of the lads urged me to smash the door down. I was just about to give way to this when I heard the thump-thump of someone coming down the stairs. The door opened and a woman in her fifties stood there scowling with two glittering hatred eyes, saying nothing. I went into the practised diatribe: 'Does Sean so-and-so live here?' but before I had finished one of my blokes charged up the stairs. She yelled, 'Sean, the fucking Brits are here for ye!' We pushed into the living room, flicked the lights on, and the other man in my group accidentally pulled the rail off the wall as he closed the curtains. 'Why don't ye wreck the friggin place?' she screamed. Her daughter came in and immediately launched into a viperous attack on us. I pulled out the white card that had been issued to us and read the words out: 'Under the Special Powers Act of 1922 I arrest you . . .' I was that nervous I fluffed it a couple of times. The mother and daughter were screaming at each other as the old man jammed on his flat cap and looked at us expectantly. We waited until the soldier upstairs had finished his cursory search and proceeded to leave. The missus calmed down, said her goodbyes, and we rushed him to the rendezvous point and threw him in the Rover. There was already an internee on board. They nodded to each other.

Sergeant, 2 Para

I'd known something was going to happen because all the warrant officers and above had smirks on their faces. Our man wasn't in, and my patrol walked back to base along the Springfield Road. The whole of Belfast was waking, the dustbin lids were banging, and as we got closer all the patrols were meeting up. A colour sergeant across the road hadn't got his man either, so he came over to talk, and we went together, full of ourselves, chatting away. Ahead of us was a telephone box, a woman inside and outside a man, an oldish guy, fair-haired, with a cap on. He turned away, and if he'd turned away a split-second longer I'd have lifted him. But he didn't, he turned back, he did that double-bluff, gave a sort of smile – he was a trained guy, you see – and I didn't think any more of it. Three days later, on the Thursday, Joe Cahill, the OC of the Belfast Brigade of the Provisional IRA, gave a press conference in Ballymurphy saying that no one in the Belfast PIRA had been arrested. He was the man outside the phone box. The CSM and I both went, 'Jesus, that was him.' The Intelligence, the big picture, just wasn't there in the early stages.

Captain, 1 Para

The IRA's reaction to internment was instant and violent, and the level of violence that day was so much higher, another dimension on the scale of the conflict. The boys of course relished it. One wants to be clear about that. To the professional soldier the whole question of operating in a constrained environment, as Northern Ireland must be, is very difficult: if, for whatever reasons, some of those constraints are removed, and certainly during internment the constraints were removed by the actions of the opposition, the better they liked it, because they felt able to operate in a more open environment and hence more as soldiers and less as policemen. What they did was respond, if you like, to the greater opportunity for engaging the enemy, as they saw it, which was thereby presented. It was a remarkable day and a remarkable week, no doubt about it.

Corporal, 1 Para

Come the Sunday night, away it went. West Belfast was the first place to get hit. As a reaction against internment some areas had declared themselves 'free': Ballymurphy and Ardoyne had dug themselves in with all their defences pointing towards the city, expecting us to come that way. But we fooled them, we came in off the Black Mountain and took them completely by surprise. The operation began at half past two that morning. Four of us went in to recce Ballymurphy beforehand, from the back, from the mountain. We got down and looked over the barricade. They'd been quite clever: they'd actually got JCBs (mechanical shovels) and dug trenches, and covered the road behind with broken glass so anybody walking on it couldn't do a silent thing. And there was four guys patrolling around, three with Thompson-type machine guns, the other with an M1 carbine. We could hardly believe our luck. But we couldn't spring anything because the battalion was waiting on the mountain, so we went back up and briefed the company commanders.

We took the Pigs and the Macralon Land Rovers along the track over the top, cut the engines and in the pitch black freewheeled down into Ballymurphy. We stopped short, still dead silent, dismounted, and crept up behind the barricade, knowing those four gunmen were still there. There was only four of us, too. The 21C said, 'Right. On my word, stand up.' We stood up, the gunmen saw us, reacted, and we fired. Three of them went down. The fourth guy, the man with the M1-type carbine, was hit too because he fell, came back up, set off running, mounted the pavement and went into a house. My mate jumped straight over the barricade, ran across the broken glass after him and into the house, almost taking the door off its hinges. The guy was lying in the hallway – I was right behind – in a pair of jeans and a white T-shirt, and running up the stairs was a girl, with his weapon. All my mate had was a pistol. He hit her, poleaxed her, took the weapon and we dragged the injured man onto the pavement. He'd been shot through the side and all his kidneys were hanging out. Even though we had an armoured ambulance waiting, we couldn't get him away because of what was going on. We were just about to drive off with him when he died.

Private, 2 Para

We moved into the Clonard, which is a small enclave between Springfield Road and the Shankill Road. Everybody was stood on the pavements, looking at their watches, waiting for the go. The brief was to knock on the door and say, 'It's the Army, a routine search.' We just kicked the doors in. As soon as one person went in, we all went. I remember running upstairs and this woman was lying in the bed screaming her head off. I said, 'Where is he?' and she replied, 'He's moved out. He's living with the woman next door.' So we ran downstairs and the lads round the back caught him running out of the next house trying to put his trousers on. We just grabbed him, handcuffed him and threw him in the back of the four-tonner. And that was the last I ever saw of him. I can't even remember his name now: away he went to Crumlin Road Jail.

We thought that'd be it, but all of a sudden the women were out in the streets banging the dustbin lids – we used to take the mickey out of them, we used to tell them to 'get a rhythm, get a rhythm going', take the dustbin lids off them, bang out a tune and then give the dustbin lids back: they thought we were mental. Anyway, I always remember we were stood there lined up along the peace line with all the women banging away when a man with two sheepdogs come through from the Protestant side behind us. All the women just parted, he blew a whistle and the shooting started. The shooting started in earnest then.

Corporal, 1 Para

We then moved from Ballymurphy up to Ardoyne. We went in from the Crumlin Road through the corrugated-iron fence there, and the first guy inside fell over a seventeen-year-old kid who was dead, lying on a piece of waste ground, with his chest blown out. My job was to go down Butler Street, on my own, and guide the company coming down from the Black Mountain in. A strange thing happened then: I was standing crapping myself with fear by this big barricade, a burnt-out bus, crates of nail and petrol bombs all round me, when a youngish woman in one of the little terraced houses opened the window up about six inches, and put four Penguin biscuits on the sill. She whispered, 'For God's sake don't let anybody see.' Ardoyne was a very strong IRA place.

Then the first Paras down off the top came in and the long shooting match began. As they came running down the middle of Butler Street, a guy up behind a chimney stack opened up on them. They just stopped in their tracks, the three of them, and blew the chimney away. They found the body in the back yard behind; he hadn't been hit by the rounds, just lumps of brick, and the chimney disintegrating around him had knocked him into the yard. The next obstacle was a barricade further on. The platoon commander leapt it, but on the other side tins of paint had been poured all over the road, and so of course he slid all over the place, covered in light blue paint from head to foot.

We got to the top end of the Ardoyne, by the bus station, and the houses burnt out the previous Wednesday were still smouldering, like a bomb site. At first light, about six o'clock, we reached the primary school. We knew it was being used as a hospital – a 'refugee centre', as they called it. I was the first one in. I bust through the double doors into a deep porchway which led to a cloakroom and another set of double doors, and when I bust the second doors open this guy was standing on the far side with a weapon, blocking the way. He was six foot plus, I'm five foot six – no matter how hard I try I can never manage to make myself look bigger – and all I did was just shove, and because of the momentum he went flying down the corridor. And away we went through the school and up the stairs where we found the bodies of the people that had been killed there during the night. They had them laid out in the classrooms in coffins draped with tricolours, and the old vigil was going, candles and prayers. When we burst in and started to check the bodies against the files of known IRA guys they didn't like it at all.

By then it was about seven in the morning. We'd taken the place, for want of a better word. It was all finished, over and done with. I sat on the pavement outside the school with my head against the wall and brewed up.

Private, 2 Para

That night the IRA mounted a full-scale attack on B Company's base at the Henry Taggert school in Ballymurphy. I remember at teatime we were sat in our location in North Howard Street having a meal and getting a quick glance at the television. ITN was showing it live on the news: people were throwing petrol bombs and the blokes were responding with rubber bullets, and we could see it was escalating into something bigger. There was a woman stood in front of the cameras with her daughter, who was about sixteen or seventeen. She pulled the daughter's dress up and showed a big bruise right in the groin where the girl had been hit by a baton round, and said to the reporter, 'What do you think my daughter is? A fucking whore?' We had a Catholic padre with us at the time and he was up in Ballymurphy, in uniform, unarmed, trying to quieten things down. The IRA got a message to the CO telling him to get the padre out of there for his own good, because the tension was obviously building up, and they would have lost a lot of face killing a priest.

Private, 2 Para

It was six o'clock when the shooting started, after the civvies had come home from work: they must have had their tea, and then did the business. I was sent onto the roof of the Henry Taggert, which gave me a very good view of the attack. Our area of responsibility was from the flats at the rear of the base to the open ground at the far side of Springfield Road in the front.

The first shots came from a privet hedge alongside a narrow alleyway behind a row of houses. A gunman was firing from behind a dustbin, and of course the first thing we did was put down fire into it – that bloke ceased firing, he was a sitting duck. There was also a woman there, firing a pistol, and she was taken out too. I know it perhaps sounds callous, but the enemy is the enemy, whether a man or a woman: if she's got a weapon in her hands and she's going to take me out, do I take her out? Of course I do.

The gunmen started coming across the open land at the front, shooting. A couple would run out, then another couple, then two more. It wasn't an organised section attack as we would do, with one foot on the ground and the other loose. I don't know what they hoped to achieve. They didn't even reach the dip, the dead ground on the other side of the waste ground. The Springfield Road was in full view, and they'd have been taken out for sure as they crossed it. And even if they'd managed to get across, they'd never have cut through the wires surrounding the base.

We talked about it afterwards. They were fighting for their ideals, I suppose, retaliating for us lifting their men, but six or so blokes running across open ground in broad daylight trying to take out scores of soldiers behind sandbagged positions – ludicrous. The IRA never made a section attack again. They learned their lesson then, I would say.

Private, 2 Para

That attack was excitement, but in some ways it disturbed me. I was still young then, my parents were Irish, a lot of my friends were Irish. I'd joined the Army to get away from Northern Ireland, and my first posting was back to Ireland. And at that specific time, when that attack started, my younger sister was staying with her cousin and my aunt on a housing estate by

Ballymurphy, just down at the bottom of Henry Taggert, two hundred yards away. The estate was mixed, and getting messy, and I was running around in circles trying to find out if any of the patrols had checked they were safe. Nobody knew, and no way could I get down there. I was worried.

Private, 2 Para

When I got back to Birmingham after the attack on the Henry Taggert I was sharing a bedroom with my two younger brothers, and I used to sleep a lot. One morning my mum grabbed hold of my arm to wake me up, and I went 'bang', punched her.

Corporal, 1 Para

On the Wednesday after internment, we came down from Bally-murphy along the Shankill Road and the pavements were lined with Protestants cheering us, throwing us packets of cigarettes, waving Union Jacks. Our driver, a Jock – whether Catholic or Protestant I couldn't tell you, it didn't matter in the regiment – stopped the wagon and shouted at them, 'Don't you start, you bastards. Because it's your turn next. It'll happen to you as well, because you're just as bad.' And it was true, a year later it happened to them. We knew there were stacks of weapons in the Shankill, we knew about the UVF, we knew all about the Protestant bad boys.

Private, 2 Para

During internment week a guy came up to us on the Springfield Road and started hitting me, and as he was hitting me he was saying, 'Arrest me, arrest me. Two guys behind are after me. I'll tell you anything.' So we arrested him. He was scared as hell. The hoods were chasing him for their percentages, and he didn't have any money: he couldn't afford to give them that ten per cent of what he earned.

Chaplain, 2 Field Regiment

Long Kesh internment camp was really a prisoner-of-war camp, just Nissen huts in a wire compound with gun towers. For the soldiers guard duty amounted to standing there watching prisoners walk about. Escape attempts provided the only excitement. Digging was the most popular method. There are all sorts of technical means of trying to detect tunnels but as far as the soldiers were concerned, it boiled down to irregular searching of compounds. These searches would start with a dawn move into the particular compound under suspicion, and the prisoners would be taken out of their huts one by one, identified and re-photographed, and then stood leaning against the wire. Their hut was then searched thoroughly: if any tunnels were found they would be filled in, and anything else of interest would be taken. The prisoners would always be trying to brew their own alcohol, occasionally they'd make imitation firearms, and a lot of communist, or extreme socialist, literature tended to be found. Then the prisoners would be allowed back in and they'd carry on their business.

There were Protestant compounds as well as Catholic compounds. The only real difference was the Protestant compounds were run on very military lines. They very obviously had their own hierarchy, and they'd do foot drills every morning, they'd clean out their rooms, polish the concrete floor of the Nissen huts – like an over-militaristic army, really. The Catholics tended to the other extreme. An absolute shambles: their places stank, you always got fleas after you'd searched them. It was the two ends of the spectrum, the Protestant areas in Belfast were the ones with the scoured steps and shiny little fronts of the two-up and two-downs, whereas Catholic areas tended to be more untidy, much more slums.

Escaping on the part of the prisoners and getting in on the part of the staff seemed to be the only events of any interest, but each morning the officer or NCO on duty gave a general intelligence brief to the assembled officers, including the CO. It was all happening in Belfast, on our doorstep, but we had to get the information from the radio. The duty officer would listen to the seven o'clock news and take notes, and more often than not he couldn't get it all down. Somebody suggested using a tape recorder, so the duty officers started recording the news, but more problems then occurred because the bulletins were never deleted. After a while people flicked around the tape, never quite sure which news they'd found, and on several occasions the same incident was reported on three or four successive days as a new occurrence. The CO believed it was a terrorist plan: 'That's the fourth incident in the same place, must mean . . .' Moments like that enlivened the tedium.

Sergeant, 1 King's Own Scottish Borderers

After internment the Catholics went on a rent strike, and there was talk about shutting off the water and electricity if they didn't pay up. So what did Paddy do? He went round to the local betting shop, held up the cashier, raked in a few thousand quid, then went round to the first house in the street and asked, 'How much do you owe?' 'Forty-seven pounds and twenty pence.' 'Here's the money.' And he went down the whole street with the cash and paid them out. The rent man came, knocked at the first house: 'Mrs Murphy, you owe . . .' She paid it all, the book was signed, and so on down the row. The rent man got to the last house, well pleased he'd got the money off all the street – and Paddy was standing there on the corner: 'Hands up.' Took all the money off the rent man, gave it back to the bookie, and that was it. You had to admire that: brilliant.

Major, 1 King's Own Scottish Borderers

Detention without trial seemed a reasonable move at the time, and I still think something strong had to be done. But, as with the Falls curfew the previous year, there was always a conflict between the short-term military goal, which could always be achieved, and the cost in the longer term. Internment had been sold as a potential solution, and to be absolutely fair to the Stormont government, the introduction of internment in 1956 had been instrumental in signalling the fate of the IRA's border campaign. But on that occasion, of course, the Irish Republic had also introduced internment, whereas in 1971 they were not at all tempted to do so. And so, with hindsight, the policy was perhaps ill-judged, and its ultimate effect was certainly to fuel the longevity of their cause.

Sergeant, 2 Royal Green Jackets

Strabane was a small, relatively quiet border town twenty miles south of Derry. We rushed down there, the whole company, in four or five four-tonners, and came rolling in at about nine o'clock at night. All along the high street – a typical, straggling, Irish high street – smoke was billowing out of shops, and the roadway was strewn with fridges, food, every sort of goods. The civil population had taken the law into their hands, run amok, and the police had had to barricade themselves in. I thought, 'My God, is this the United Kingdom? We are no different from Guatemala, Egypt, anywhere else you care to name; this is the good old UK citizen at his very best.'

Corporal, 1 Coldstream Guards

It was dusk when we got off the LSL at Belfast Docks in October and boarded this doubledecker bus to drive to Ballykelly, Londonderry. We thought we were going to war. The first time you go over there you think that literally as soon as you get off the boat you're going to be dodging bullets. Only one bloke on the bus had ammunition: he'd been issued with five rounds, so he was our guard. The bus had no protection, it was only a normal commercial model, and everybody was scrambling to get seats. Normally people want to sit at the front, or next to the window, but we were fighting for the seats on the inside so as not to sit by the windows, and the slower ones piled their kit bags and lunch packs up against the glass. That was my first taste of Northern Ireland: a hairy journey through Belfast.

The other striking memory I have of that tour is that supposedly you were in danger all the time, and yet the countryside was beautiful: rolling green hills, lovely open roads, hardly a car in sight, cows in the field – like being a farm boy. You'd stand on a VCP outside Derry thinking: 'What the bloody hell am I doing here?' I mean, everybody spoke the same language as you, you could buy Weetabix, Corn Flakes, things like that. It wasn't a foreign country: under normal circumstances you'd pass these people in the street and not think twice about them. And yet you were armed to the teeth stopping people outside the areas where it was all going on: What did they think? How did they feel?

I certainly found it difficult to understand why I was stood there, an Englishman amongst fellow Englishmen – well, we do that, don't we?, tend to call it England when we mean the UK.

Sergeant, 2 Royal Green Jackets

We got posted back into Derry in late '71. On the interface between the Protestant city and the Catholic ghetto was a warehouse, a Protestant business, and the Catholic kids had attempted to set fire to it. We rushed out and threw up a cordon while the firemen hosed the place down. Things were quietening down when the kids on the building site next door started dropping planks. As each plank fell, the foremost part of the timber hitting the ground would give a crack, and as the rest slapped down, it gave a thump. So of course we began ducking and taking cover, acting as though we'd been shot at. We repeated this game about five or six times and then eased off, thought no more about it.

I was standing in a cordon, in the dark, with the company commander who was giving orders over the radio, when all of a sudden he clutched his stomach, shouted, 'I've been shot,' tottered forward and collapsed. We all scattered into the shadows, and immediately every man in the company, 120 men, cocked his weapon. The crash of rifles being cocked was tremendous and the kids went very quiet. For that split second, if someone had said 'Fire', there would have been a massacre. The blood went straight up, and anyone shadowy enough would have been so easy to determine as a gunman. Quite frankly, we could have killed dozens.

Thereafter, whenever we went on the streets, the crowd would taunt us: 'We've got your major, we've got your major.' He was ill for about three months, and died at the end of January. When the death was announced, then it was a case of, 'We killed your major, we killed your major.'

Corporal, 1 King's Own Scottish Borderers

It was just a big game in Turf Lodge. There was one there, let's call her Mrs Black. She was marvellous. This girl could curse and swear, just really blue with her language, awful – the whole community reckoned she hated anything in uniform. If we were passing, one of us would always knock on the door and say,

'Hello, Mrs Black. We haven't had a chat since yesterday, and we know you want to offer us a cup of tea,' and the dogs would be set loose, everyone would run out into the streets. It was just a game because in fact she was on the side of the soldiers. We made her day. Before we turned up she had nobody to talk to: she loved the soldiers coming round. And not only her: a lot of people would deliberately show the aggression that was required of them, because Turf Lodge was a very strong IRA estate. They would come out to demonstrate, but there was nothing in it.

You had to develop your own tactics, use your initiative out there. One night a patrol doing a house search had caused all sorts of nausea, and we were being pelted with bottles and bricks, all the rest of it. I said, 'Right. This is the answer', and walked across the road to a house I knew was owned by a man in the Official IRA. I stood there, they threw the bottles and stones, and broke all the windows in the front living room. Then I moved two doors down, he was in the Provisional IRA, and all his windows got broken. I was playing them at their own game, and after about four houses they stopped: they realised.

It was a relationship. We'd chat to anybody and quite soon no one was allowed to talk to any member of my patrol. That came down from the IRA, because people were giving us information, kids as well. Kids walking about the street, what did they know? They knew a bloody lot. I walked into an empty flat in one of the blocks in Turf Lodge, and the oldest one playing in there was ten years old, the youngest maybe seven. He had a demonstration model of an airbomb: six-inch nails and putty. In the back were crates upon crates of empty milk bottles. The information didn't necessarily start from a grown-up person, so we used to talk to everybody. We even used to pat dogs as they went by.

After a while you didn't get surprised out there. One particular night in Turf Lodge two lads I'd never seen before came out of the CESA (Catholic Ex-Servicemen's Association) club. They'd both had a few, but we approached them anyway, and I said to the big one, 'Hello, mate. What's your name?', and he said, 'Willy.' Now, you knew when someone said 'Willy', it wasn't going to be a good night. It was drizzling, starting to rain hard: definitely it was not going to be a good night. I said, 'Okay, Willy, what's your second name?' He said, 'Woodbine.' 'Fine. What's your mate's name?' and he said, 'Joe Soap from 3 Slippery Way.' You see what I mean? Well, after a wee while they were soaked, sobered up, and off they went.

Now, this sort of thing developed all through the evening, and much later we were going along Norglen Road and there was a guy walking up with crutches and a stookie (plaster cast), a great big white stookie on his leg. I wasn't happy with that stookie at all, I didn't like the size of it: a leg was the last thing I thought would be inside. I approached him: 'I realise the predicament you're in, sir, but I haven't seen you about these parts before. What's your name?' He said, 'Mr Dillon.' You remember that cowboy Dillon with the wooden leg? Now that wasn't a funny joke at two o'clock on a miserable wet morning. I was tempted to give him one when the word came back on the radio – his name was Dillon, he did live in Norglen Road: he'd stepped on a mine and just come out of hospital that day. Of all the guys I met that night who caused problems, he was the only innocent one.

You needed a sense of humour. We sometimes checked the Martin Forsythe club in Turf Lodge: every Saturday night was dance night, and once when I went in they stopped the band and played 'Whispering Grass'. It was brilliant. I loved that: that was magic.

Subaltern, 1 Coldstream Guards

When we were on the edge of the Creggan in Derry we saw real hatred, not only directed at us but at themselves as well. Over Christmas '71 my company was based in the old library there and the cooks used to help with meals-on-wheels. They'd been dishing out suppers to one old lady, and her two grand-daughters, aged twelve and thirteen, left a half-bottle of whiskey at the gate for the cook-sergeant. They'd obviously been seen, because later that same night they were tarred and feathered, their heads shaved, and they were tied to the bottom gate with a placard saying: 'Don't Help Soldiers'. Luckily one of the platoon sergeants – I say luckily, because he was older than the rest – he found them, and there wasn't a dry eye in the patrol. That was something we couldn't understand, something totally new. It was very, very testing, not to beat the living daylights out of the next Mick you met after that.

Fortunately those two girls managed to get away from Ireland. I still get Christmas cards from them. One's living in Bristol, the other not far from my home in Lancashire. They've both married, they both have children.

'Bloody Sunday'

30 January 1972

Captain, 2 Royal Green Jackets

It was fascinating to see the differences in attitude between the Army in Londonderry and Belfast. One hobby-horse of mine is that if ever the Army got it wrong, they got it wrong on Bloody Sunday. And on the Sunday before that, at a place called Magilligan. There was a protest march from Londonderry to Magilligan Point at the mouth of the Foyle, where a new internment camp was being built. Two companies of Green Jackets were deployed, with a company of 1 Para as reserve. The marchers came down the beach, the wire didn't quite extend far enough, and they came around the end towards the internment camp. The Paras were called forward to stop them, and in my opinion did so in a manner far too aggressive for the situation, in a way perhaps more suited to Belfast. A series of unpleasant incidents was shown on television, of people knocked to the ground, an old man being thumped with batons.

Captain, 1 Para

'Bloody Sunday', as people call it, was, it's fair to say, a high-risk operation. What was intended was very clear. For a number of weekends there had been larger and larger so-called civil rights demonstrations in the Province – this was a good year on from the demise of what I regarded as the genuine civil rights movement, and by then many of the participants were somewhat suspect. All the marches were illegal, all banned. It was known that a very large protest march would take place in Londonderry on 30 January 1972, and the authorities decided that a complete stand was to be made. The aim on our part that afternoon was to make maximum arrests of the hooligan element in the crowd. The arrest operation was to take place within a very limited area, beyond what was then known as the 'containment line', the near side of which the security forces were happy to operate, but on the far side of which they were not. That might seem remarkable now, but that was the policy then. It was our task to make a limited incursion of about two to three hundred metres beyond the barricade and round up as many hooligans as possible and whistle them off to the local nick.

The gut feeling was that it wouldn't be as simple as the orders in black-and-white suggested. There was no hard intelligence, but it was felt that the opposition would not, and could not, permit such a clear violation of the rules pertaining to the containment line, beyond which they had full reign in the no-go areas of the Bogside and Creggan; that they would be bound to react; and that the problem wouldn't be the hooligan element, but gunmen – two rather different categories of opposition.

Corporal, 1 Para

The political side, which is always interesting to a soldier, was obviously human rights. Human rights are great, fine, and there had to be a mediator, but the IRA had infiltrated the organisation and were leading a lot of people up the garden path. Manipulating the marchers was a really bitter way of doing it, because those people were decent people. They might have been singing Republican songs, but they weren't IRA. They were hoodwinked, conned: that was the sad thing.

Private, 1 Para

We'd known something was going to happen because all the windows had been blacked off in the company offices, but we went into Londonderry expecting just a riot. Even when we moved forward to make the arrests we still expected ordinary rioting. There were hundreds of people – we couldn't have busted it up. The rioters would surge forward, stop and then go back. They'd charge the barricade, we'd fire rubber bullets at them, they would stop, cower and then back off. It seemed as if they were trying to draw us into it.

Captain, 2 Royal Green Jackets

Down on Barricade 14, in the next street, there was a certain amount of stone-throwing but as far as Londonderry was concerned nothing in any way excessive. CS gas was thrown, actually by the rioters, but we used the water cannon and all went quiet. It was just after that the Paras went in.

Captain, 1 Para

It was about half past three, quarter to four, when the marchers came off the top of the Creggan Estate and headed down the hill towards the old part of the city centre. The rioting had started against the barricades, missiles were thrown, and the security forces had replied with gas. At about ten to four we were given the order to execute the pre-planned arrest operations. We moved through the troops manning the barricades and passed beyond, three companies on three different axes. The idea was to get beyond the rioters and scoop them up from behind. That was partially achieved, but not completely: a lot of the crowd started running back once they saw what we were doing. Events then took their course.

Corporal, 1 Para

We started dealing with the situation exactly as we would have in Belfast. The weapons were never really out of the vehicles. We dispersed the rioters just by using batons – shields we didn't bother with because they were too cumbersome. I captured a few people who were throwing stones. One was an American sailor, United States Navy – he was in a lot of trouble.

Then we were fired on. I know in my heart of hearts, and I'll take it to my grave, that we were fired at first. At that, of course, the weapons were given out from the backs of the vehicles.

Sergeant, 1 Para

I was crossing the open ground in front of Rossville House, trying to reach the high end of the pram ramp by the shops underneath the flats, when I first heard shooting. A guy on the corner of Rossville House opened up on us with a Thompson; the rounds were way above our heads. I saw him go down, shot by one of our troops over on the right-hand side of the open ground. He also took out a gunman firing from one of the windows in the flats; I think we took two casualties from a machine-gun attack from there. Acid bottle bombs were being thrown from the top of the flats, and two of our blokes were badly burnt.

By that time there were lots of running crowds. It was very busy, very chaotic: panic had stricken. People were running in all directions, and screaming everywhere. Innocent people were being bowled over – we were running past women and children, shouting at them to get out of the way. At first they wouldn't believe us, but very soon they were putting up white handkerchiefs, to show they were peaceful, not armed.

Private, 1 Para

I was to one side of the open ground, down an alleyway; I'd heard shots but didn't know where they were coming from. The corporal with me had the rifle, and I had the rubber-bullet gun. There were odd little riots in the side streets, so I thought I'd arrest the troublemakers. As I was running towards one, a man came out round the corner thirty metres away with a pistol, probably an old Webley. I fired a rubber bullet at him, and I turned round to the corporal when I heard 'ping' on the wall above. We chased him up the street but lost him. Further along the road somebody else must've got him: by the way he was dressed he was one of the dead picked up later. His tactics were very poor. He didn't really use fieldcraft, or urbancraft: if he'd hid himself and waited for a target he could probably have shot some of us, but he was just running around firing, which led me to believe he was a novice. The gunmen in the crowds seemed to have pistols that could be hidden, and the riflemen would probably have been firing out the windows of the buildings.

Captain, 2 Royal Green Jackets

The reaction down on Barricade 14 when we heard three people had been shot was one of complete surprise. It had all happened just round the corner, and yet we hardly heard a thing. And when it ended up with thirteen dead we were totally amazed.

Private, 1 Para

The shooting seemed to be over in about ten minutes, but perhaps it lasted half an hour. It wasn't continuous – more like a skirmish. When the gunmen realised they'd got the worst of it, they packed up and left. Once the people in the streets started seeing dead bodies, the rioting stopped – they were petrified. It all died down very fast, and we went on a body-collecting patrol. There were three dead by the barricade; the others were round corners, up the alleyways. We loaded the bodies into the back of a Pig and took them to the hospital in the city centre. We carried them up the steps: the nurses were fainting at the blood. The bodies were laid out in the hallway, and when we got to the tenth I thought, 'Bloody hell!' People were starting to worry then: I couldn't see why, but that was the most that had been killed by the Army in one day in Northern Ireland.

Sergeant, 1 Para

We thought it a huge success: morale was bouncing off the ceiling. When we got back to our base, a factory at Drunahoe a few miles outside Londonderry, as we stepped out of the wagon we were literally put upon soldiers' shoulders and carried in like conquering heroes for the great job we'd done. We were taken to the school across the road and all the village ladies gave us tea. And sitting in the factory that night we had the first real inkling of instant reporting: there was a two-hour programme on the entire history of the Parachute Regiment on television.

Captain, 1 Coldstream Guards

My company was positioned down by the cinema in Derry, which was showing *Sunday, Bloody Sunday* that day. The first time I heard the words 'Bloody Sunday', I genuinely believed that was the reason.

Sergeant, 1 Para

They said we killed thirteen, wounded sixteen, all the rest of it. There is a distinct possibility that we took out more. All we could count were the bodies we could actually get to. We didn't assume anything: I'd have put the body count at thirty, not thirteen. I believe the extra bodies were whisked across the border. We know, on the grapevine, from friends in other units, that graves were found on the other side. I believe those bodies were taken across because if they had been recovered, forensic tests would have proved without a shadow of a doubt that those people had been firing weapons. Those bodies would have shown that the marchers had been infiltrated, manipulated. Instead, the IRA were able to turn it into a great propaganda exercise, which worked, in my opinion. I think that as a result, the Army had to reconsider its role in Northern Ireland, and its handling of the situation has been different ever since.

Corporal, 1 Para

We were stopped that day. We were poised to go further in, into the Bogside, but they pulled us out once they realised the body count had gone thirteen. We were stopped from high up, because we were ready to carry on. The main tower block just as you entered the Creggan, they reckon it had been set up as a field hospital and clearing station: the IRA were expecting a big confrontation that day. I know, knowing what I know now, that the Army could have nipped it in the bud then, by going in hard and sharp. In 1972 the IRA were known, they were all known: the Belfast mobs, the Londonderry mobs, even the ones in Dublin.

Private, 1 Para

Nobody was ashamed of anything; nobody felt any guilt. We'd done our job, and they'd done theirs; we didn't open fire until the gunmen started. Nobody was about to break down and cry, or feel bad about it. But next day a TV cameraman came and filmed us individually on parade, on behalf of the Army. I remember me and a few other lads wanted to turn away, but the boss man said to us, 'You've nothing to be scared of.' He was right: we just stood our ground.

Private, 1 Para

We'd only fed a little bit of fuel into the fire. It was like anything else: if you are achieving your aim, people in their politics will kick up as much fuss as they can to get rid of you.

Warrant Officer, 2 Royal Green Jackets

I don't think the Paras did us any favours, did anybody any favours. In our eyes, it was playing into the IRA's hands. One of the saddest consequences was when a lot of Catholic ex-servicemen who'd served in the Second World War tossed their medals onto the war memorial in the Little Diamond as a protest. Of course, we didn't know how much they'd wanted to do it, and how much they'd been pressurised, but it was sad. All the no-go areas started then, and the situation became worse. That Sunday in Derry set the whole thing back by years, I reckon.

Captain, 1 Para

It wasn't an easy time, because so-called 'Bloody Sunday' was world news. It was clearly the catalyst for some very important events – the prorogation of Stormont took place some two months after; perhaps it was the single most seminal event in the history of the British Army in Northern Ireland. And it remains a contentious issue, a subject of enormous controversy. All of a sudden the battalion was being accused of losing its head, running amok – emotional phrases of that nature, which to us didn't make sense, but nonetheless were being said, and so there was a case to be answered.

To my mind 'Bloody Sunday' was us doing the best we could, within the constraints of the game, and within the circumstances presented to us. In other words, we were engaged by fire, and we returned fire. I thought that answer was sufficient, but like any innocent man charged with murder we were worried until acquitted. One could get into an arcane argument as to whether the boys were within the laid-down rules of returning fire, and a far cleverer man than I ruled on that: the Lord Justice Widgery was invited to exercise a judicial mind on the factors involved, which he examined in great detail, and his judgement was extremely balanced and carefully thought through. Widgery accepted that on the whole our soldiers were within the prescribed rules; he pointed a finger at one or two soldiers, describing their actions as 'bordering on the reckless', but basically he acquitted the battalion of unprofessional conduct. And, of course, there was relief and pleasure in that decision.

Looking back now, fifteen years on, I think perhaps Widgery was less forthcoming on how sensible it was as a complete operation. Others might argue that matters had to be brought to a head, and whatever way that confrontation was achieved it was bound to be ugly, at least temporarily world news. My epitaph might be that the operation was properly executed, but perhaps less surely conceived.

'A War Situation'
1972

Sergeant, Royal Military Police

In the early seventies, before I joined the Army, everyone was involved in an organisation round Belfast and on several occasions as a youngster I went up against the Army. The one occasion I'll always remember was against the Paras – I was sixteen at the time – during the first Loyalist workers' strike in March '72. This was after direct rule had been imposed by the British government. There were no pubs open, nobody at work, no buses, no public transport of any description, especially in East Belfast, our side of the city. It was very eerie. Nobody knew what was going to happen: the feeling was that that day it could have gone to civil war. Rather than staying in the house, people went out: at least if you were out on the street you could get into the flow of whatever was going to happen. All the men were stood on street corners outside the closed public houses; there were no cars on the roads – the bloody thing would be taken off you.

In the city centre the boys came up in their UVF uniforms and passed us the word to stand outside the police station. A good crowd developed so the police called for the Army and a company of Paratroopers came down. The Paras lined up outside the police station and we lined up opposite them about six feet away. I was at the front – I was only a little git at the time – and I'll never forget the Para stood facing me: he was big, broad, with a shaven head, ugly, and really mean. He stood there in his combat gear with this bloody three-foot baton, tapping it in his hand, looking at me, his facial expressions changing every minute from growls to grins. I pretended I wasn't impressed, couldn't get worried about it.

We just stood there looking at each other for a couple of hours, and then the whole thing died a death for some reason, and people started drifting away. We ended up talking to the Paratroopers, and this particular guy said to me, 'You know, if it had started, you'd have got it.' I said the usual crap, 'If it had started you'd

78

have got a sore head', and we got in the back of their Land Rovers and sat talking. In those days the big thing was to collect loads of UVF badges, Orange Widow badges, and I had them all on. We were having tea and they started on 'Give us that badge'. At first I wouldn't, but when I came out of that bloody Land Rover I hadn't a badge left. You see, we never went around with the intention of fighting soldiers or policemen because from the Protestant viewpoint the soldiers and police were always on our side.

Corporal, 1 King's Own Scottish Borderers

I came back into base off an operation to find hardly any of the company there. The guards told me that all the boys had slipped off for a going-away party at Mackies. Mackies was a big iron factory just off the Falls and it had a working-man's club, quite posh; although maybe fifteen per cent of the workforce was Catholic, none of them ever went to the club, they just didn't go to it. But the sergeant major said to me, 'You're a Catholic, aren't you? You can take the padre round. Everyone's invited.' I said, 'There's no way I'm taking a Roman Catholic priest into Mackies social club.' I wasn't happy about it at all – he even had his dog collar and garb on. But the company commander looked at me daggers and started whispering to the sergeant major, so off we went, me thinking, 'That's it, man. My career's ended, taking a priest into a place like that.'

Of course, the whole place went dead when they saw him: it was utter silence. I was sweating cobblers, but he took his accordion out and sang 'The Sash' from beginning to end. They began to join in, and within an hour they'd sung all the Protestant war songs you could think of: the priest knew the whole lot. They were buying him pints, and he said, 'Right. We've had some of your songs, now we'll sing some green ones.' He started off with 'Kevin Barry', and by the end of the evening they were all singing rebel songs, going, 'What a night we've had. What a night!' He was getting invited to come back: 'You can drop in here any time you want. What's your name again?' 'Father Brady.' 'Never mind the Father. What are you, John or Willy? You come round again. And bring the squeezebox.' They wouldn't call him Father, but they accepted him, they accepted him.

Lieutenant, 1 Royal Regiment of Wales

When we arrived in the Ardoyne in March 1972 there was hardly a man on the streets. The Green Howards from August '71 on a four-month tour had locked up the bad boys and for the four months after that the Light Infantry had continued the process. So patrolling at first we hardly ever saw anybody – they were all behind bars. Then Whitelaw arrived on the scene with a peace initiative, and within three weeks we were told to sling our rifles over our shoulders, look like policemen, blend in with the community. The brief was to be as helpful and as kind as we could: buy ice cream for the children. But as the weeks went by more and more of the bad boys were released with appeals from wives and girlfriends etc., and the big frustration set in. It was the dear old soldier in the middle who had to bear the brunt; he was the actor on the stage.

The men felt very much that they were being used. The Loyalist barricades were going up, they were getting tremendous abuse from both sides, and they saw all their hard work going for a ball of chalk when the gun battles started to increase as the internees came out. They were held back all the time, with no chance of getting any decent intelligence to put any of the bad boys back behind bars, or find some weapons, or make a contribution to the military situation. I think at that time the boys had a complete mistrust of politicians. Mind you, I think soldiers get used to that. It's so often the case: the British soldier in a far-flung post somewhere, where the climate is bloody awful, the equipment they need doesn't arrive, the press they get is bad press and the politicians at home don't care anyway. There's a tremendous 'useful resignation' about the British soldier.

Marine, 42 Commando

We used to go out on patrol every night and have a gunfight, every night, guaranteed. You'd go round next morning doing the daytime patrols and you'd get a character standing at a doorway saying, 'Get any of us last night? Try again tonight.' And you knew he would too. The politicians would come across from time to time on big visits, had to meet the soldiers, and so you'd be pulled off the streets. We were in a hide on a long operation, been in there for four days, when we got the word: 'Pull out. Get back in.' There was a big flap on, a patrol came round to pick us up, we go back in, and the only reason was to meet Whitelaw. And all he said was, 'What do you think of the situation? You're doing a wonderful job.' And you weren't. You knew you weren't because people like him were stopping you.

Private, 1 King's Own Scottish Borderers

On the '71/'72 tour there were hundreds of incidents in Turf Lodge. Mostly they repeated themselves over and over again, so we had to change tactics accordingly. We stopped using vehicles because with the petrol bombs it became too dangerous, and had to go by foot. And then instead of walking around the estate we had to run because shootings were becoming more and more frequent. The form was normally one shot and away, but occasionally a gun battle developed, which might last up to about five minutes. Myself, I never killed anyone – or I don't think I did: usually there was no follow-up so you couldn't be sure. If somebody was killed, the next thing you knew about it would be a funeral cortège coming out, and that would be the end of the matter. After you'd pulled the trigger you just had a blank feeling. You didn't know if you felt guilt or elation, because you didn't know what effect you'd had.

Marine, 40 Commando

Then you had all the no-go areas like the New Lodge, Ballymurphy, Andersonstown in Belfast, the Bogside, Creggan in Londonderry. Anybody inside there could be the enemy. It was a war situation.

Corporal, 2 Royal Anglian

The hardest tour we had as far as casualties and the workload went was 1972. When I say workload, we patrolled probably as much on subsequent tours, but it wasn't as deep, you weren't as conscious of the dangers. In '72 we were constantly under threat. Not that we aren't now, but then it was far different. In those days a battalion was responsible for probably what a company is

81

responsible for today: that is the equation. And there were an awful lot of shooting incidents, whether at somebody close by or at your own company. I personally felt my adrenalin pumping from the moment I walked out the gate until the moment I got back in.

Sergeant, Royal Military Police

When I think of some of the things we did in blissful ignorance, I cringe. Bombs for example: any bomb was a problem, but particularly car bombs. Very often they started with just a shout for a warning: somebody'd come up with: 'Hey, mate, there's a bomb in there.' We were on patrol in Lisburn in March '72, on the day the first ceasefire ended. The RUC were quite worried about a car in the main street, so we helped clear the area. Having done that we began to wonder why there were no other security forces people around. So I got on the radio and said, 'We're sat here all dressed up and nowhere to go. What are you doing about the car? How about organising a bomb disposal man?' 'Oh no,' they said, 'we don't think there's a bomb at all. We'll need a description.' In blissful ignorance we jumped into the Land Rover and went out to look at the car. All the door handles were tied down and a wire was coming out of the dash, right through the car and into the boot. That looked significant, so we started putting up spotlights to illuminate it. We thought we were being a bit clever, got out of the vehicle – and then the bloody thing went up. All three of us were lying in the road, gently smoking. When the chaos stopped I thought, 'Bloody hell.' I could see, I could move my fingers; I looked round, had a feel and everything seemed all right; looked down at my feet, and there was a smouldering hole in my boot. It didn't hurt at all. I thought any minute now it would start – you know how you do. My colleague was just coming to, out of the shock, and he said, 'Hang on, I'll help you.' He stood up and fell flat on his face: he had a piece of metal through his leg and didn't know it. We were stupid, bloody silly, blissfully ignorant: young soldiers very early on in the campaign, who just didn't know any better. It was a steep learning curve.

Staff-Sergeant, Royal Army Ordnance Corps

The car bomb was just coming into its own in the early seventies, and every car that was stolen in Northern Ireland by joy riders became a potential bomb. The police wouldn't go near them, we were tasked to almost every one, which led to some amusing incidents. The cars I used to hate were the Austin Westminster and Cambridge, because they had a huge piece of chrome round the windscreen. My favourite way of getting in in those days was literally to take the windscreen straight out in one piece, because it couldn't be booby-trapped without being visible. One morning at two o'clock I was called out because the police were unhappy about an Austin parked outside a pub by the dockside. Behind the radiator was a one-gallon can, which I thought was probably his spare can of oil, since Westminster drivers often made use of the shelf behind the grille, but all the same I had to do the job. I'd been working on the damn thing for about an hour, had taken the panels out round the sides and was about to tackle the engine compartment, when a car pulled up outside the cordon: 'What you doing to Mick's car?' The police inspector said: 'We're suspicious, so it must be dealt with.' 'Oh dear, Mick will be annoyed. He thinks he's been drinking too much lately so he left the car keys with the barman across the road and decided to walk home.'

Subaltern, 2 Royal Anglian

The Army's got wonderful training organisations now. But going over in May '72 we trained for Belfast in the forests of Germany. We'd pretend the forestry rides were streets, trees the sides of buildings, and doors would be marked off with white tape. On the ranges, you'd paint something on a piece of hessian screen and then run round the bottom of the range with it. We didn't have all the electronic targets they've got now, but that training was probably just as good.

Lieutenant, 2 Royal Green Jackets

Our build-up in Germany was all Heath-Robinson. We would exercise one company against another, and we had more injuries with homemade petrol bombs and bricks than in life, when you were actually out there. It was difficult because there was nobody who could instruct us properly. I remember being trained how to search cars by somebody who obviously thought he knew something about it, and I asked the obvious question: 'What does an improvised bomb look like?' I got rather short shrift: 'Don't ask silly questions.' I remember also endless hours spent poring over photographs of wanted terrorists. All right, there are some people who've a memory for that sort of thing, but certainly I haven't, and I suspect an awful lot of my soldiers hadn't either.

Corporal, 2 Royal Green Jackets

In July we went into Belfast from Derry as reinforcements because there'd been trouble with the UDA. That was the first time we'd come across Protestant animosity towards us, which was very significant, because as a result the men's attitude changed a lot. Before, most English soldiers were not really aware of the Protestant/Catholic divide; that was a political issue. They didn't like the Catholics because the IRA came from there, and because they only saw Catholics in conflictual situations, but when they faced the Protestants in Belfast they began to see the other side of the picture, to understand the ways in which Catholics were discriminated against. I think the men developed a more . . . not a more even-handed approach, because their approach was always pretty even-handed, but more sympathy for the circumstances in which Catholics had been living, although no sympathy at all for the IRA.

Corporal, 1 Scots Guards

My overriding memory of 1972 is of seeing bodies being dragged out of a blown-up house and the people on one side of the road screaming and laughing and the people on the other sympathetic. That really affected the way I felt. It always seemed it was Catholics versus the Army. Although I know that wasn't actually the case, it did seem that way at the time.

Corporal, 40 Commando

The second PIRA truce began at midnight on 26 June, and for the three hours prior to that all hell was let loose, with running gun battles throughout Belfast. My most horrifying experience in Northern Ireland was at ten o'clock that night. We were trapped in a back alley with a Thompson firing at us from one end and an Armalite from the other. All we could do was press into the back doors and try to get into the gardens behind. The rounds were literally six inches in front of our faces. The Armalite gave a high-pitched crack as it went past, while the Thompson – a big .45 Thompson bullet is about the size of your thumb – was like a bumble bee, a very fast bumble bee, it buzzed as it passed you. But because one end of the alleyway was the Tiger Bay, a Protestant area, and the other end was the Catholic New Lodge, it was quite possible that the guy with the Thompson was firing at the guy with the Armalite. We never did know if they were trying to hit us or each other.

In comparison to the previous two weeks which had been heavy, the ceasefire itself was an anti-climax. Because we'd become acclimatised to rioting, acclimatised to gun battles, to be honest it was a little bit boring. During the day we'd spend four hours on the ground, or six hours if we were mobile, and nothing would happen. First thing in the mornings we actually used to go right up the Antrim Road to Belfast Zoo and play chasing rabbits with Land Rovers, trying to hit them with batons.

I never believed the truce would last. It could only be temporary, a consolidation. After dark the atmosphere was very thick, unnerving. The street lights were out, and no one was on the streets at all. It was like being at the edge of a fog; you could almost taste the tension. You knew something was going to happen, you could tell it had to break. Walking down the New Lodge Road was like 'High Noon'.

Corporal, 2 Royal Green Jackets

There were various truces that year, in March, in May, in June into July. Everything changed during those truces. We took our flak jackets off and sat in the Land Rovers: instead of facing out, ready for action, we'd just sit. We had to adopt a non-aggressive posture. There was a truce with the Official IRA and a truce with the Provisional IRA. It was unreal. I personally wasn't very happy about the Provisional IRA going to Westminster. I don't think one should give in to excess force. Even though they had what some people might have considered to be a reasonable cause, I don't think there was any excuse for their violence whatsoever. However, they did talk to the politicians, and the truce didn't last very long. No one who lived there could possibly have expected it to.

Marine, 40 Commando

After the PIRA truce ended in July, we were in a gun battle in the middle of Belfast city centre. We didn't really know where the fire was coming from, so everybody was down to ground looking for a target. There was sporadic gunfire all around and people shopping were walking over us. I mean, we were down in a doorway, and the women were stepping over our legs, just carrying on. I got the impression that their attitude was that it was nothing to do with them: 'You're the ones in uniform, you're the ones with the rifles, it's your war and not ours, so sod you. You've got your thing to do, and we've got ours.' They just weren't interested.

Belfast was two separate worlds. In the city centre, bombs could go off in one street, and there'd be panic and chaos in the streets immediately adjacent, and yet four or five streets away people were still shopping. It had already become a fact of life for them.

Corporal, 40 Commando

I think the most surprising thing to me was that the people there had grown up with violence. It was nothing new to them, but I'd come from a fairly sheltered middle-class background, and the shock was enormous. I'd be on the streets, and someone would be trying to literally take my life, for no apparent reason. It was a weird feeling, very, very strange. I mean, that didn't happen to a normal person. And I don't think I ever adjusted to it. It was like getting kicked in the head: you get used to it. It was just nice when it stopped.

'A War Situation'

Sergeant, 1 Royal Green Jackets

We had a guy killed and two others injured by a single shot through the back window of a Saracen. The round passed through the head of the first man, killing him outright, took out an eye and damaged the nose of the second bloke, and ended up in the third guy's ass. The gunman had lain down on the table in the back kitchen of a house they'd taken over, propped up the letterbox with a pencil and fired through the whole length of the house, out the door and into the back of the passing vehicle. It was either a very lucky shot, or the gunman was very good. The Belfast IRA had a guy we nicknamed 'One-shot Willy' working for them at the time, and we always reckoned he might have done it.

Corporal, 1 Para

Nobody says anything about 'Bloody Friday', 21 July, any more. They call what we did in Londonderry 'Bloody Sunday', but what happened in Belfast's all forgotten. I saw the consequences of those IRA bombs – twenty-six explosions in the city centre within an hour. Eleven people killed at the bus station waiting for a bus. I'll never forget that.

Sergeant, Royal Military Police

The Oxford bus station, that was dreadful. They planted a bomb in the bus station, and a little boy was killed. Dreadful: it upset my lads a lot. A little shoe, the bits and pieces, we had to put them into plastic bags; and we had to photograph the bodies in the morgue. That was the worst incident I've seen in Ulster. I'd seen Chinese blown up during the Korean War but you got immune to that. It felt different when you saw your own country-men being killed that way. I mean, I classified it as my own country.

Corporal, 40 Commando

The longest period I had on duty was on 'Bloody Friday'. We were rent-a-trooping in Brown's Square, just off Unity Flats, and of the twenty-six bombs that went off in the town centre, thirteen were in our area. We spent fifty-three hours on the ground and by the latter stages it was starting to get dangerous. The guys were almost walking zombies under the constant pressure: the bus station would go up, we'd drive in from somewhere else, then another bomb going off, we'd drive to that, and so on. Awful long hours on the ground, and after the first few you become inured. I know it's very callous to say 'Another person killed', but after a while they just become numbers. You'd think, 'God, another bomb. We've got to go back out yet again.'

Corporal, 2 Royal Anglian

We were down round the Divis area. All I remember being conscious of was a number of explosions, this high tension, and then waiting for the reports to come through. It made no more difference than that to normal life on the Springfield Road. 'Bloody Friday' was just another incident, and incidents were just a part of the day. There was nothing said like, 'Oh wow, there goes a bomb.' It was just another bomb, or another shooting.

Corporal, 2 Royal Green Jackets

Our part in Operation Motorman in late July was to take back the Bogside and Creggan, the no-go areas of Londonderry. The talk before was that we were going to fight to the death, but I never believed the IRA would fight, not for a second. It was not in their interest. The IRA always considered themselves guerrilla fighters, and knew they could never take on a military force man to man. They were more than well aware that we were coming in. For days before, scores of Saracens still painted a sandy colour for the desert were driving around outside Londonderry; extra troops were drafted in; VCPs everywhere.

We went in at about 0300 hours and took the place back. It was a very quiet operation. We had two contacts, killed one gunman in the Creggan graveyard: he must have been left behind. Everyone who was anyone had got in their cars and gone over the border. The main thing we picked up on was that by and large the civilians were glad to see the back of them. Many did support the IRA, but at that time lots of the gunmen were just thugs, firing weapons off and bullying people. They were glad to see the back of them, and also it was inconvenient living in an area cut off from everywhere, with no points of exit and entry, and constant rioting. People don't like that.

Marine, 42 Commando

We were in Belfast for Operation Motorman and the briefings for it were horrendous. It was going to be machine-guns in windows, people throwing grenades, storm-troop tactics. The operation was supposedly top secret, completely hush-hush, direct from Whitehall. We were to take out the high-rise blocks in the New Lodge – Artillery, Templar, and Churchill. The aim was to get on the roofs and dominate the town while the rest of the unit sealed the streets and did house-to-house searches.

The adrenalin was running very high. We were wearing running shoes so as to get in as fast and silently as possible. Everyone was nervous and alert, chewing gum and Polo mints at the same time. The sun was just coming up when we went across the wire and dashed up the stairs like idiots, clearing all the way up, all sixteen storeys. We got out onto the parapets, and there was the press waiting for us: BBC, ITV, everybody. They'd obviously been briefed as well, because they were walking around as though we weren't there. I rushed out, adopted the fire position in one of the pistol ports the IRA snipers had used, and there was a boom mike and a cameraman next to me. So it was a bit of a farce, a waste of space really.

Corporal, 2 Para

We had six hundred blokes in the Murph and Whiterock, virtually a battalion in what had been a company area. We swamped the place, they were petrified. People were either running for the border or had gone over to England for a holiday. We were digging up guns – well, we didn't even have to dig them up, we were finding them in the roadway that morning, in hedges, in gardens, just laid there. People had just thrown them away.

Northern Ireland: Soldiers Talking

Corporal, 1 Para

During Operation Motorman I was living at Tennent Street police station. A bunch of young teenagers, Protestants, came in one day, and one of them I recognised as a young kid I had known well in '69. I spoke to him: 'Hello. How's it going? What you doing these days?' He was friendly, shook hands with me, and said: 'I'm fucking trying to kill you bastards.' It was as straightforward as that. He was deadly serious: he wasn't joking.

Sergeant, 1 Royal Green Jackets

A week after we got to Belfast it was the anniversary of internment. On my first patrol, walking round the Lower Falls, getting a feel for the atmosphere, I gave a little boy, four or five years old, a wink. He said, 'Do you want your fucking bollocks cut off and sewn up?' I was appalled. To me that summed up how the terrorist had forced a decline in human values in Ireland. People don't know what terrorism is: when they hear the word terrorism they think of a plane being hijacked, something of that nature. Knocking on people's doors at two o'clock in the morning and ordering eighty-year-old people to come out and riot, that's terrorism. When your kids come home from school with black eyes because you didn't take part in the demonstration the night before, that's terrorism. When your wife's tick at the shop stops because she doesn't agree with some particular aspect of it, that's terrorism. When you're threatened with knee-capping because you were seen talking to a policeman or a soldier, that's terrorism.

I felt sorry for the people there because of that, and acutely sorry for them because of the conditions in which they were living. The Lower Falls was like Coronation Street: no baths, outside loos, houses that had never been repaired, deterioration everywhere – a terrible, filthy place. In those days we used to do the search at two o'clock in the morning, at random: we didn't have to have proof, we just searched a house for no better reason than it hadn't been done before. And if the door wasn't answered within thirty seconds, we kicked it in, because otherwise people would have time to escape. It was nothing to find four or five people sleeping in a double bed; women who you thought were fantastically attractive in the day time, you'd see them in a nightie with no shoes on and notice how black their feet were. It undermined their self-respect for you to see them like that. I don't think anyone lived happily in the Lower Falls. Motorman had just gone in and cleared the barricades, so they had their backs to the wall. In those days they had very few rights, they were hounded continuously, there were soldiers motoring around constantly, a soldier on every bloody street corner.

Lieutenant, 3rd Regiment Royal Horse Artillery

There was a lady called 'the witch of Hardinge Street' living in one of the streets that runs parallel to New Lodge Road on the eastern side. Every day throughout the tour she would spit with her milk bottle, shout obscenities and generally be a pain. Throughout the tour. On the day we were leaving she gave me fifteen pounds and said, 'Buy the boys a beer.' With logic like that, how could we beat them?

Private, 1 Para

When we got to the Shankill, because the battalion had been stationed there in 1969, and because of 'Bloody Sunday', we had a very good welcome. Then we started lifting well-known UVF and Ulster Defence Association guys, they reacted, and there were riots. The Prods always said they were Loyalists and wouldn't fight the Army, but from there on relations went downhill.

Corporal, 1 Para

No patrols had gone out all day because there'd been trouble the previous night. The Protestants had been threatening to kill British soldiers for alleged brutality on the Shankill Road, and my patrol was told to take a look round. I didn't like it, because there was something in the air: you could sense it. We drove down to the peace line near the Falls Road, and there was not a soul, as if a curfew was on. There were always people in the Shankill, but when we crossed over the Shankill Road at the top end there was nothing in the street. So I stopped our vehicles, got everybody together, and said, 'Right. Helmets on. There's something very odd here.' We drove up the Shankill Road again and stopped at a T-junction just above Butler Street. A crowd of maybe fifty UDA guys with batons and little tin shields, all dressed in Belgian camouflage kit, hats, face veils, scarves, came running round the corner and started charging us. Behind them there was another large crowd throwing missiles over their heads. So we deployed, waded into the crowd totally outnumbered. We were going to get slaughtered and they were trying to slaughter us, but we just went berserk, like Viking warriors. We were slapping people down with batons because we knew that they were going to kill us, that if we didn't fight like hell we would be overwhelmed. They started to withdraw then. They had no bottle, those people: hard pub drinkers, but man to man they were nothing.

The riot was practically over when all of a sudden a Bren gun opened up from Butler Street across the other side of the Shankill Road. A couple of the lads fired back at where they thought the gunman was, which was correct, because he didn't fire again. It just went on from there, lots of silly fire. One fella in a car would drive across the Shankill firing a Sten gun. I couldn't believe what those people were playing at: of course, the next time he came across we all fired at the car, and he didn't appear again. After that it just escalated.

These were Loyalists, so-called Loyalists firing at British soldiers – great Loyalists, all Union Jacks and spitting in your face.

Captain, Royal Army Ordnance Corps

I often felt a lot of anger, because working in bomb disposal I saw the results of vicious terrorism so frequently. I went to one incident where two little girls had been blown up. It was Halloween night, 1972, and some Protestant, in inverted commas, terrorists had driven a mini loaded with explosives to outside a pub used by Republicans down near the docks. They had lit a very short fuse and buggered off, regardless of the fact that, being Halloween night, there was a bonfire in the street and a lot of children playing about twenty yards from where they parked the car bomb. By chance, within the next five minutes most of the children left, apart from these two little girls, who were burnt to pieces. When I got there to look for evidence I could hardly find traces of either of those children. It was appalling, I was utterly appalled, and on the way back to our base I called in at the sergeants' mess of the local Territorial Army unit and had a quick drink. Somebody asked me what I'd been doing, so I described this enormously unpleasant incident, and explained how I felt about it. And quite rational, or otherwise rational, people in the bar made comments like 'They'd only have grown up into the sort of Fenians who produce another ten Fenians.' I found that sort of absence of any sympathy awful, black beyond blackness. I could not understand then, and I still do not understand now, decent people reacting that way, which they do, which is what's so desperately wrong with the Province. So when people talk about reconciliation in Northern Ireland I'm afraid I can only think of my own experiences, and I don't believe things have changed significantly since then.

Captain, 2 Royal Green Jackets

Someone in the battalion sent the IRA a Christmas card in 1972. Their card to us came by return of post, and said, 'We reciprocate your greetings, and hope that by this time next year you'll be back in your own country.'

The Changing Role of the Army
1973–9

Sergeant, 40 Commando

To my mind the biggest change from '72 to '73 in Belfast was atmospheric. In '72 houses in the New Lodge were still lived in after being petrol-bombed, the lace curtains still hanging up, but by the autumn of '73 an awful lot of houses had been boarded and breeze-blocked up. In some terraces only every fourth house was occupied. In '72 there was in the heart of the New Lodge a cinema, and that had been burned down by '73, and also many of the clubs. I suppose the owners of cinemas and clubs just didn't think it worthwhile rebuilding, that the return didn't merit the expense, and so the people in the area had very little to do with their lives.

Marine, 45 Commando

We went over to Belfast in February 1973 for four months and had three serious casualties, one fatal, in one small part of the New Lodge alone. The first guy had his legs taken off by a remote-controlled bomb in a doorway in the New Lodge Road at night. First thing next morning the company commander apologised to everyone in the neighbourhood for the explosion blowing their windows through, which we couldn't understand, because the control wires was literally fed through four rows of houses and across the next street to the firing position two streets away. It was reckoned that one of the Fianna na h-Eireann, the IRA youth movement, was stood on the corner and by taking a drag on his cigarette gave the signal to a man two streets down, and the bloke that pushed the wires never saw what he'd done.

Then speed ramps were put in at the top and bottom ends of the New Lodge Road. That was an agreement between us and the representatives of the local community. They said they were frightened the Prods would come screaming down and attack the

Starry Plough with a quick bomb in the door or a machine-gun burst, so the sleeping policemen went in. It only took the opposition ten days to work out an ambush. Two company vehicles were driving over the ramps when a lance corporal was shot stone-dead through the heart from the top of the burnt-out cinema and a sergeant had the side of his leg ripped off in a ricochet that went through the side of his Land Rover. We were bitter about that, because the ramps were put in on their say-so, and it worked for them, but not for us.

Corporal, 40 Commando

We did a house search in '73 at dawn and one of the girls in the family went into the back yard where the cordon party was, pulled up her nightie, squatted over a drain hole and went to the toilet in front of them. In another house the dreaded understairs cupboard had been battened off, hardboarded up and wallpapered. We thought, 'Ah, a hide', so we took all the decoration off and opened it up. It was full of dirty washing – chock-a-block. How long would it take you to pull out, say, a dhobi bag full of washing? It took us ten minutes to get all those clothes out. They were crammed in that much they'd become hard. There must've been two or three thousand quid's worth of clothes in there. Very strange people.

Private, 3 Para

We were on a patrol just off of Flax Street, on the Etna waste ground, and we stopped this guy and did a P check: take the name and address, and sent it over the radio for a report. The corporal was brilliant at the chat routine, and asked him, 'Where are you going, then?' The guy replied, 'Across to the gym.' 'You're a sportsman, are you?' He was a big guy, this bloke: 'Yes, I'm a boxer.' The corporal said, 'What a fucking coincidence,' remembering I was a young soldier, eighteen, and I boxed. He shouted, 'Flanagan! Over here! Put your weapon down.' So I put me weapon down, he trod on it and then said, 'Right. Three rounds with this guy.' The Paddy cried, 'Oh no,' to which the corporal said, 'You either box or we take you in.' So there we were, all met in the wasteland, I've got a flak jacket on and we started

95

boxing. He hit me a couple of times, and I thought, 'I mustn't hit him,' because I was fairly good. I just stood there, but he was hitting me, so I punched him three or four times in the guts and head, downed him. When the guy got up the corporal said, 'Get off to your gym and keep your mouth shut, else we'll be round your house.'

As we were coming to Flax Street Mill at the end of the patrol, guess who we saw walking out? The guy had been in and reported the incident to the powers-that-be. But we got away with it.

Private, 3 Para

In 1973 I was attached to the Int section as an Int collator. We had an OC at the time who reckoned he would pacify the Ardoyne, which was a bad little place at the time. We were to stop all the cowboys, and the OC decided to write personally to each and every person on the estate, about 13,000 people, saying, 'I'm the sheriff. You play by my rules.' To do that he had to get clearance from HQ, who said, 'Draft a copy, we'll print it, you deliver it.' He drafted the letter and off it went. About three weeks later a bloody great truck arrived full of cardboard boxes, all addressed to the Int section. We thought they were stationery, pencils and pens, but they were full of these letters. The IO (intelligence officer) opened up the first box and went upstairs to the Ops room to show the CO while we lugged all the boxes and stacked them in the corridor – there were thousands and thousands of boxes. The CO was one of those cigar-smoking Patton types, very flamboyant, a load of crashing smoke, and he took one look and spluttered: 'This isn't what I fucking wrote. This isn't the letter I drafted.' What they'd done was accepted his letter but rearranged the wording to their type of language. 'Burn the lot, burn the fucking lot,' he cried. We'd got boxes to the roof, 13,000 letters, they'd only just arrived on the truck – there was still exhaust smoke in the yard. We had no incinerator in the place, all we had was a fucking dustbin. It took us a week to burn those letters.

Corporal, 40 Commando

The IRA manipulated the crowds to gain kills. They would manufacture a disturbance to draw the security forces in, and then withdraw the rioters and carry out the shooting. I remember one classic example in the New Lodge in '73. There was a club called the Wolfe Tone which had fallen derelict, and the locals used to take the bricks from inside the building as ammunition. Once a riot had finished, they would collect all the bricks off the streets and replace them for the next time. So the powers-that-be decided that the building was to be bricked up, and the Engineers came down with breeze blocks and cement, and sealed the building up. My patrol and another lad's then had to stand on either side to prevent anybody pushing the breeze blocks in while the cement was soft. The street in front of us was packed with people, when all of a sudden all went quiet: everyone disappeared – there were no dogs, no kids, no women, nothing. I thought that was strange, but it didn't actually click there and then. All of a sudden an Armalite and a Thompson let rip at the lads on the other side of the building and the rounds were hitting the wall about three feet above their heads. We all disappeared down the side streets to get away, but one lad on the far corner ran out into the middle of the killing zone. That was his training, to be aggressive, and there he stood, in the middle of the street, looking for the gunmen. Luckily it was cowboy shooting: one burst, and gone.

Corporal, 2 Para

Officially we'd carry full mags with empty chambers, but I always kept one in the spout, always. From the second tour on I never went out without one up the spout, which was strictly against the law, but lots of blokes who had been there a few times did so. Many times I got the feeling in my water that somebody was watching me over the sight of a weapon and other blokes I've talked to have felt it as well. One example was in Newry in 1973. We were going down this street and stopped outside a Republican club, and they started gobbing off at us, throwing stones and giving us a lot of verbal. One of the other boys felt it first, and he just tapped on the side of his mag. I looked round and he asked me if he could cock. I said okay, 'cos if he'd got the feeling perhaps I'd missed it or maybe I'd been there too long. The three of them just cocked as one, and we never got any problems. You might think it was just us being tired, bollocksed, over the top, adrenalin or whatever, but I'm firmly convinced that feeling kept us alive.

Sergeant, 2 Royal Anglian

You couldn't really please or satisfy the people in Derry, no matter what you did. You were the middle man. In '73 my platoon was on the junction of Bligh's Lane and Central Drive in the Creggan, surrounded by half a dozen screaming females. One said to the guy on my right, 'We don't want you bloody people here. Why don't you bloody go home and leave us alone?' This guy remarked, 'I would like nothing better than to be at home with my family.' Then, in her next breath, she said, 'There you are, you bastards. You're only interested in yourselves. You don't care what happens to us.'

And the IRA were callous. One of our patrols was on Creggan Heights when they saw somebody walking about in an empty house. Two boys were sent in to check it out, and found a guy fixing a Yale lock on the front door. They all went upstairs, and a trip wire across the top of the stairs set off a charge. One lad was only covered in white dust, in shock, but the other lad's calf was damaged in the blast, and the repair guy had his leg blown away. When we went back in '74 he was hobbling around on crutches and a false leg.

That was the sort of picture I had of the IRA then. He was one of their own community, and perhaps it was a case of the left hand not checking what the right hand was doing, but I became more and more conscious of their disregard for their own, and their lack of common sense as to why the Army was there. I didn't think they'd ever achieve their aims by the bullet.

Captain, Army Air Corps

Picture the Orange Order marches: I'd just sit over Belfast in the helicopter watching the sheer numbers able to get on the streets. There'd be a great long column and then you'd see the odd troublemaker nipping around the side streets and coming in. You didn't get any feeling of atmosphere in the air, they were just cold objects, rather like watching a silent video of a football crowd. You'd sit there in your helicopter, see a problem, relay what was happening to the blokes on the ground, and move a unit in to cope. It was rather like manipulating chessmen: you'd sit there virtually having a game of chess – the same cold detachment.

Lieutenant, Army Air Corps

A lot of flying work in the seventies involved pure observation, sitting up overlooking Belfast, watching, or doing top cover day and night for the security forces in the city. The soldiers on the ground often had difficulty in telling you where to shine the nightsun. So we used to say, 'Just tell us to move the light two hundred metres north, two hundred metres east, instead of right or left, because you don't know which way I'm facing.' But they never seemed to get it. I was with the UDR just outside Belfast where they found a guy who had been topped lying in a ditch, and they wanted light to see if the body was booby-trapped. After much difficulty I got through on the radio to their patrol, who said, 'Put the light on now.' So I shone down on the general area, and there was a long silence: they obviously weren't quite sure what to do. Eventually I asked them what was needed, and the reply came back, 'Fly to the moon', which was seemingly the only reference point they had.

Private, 1 King's Own Scottish Borderers

Christmas 1973 wasn't a Christmas, but morale was high because we still had a traditional Christmas dinner. The sergeants and officers served the turkey: that made all the difference. On New Year's Eve I remember we were lying in ambush, and at midnight mixed in with the bells were explosions all over Belfast. For a Scotsman, New Year's the great thing, and we all had a good laugh, looking at our watches and lying there hearing the bells and bangs. No 'Auld Lang Syne' that night, just bombs from the IRA.

Corporal, 42 Commando

At six o'clock on the morning of 15 May 1974, the Ulster Workers' Council strike started, as we'd been warned it would. The Protestants closed off the estates, cars were overturned to make barricades, and all the Prod areas became no-go. We actually thought that it was going to be the big one because the Prods were truly up in arms, no two ways about it: we were having to ram our way into, for instance, the Rathcoole Estate, which then was the largest housing estate in Europe: they started petrol-bombing the Catholics out of the area, they had their own mobiles set up, they had OPs dotted around the blocks. It got pretty ugly at times. Just down the road was the Bawnmore, a real hard Catholic estate although very small, and when the UWC strike began they were the first ones to turn up at the gates asking for extra patrols, because they were frightened of what the outcome would be. Reports from the rest of the unit showed a similar attitude. In the New Lodge the Catholics were totally back to 1969: they were giving the lads sandwiches and cups of coffee, because they were so pleased at the presence of the troops. Yeah, the UWC strike was quite something. We ended up doing a big operation taking out the no-go areas, and that was a total turn-round from 1972. Then I'd been on Motorman clearing the Catholic ghettos, and in '74 I was doing it on the Prod estates. There were a lot of marches, smaller riots, and we thought it was beginning, that it was going to blow up and really happen. But it faded away.

Major, Ulster Defence Regiment

The great fear the UDR had during the Ulster Workers' Council strike was that the regiment would not function, because of the way the strike was being organised. It happened so quickly, and everything stopped. Union activity, militant activity was such that people were intimidated by the mere word, not necessarily by the presence of the militants; the fact alone that they were talking on the radio kept everybody inside. But as far as my company was concerned, they turned up to a man and did their job as soldiers. We had no major problems, and we got a great sense of achievement that we, the regiment, played our part in supporting the security forces to keep the routes open, to keep vital services functioning, and to guard all the key installations for which we were responsible. It was very tense, a time when the full weight of military law, with small capitals, took over.

I was also involved on the civilian side in that I was employed in the energy business, managing the delivery of petroleum spirit to filling stations. So I could see the problems and logistics from both sides and in my capacity as a soldier I was able to assist the Army with my civilian experience because they were doing the things that I knew could not be achieved if they went in with their eyes shut. The Army learned an awful lot from that particular exercise – there are subjects about which they are out of touch. It was an interesting time.

Private, 2 Para

It was quite nerve-racking to come across the crowds. A woman tried to cave my head in with a piece of concrete sewage pipe. I was looking in a different direction, and out of the corner of my eye I saw it coming and it hit my rifle butt. I didn't notice until I got back into camp that my rifle butt was completely shattered, all split and broken. The Irish had a way of making themselves hysterical. They seemed to work themselves up into a frenzy, but a couple of baton rounds pumped into them seemed to put them off.

We still had the old rubber bullet then, and there was one case where a section fired a round which hit the roof tops and actually took a chimney pot out, much to everybody's mirth. The orders for opening fire were the early version of the Yellow Card. The way it was written I never did understand. The terms were very misleading. You could read into it what you wanted to, so the basic guideline ruling, that you could only fire if that was the only way to stop them after due warning, was really the section commander's responsibility.

Sergeant, 2 Royal Green Jackets

We got there in December '74 and patrolled exclusively Protestant areas. The Protestants were involved in some internecine conflict, and we had a hell of a lot of murders to deal with, twenty or thirty at least. Most were between the UDF and the UDA. Both organisations were trying to gain control of the area, protect the people, and so forth. I came across mainly UDA people. They were the most appalling thugs, they really were, involved in petty criminality of all sorts: fruit machines, stamps, drinking clubs, building-site rackets, etc. A lot of innocent people were killed as well. Three men walking down a road in the Highfield Estate were gunned down by mistake by machine guns out the windows of a passing car – exactly like Chicago.

101

Private, 2 Para

A lot of the time I disliked the Protestants more than the Catholics. If we were in a Catholic area we were going to get stones or bottles thrown at us, or on the anniversary of internment a minor riot. That was par for the course: the Catholic population just didn't trust us and didn't like us, and the fact that we were the Parachute Regiment only helped in that distrust. But down in the Protestant areas the guys in the UVF would wander around doing as they pleased and actually expect us to defend them. They seemed to think it was their right for us to protect them and nobody else. In my dealings with the Protestant population I got to distrust them more and more, far more than the Catholics. The Protestants were doing things behind our backs all the time, and we could never actually catch them at it. Even though I used to drink the tea they gave us, I didn't trust them enough to go inside their houses. A lot of the younger women were looking to marry their way out of Northern Ireland, and if they could find an eligible soldier who would take them away they would have been quite content, and I just never felt quite right with them. I still hadn't figured out what we were doing in Northern Ireland at the time, and trying to understand confused me. I was just twenty, and it certainly was a confusing time. In fact, in our platoon we had about five Irishmen from Belfast, and they were probably nastier than any of us. I suppose having been brought up there they could see what the troubles were doing to their home town. They weren't sectarian: they would slap anybody around the head.

Captain, 2 Royal Green Jackets

During the PIRA truce in December 1974 we went to Midnight Mass in Ballymurphy. I remember riding in a Pig to the CO's base at Whiterock, armed to the teeth, having a cup of coffee, then him saying, 'Right, we're off to Mass.' The CO and myself, who were Catholics, and a couple of others who I think volunteered, went along. We had a patrol hovering around, but the locals were amazed at us walking, in uniform, down the middle of the road in the dark, without flak jackets or rifles. We went into the church and at the back were the heavies, the opposition. I felt unnerved: it wasn't my patch, and I certainly detected the hostility. Actually it turned out to be quite a nice service: the singing by the women

102

was impressive. The priest was absolutely amazed to see us. The sermon he preached was perhaps not very Christian, but it was interesting, and of course a priest in a place like Ballymurphy was in a very difficult position. When we went up to the Communion rail I thought we were going to have a confrontation, that he might not give us Holy Communion, but he did. And later that night we received a couple of telephone calls from people thanking us.

Chaplain, 2 Para

One man's freedom-fighter is another man's terrorist, and an Irish priest who believes Ireland should be united might well say that a Roman Catholic soldier, or padre, is selling out his faith. As far as he's concerned a Roman Catholic in the British Army is supporting a repressive regime employing armed troops to keep their people down and shoot their parishioners. I think the big problem for a Roman Catholic priest in the 1970s, and I am guessing now, could well have been that were he to have taken a stand against the terrorist he would have felt anxious about alienating his own congregation, so it would have taken a lot of moral courage in a strong Republican area in Northern Ireland to say anything that might have been in the slightest way construed as supporting the Loyalists. Indeed, often I don't think they could have spoken out against the terrorism without it being seen as support for the union, and in many respects the tragedy of Northern Ireland is just that. Priest and citizen alike is going to be polarised whether he or she likes it or not, even to the extent that until recently the working man, the artisan, has had in effect to vote Conservative if he supported the United Kingdom, or Republican. There still is no party to represent the working man that might cross the sectarian divide, and, of course, very few marriages have ever crossed that divide. And I think the position of the Roman Catholic chaplain in the Army is even more pro-scribed. They meet their fellow clergy and do what they can, but I think again they are very conscious that they could be seen as agents of a repressive regime, and unless they completely isolate themselves from the local population in Northern Ireland they have a very difficult time indeed: one Roman Catholic chaplain was beaten up by the IRA, and another had a shot put through the windscreen of a four-tonner as he came out of the police barracks in Londonderry. If a particular car was known to be the chaplain's car it was hoped it would be sacrosanct.

Captain, Army Air Corps

On Christmas Day 1974 I was on standby in South Armagh. It was eventful: I was tasked to pick up the company commander from Forkill and fly him back for the regimental party in Bessbrook. The weather got worse and worse, it got later and later but eventually we got in the helicopter and off we went. We were so busy chatting we got rather lost. I think we went a bit too far south that night: there were some awfully bright lights below us – Dundalk, the Irish Republic!

Sub-Lieutenant, Royal Navy

The road vehicles for HMS *Rame Head* in Londonderry consisted of two Land Rovers and two Ford Escorts. All were painted civilian colours and had civilian number plates to protect our anonymity. At one point one of our green-painted Ford Escorts went to RNAD (Royal Navy Armament Depot) Antrim for a re-spray. It was returned to the ship painted maroon, and within half an hour of its return the ship's transport officer received a phone call from the IRA enquiring why RN Reg. No. . . . was now painted red, and what was wrong with 'the green'. So much for anonymity.

Sergeant, 40 Commando

February 1975 in Andersonstown was quiet. I think the PIRA had started to appreciate that they were living there and didn't want violence on their own doorstep. I couldn't blame them: I mean, if I was going to create filth and nausea I wouldn't do it in my front garden, I'd go do it in somebody else's. I think their wives were having a say too. They were getting fed up with it, all the people that lived there were. Like all terrorist organisations, the PIRA needed the backing of the local population and so they had to change their operations, become more subtle. Which they were: the days of the guy sticking a Thompson round a corner and blazing off a magazine were long gone. By the '75 tour they were well practised and very professional at their job. And the local population, the nationalists of Andersonstown, didn't object to our presence so much. You could actually talk to some of them. They'd be, not friendly, not overtly hostile, just cool. They didn't openly hate you like they did in the early seventies.

Corporal, 40 Commando

I met my wife in 1975 at a tea stop. I was in the Intelligence section then, and we had to go round and make contacts with as many people as possible. Part of our patch was Rathcoole Estate, 65,000 people and all Prods, and we had two Catholic estates close by. I was on the Catholic team and to get out of our area we used to have tea stops on the Protestant estate, and that's where I met her. Before we got married, she worked as a receptionist in the Europa Hotel. Of the staff there the hall porters and a majority of the waiters were Catholics, and most of the receptionists and telephonists Protestant. When they were working together there were no problems at all, but if they'd have seen each other in an area where they weren't supposed to be, then probably they wouldn't have been so friendly. Of course, one of them happened to catch on that I was in the services, and my fiancée was warned by a phone call to the reception that any touts or people fraternising would get tarred and feathered. She took it seriously and pulled in the RUC. I was more frustrated because I was out of the country and couldn't do anything. Fortunately nothing happened, nothing came of it.

Sergeant, 2 Para

Checkpoints were a big thing in '75, and we used to get a lot of awkward people at roadblocks. Not surprising, when you consider that in them days one man driving across Belfast might be stopped six or seven times. He soon got fucking pissed off, and the attitude of the soldier on the ground was: he's pissed off – right, get him out, seats out, tyres out, check the wheels. So the driver would be there for half an hour, getting more angry. Obviously you couldn't let people through just because they said they'd already been searched six times, you just couldn't set a precedent like that, but it didn't half get people angry, and they never forgot. They'd be late for work – leave their house at seven o'clock and get in at twelve. That was wrong – it shouldn't have happened.

Private, 1 King's Own Scottish Borderers

I went with my father in 1975. He had a two-year posting at Palace Barracks. I was ten. I used to go to an Irish school: Protestant. I made lots of friends and I just couldn't figure out why my dad didn't like the Irish. I got on brilliant with them. I used to pal with them and go downtown. We'd see a patrol pass in the street and it just never bothered me. I used to see my dad on the street. If I heard somebody had been injured, I never used to think, 'Oh God, that could be him.' I really liked Belfast. I'd go back there tomorrow, I'd go back and live there. But I joined up, burnt my bridges.

Private, 1 King's Own Scottish Borderers

When we were changing the guard in the Crumlin Road Jail we used to shoulder arms, step off together, and march round the perimeter of the prison. All the prisoners would be hanging out the windows as we passed, giving us dogs' abuse: 'Get your fucking left arm up. Put your rifle back.' They knew the score, but we just ignored them and carried on. 'Squad halt', and they'd cry, 'Fucking rubbish.'

The Crumlin was like a spider, like the inside of the old steel helmets we used to have: put it down and spread it out, and you had the centre and all the legs going outwards. Each leg, each block, would be a different unit: that leg would be UDF, that leg would be UDA, IRA, and so on. The other leg would be just normal prisoners, and at the end of the normal prisoners were the top security, the child molesters and all those people. We could see them all at night from the sangars, passing messages, bits of toilet paper down out the windows. I remember we were facing the IRA block one night and they used to shout out, 'Hey Jock.' 'Aye, what is it, Paddy?' 'Who's fucking your wife at the moment?' just to upset you. We used to give it back to them: 'Who's not fucking you, you Irish bastard.'

The best sangar was number 7, the super sangar. We used to

get into trouble with this sangar because it was the highest in the whole Crumlin and had two spotlights, real Alcatraz kit. They were shone along the dead ground between no-man's land and the prison cell to make sure no one escaped. Those beams were so strong there was a warning marked up inside the sangar not to shine the lights at a certain degree because they'd dazzle the OP on the top of the Divis Flats in the Falls Road three-quarters of a mile away. That's how fucking strong the light was. It was to be used to shine into a courtyard at 150 metres. So we'd be there at night, and at maybe three in the morning we'd pick a cell, shine it in and leave it on. I'd guarantee that within ten minutes the prisoner there – he probably had the patience of a saint – but within ten minutes: 'Hey Jock, switch the fucking light off.' 'Fuck off, you bastard. I'm awake, so you're staying up too.'

Private, 2 Para

We were in the Crumlin Road Jail on guard when one of the sangars reported Morse code messages being sent to the prisoners. We had a corporal with us on machine-gun who was into Morse, and sure enough he could make out certain letters. So we radioed the information back to base, and a patrol was sent out searching. What they found was a black plastic bag with a hole in it flapping in the wind over a streetlight. It really did sound very much like Morse, but we felt a right bunch of idiots afterwards, and had the mickey taken out of us unmercifully.

Lieutenant, 1 King's Own Scottish Borderers

In '75 we were in the Short Strand, a Catholic enclave just down by the river in Protestant East Belfast. The company had a tiny little base down there, and one night there was a lot of noise and fuss in the air. A few stones were being thrown at our patrols, the early stages of excitement, and you could feel the tension rising throughout the area although you couldn't put your finger on it. Three girls came round the corner, running, so I stopped them with my patrol and said, 'Where are you going?' They said, 'We're going to get some chaps.' And I said, 'Now, who would they be?' because I was worried about more boys coming to assist in what was maybe a riot round the corner. They looked at me as though I was from outer space and said, 'No. Fish and chaps.'

Private, 2 Para

We had the buffer zone between the New Lodge and Tiger Bay, which was a lot of Protestant estates and small Catholic enclaves in the middle. There was one called Little America, with Kansas Avenue, Vancouver Drive, Madison Avenue – the Irish seem to have a way with naming streets. One of the government/PIRA truces had only just ended, and internment was being phased out, so there wasn't a lot going on. We had a couple of minor sectarian killings, and quite a big crowd disturbance on the anniversary of internment, but it didn't escalate much.

During the so-called truce a team from *World in Action* came across to film us. The briefing was to let them wander around following us doing our normal thing. We were well plastered with camouflage because it was at night, and we were down at the bottom of Duncairn Gardens lying up in darkened doorways when the camera team arrived. Within twenty minutes you couldn't get into a doorway for the amount of people who'd arrived because the TV cameras were there. We were walking up Hillman Street in the New Lodge when one of our patrols ran across the road ahead of us, through a patch of light. I could make them out quite clearly from the Denison smock, but our platoon commander didn't see them properly or got muddled up, because he was convinced they were four gunmen, so he cocked his rifle and went after them. The camera team was following us, and as the platoon commander legged it up the street he tripped over, went down, hit his SLR magazine on the ground; the base came off, and twenty rounds rolled out on the street. By this stage we were in hysterics, and the blokes from *World in Action* didn't know what to make of it. The cameraman just switched the camera off and said, 'Sorry lads, I'm going. Don't worry, this won't go to print.' We spent about an hour picking up the rounds from the gutters and explaining to the platoon commander in various terms exactly what we thought of him.

Corporal, 1 King's Own Scottish Borderers

In 1975 we had a community relations team, purely to serve the community, to show that the Army wasn't there only to be peacemakers or aggressors, but was also there to provide a stable service to the community. We used to put on a complete cabaret act and took it round some of the old folks' get-togethers. Now, if the social was in a Protestant area the local UVF commanders would be there making sure everything was hunky-dory. If we went into a Catholic area it was a bit more dodgy, but we were given a safe passage in and safe passage out. Both sides trusted us because we weren't up to tricks, weren't trying to con people to get information. The old folks all thought the show was lovely: they'd sit with their tawny port and get juiced up, and we'd come round with their cups of tea and they'd be half-japed. They loved it.

One particular night I recognised a local UVF commander, brigade staff, sitting there, and he invited me to have a chat. 'Have a pint,' he said. 'Fine. Thank you very much.' I knew who he was and I felt quite safe because I knew the system. We were chatting away to the end of the night, he got two or three pints into me, and then leaned over and said, 'You know, I've never met a Protestant Polack in my life.' I thought I was in line for a head job. Instant: he knew right away I was a Catholic in this Protestant stronghold, and for that man the SAS was nothing. I couldn't get out of there quick enough. When I was leaving he went, 'We brought you in, so you're all right. We'll take you out. You've done your best.' I never went back again. Those blokes were real, the whole lot of them: they looked after their patch. He knew he had me on a fine string, and he knew how far he was going to go. I didn't.

Corporal, 1 King's Own Scottish Borderers

We were doing a patrol, four of us, up Thompson Street in the Short Strand and a van came along and the guys inside started abusing us. We tried to stop the van, but it turned down Moira Street. They went into one of the IRA clubs, the brick commander spoke to the gateman, and the guys wouldn't come out. So we waited and waited, until they came out, and started questioning them. A row started, one of them said, 'Oh, you're a big man with a weapon in your hand.' All of a sudden the gateman opened the door, and everybody in the club came out and they cornered us off. That was my worst experience in Northern Ireland. They got round my mate, and one man grabbed his rifle. We warned him: two warnings, three warnings, and he wouldn't listen; three warnings and he would not listen. He opened up on us, so I had to shoot him. The force of the round threw him back against the wall, and his hands snapped free of the weapon. Afterwards they took me off the streets for two weeks. When I went back they still called me a murderer. The memory is bitter.

Sergeant, 1 King's Own Scottish Borderers

There was a really major funeral in 1975. The procession first of all lined up just outside Turf Lodge in the Glen Road and headed downhill towards Milltown Cemetery. They were becoming much more sophisticated, people in the IRA had cameras there, and since I'd got fairly well docked I hid with a few other guys about fifty metres away from the road. I saw this brat, a young kid, coming towards the mourners with a carrier bag. The system was that the bag would have been passed on to the kid to come across with because inside were the half-dozen pistols for the funeral, for shooting over the grave. I missed the kid by about a foot, just couldn't get there in time: as I was getting to him the pistols were taken from him and passed along. We couldn't do any more. The only part of funerals we got involved in was the start, from a distance, seeing it go into the cemetery. Anything else was just asking for trouble. They were making their show of strength, and we could do nothing about it.

Captain, 1 King's Own Scottish Borderers

The Republican funerals were innumerable people and carefully stage-managed. The family itself was rather pushed aside, taken over by those orchestrating the event. In the mid-seventies the processions going to the Milltown Cemetery were enormous. They'd always fire volleys over the coffin, and the Army would be criticised for allowing that to happen. But did our critics realise what the end result of trying to arrest those responsible would be? Usually there were upwards of five or six thousand people around the grave: how many forces would be required? How would we physically get to the middle? How would we find those pistols? How would we search all those people?

The Changing Role of the Army

Warrant Officer, 1 King's Own Scottish Borderers

As resident battalion we could be deployed at very short notice if a problem with car bombs or murders or whatever reached an unacceptable level. You'd parade your platoon, get your three or four armoured Pigs ready to move and trundle off down the Sydenham by-pass. I used to look over my shoulder and all the guys would be sitting there in the back with their helmets on and visors down reading *Playboy*, comics, anything. You'd get down into Belfast, they'd all get out, you'd brief them, and their principal aim then was how much loot they could acquire: I don't know how well you know the Army, but everybody is hell bent on getting their hands on your kit. They would all be immediately switched on to the prime role of stealing as much property – eating trays, torches, etc. – from the unit you were relieving. The spoils would be slung in the back of the Pigs, they'd say, 'That's the main job done,' and then go off to confront whatever the problem was. There might be riots, petrol-bombings, car bombs, people cut in half by flying glass, shot to pieces.

At the end of the day the trouble would die down and you'd trundle back up the Sydenham by-pass. I'd look over my shoulder and all these young impressionable guys who'd been exposed to riots, people cut by flying glass, gunshot, whatever, would be back to reading the *Dandy*s and *Beano*s. You'd get into Palace Barracks, all the ammunition and kit would be checked, and half an hour later the place would be totally empty. No one would be saying, 'Oh God, what a day', nobody was mentally or physically shattered. They'd all been straight to the showers and down to the disco. It hadn't even occurred to them, the sort of things they'd been witnessing. There are now thousands of those young guys running round Britain who experienced all that with no apparent ill effects.

Corporal, Royal Military Police

When you got called out to the shagging riots, as soon as you were out of the gates the adrenalin was pumping because you didn't know what you were going to. It could be a full-scale riot, or it could be snipers waiting for you to show up. You used to think, am I going to be alive at the end of this? Am I going to come back? That sounds melodramatic, but it did go through your brain. To try and take my mind off that, I would sit there wondering what the others were thinking. I'd look at each one in turn: 'Is he thinking about his missus? Is he thinking about his girlfriend back at the camp? Is he thinking about his mother?' That's what I used to do, and they were all probably doing the same. We never spoke. As soon as you got in the Land Rover you went, and then it was every man for himself, to his own thoughts. Of course, once you got there that was all forgotten, you did whatever the hell had to be done, but there was always that initial journey: you hadn't a clue until you got there what exactly you were letting yourself in for.

Sergeant, Royal Army Ordnance Corps

Statistically 1976 was one of the busiest years in Northern Ireland that bomb disposal ever had. There were four teams in Belfast, and on an average weekday you'd find seven devices. Perhaps three would be dealt with, and four would go off. We used to have an ammunition technician based permanently at the Forensic Science Laboratory in Northern Ireland and his job was to produce what were known as Quick Look reports. For example, we'd get a device turn up which would have a mercury-tilt switch or a light sensitive diode incorporated in the circuit. We'd rattle off very quickly to the Forensic Science Lab, they'd look at it, work out how it worked and write out a Quick Look report. Every ammunition technician in Northern Ireland would get a copy of that report within twenty-four hours, so they'd know how to deal with one if that type of bomb turned up again. That was a full-time job up until, say, 1977, '78.

Captain, Army Air Corps

The Army Air Corps had its own little set-up at the Maze Prison: a hangar for the helicopters, an Ops Room and a refuelling bay. The regular guard force kept looking at us to take on extra tasks, like providing riot squads. Now, the Army Air Corps aren't renowned for that sort of thing, but if there was a riot in the Maze, the boys had to go in. And when they had the big break-out in May '76, when they burnt the place down and nine Irish Republican Socialist Party members made a break, four were captured by an

Army Air Corps patrol – purely by accident. It was at night, the Army Air Corps were called out, and roared round in the Land Rover. They went up and down, didn't see anything, and stopped because the lance corporal in charge was bursting for a pee. He cocked a leg over a trench, and below were four of the boys. So they picked them up and put them away – I'm not sure if they were exactly captured.

Private, Ulster Defence Regiment

I was only part-time in the UDR then, and one night a car followed me on my way to work at half seven. I had the wireless on, and didn't know they were firing at me; I thought the noise was stones on the tarred road. It was only my third evening on night duty and as I drove in, a car come in behind with sidelights on. As I got out I looked over and saw one man in the front and two in the back, one lad crouched halfway down. I said to myself, 'That's funny,' and as I locked my car the boy jumped out, pulled his coat back and fired five shots from an Armalite into the car. There was no place I could hide; he followed me right into the hospital. The entrance was usually locked at night but some of the nurses must've known what was planned and had left the door open. If that door hadn't been open I wouldn't be here today. He ran after me down the corridor, firing: every time he put the gun up, I zig-zagged. He got me in the arm. He fired twenty-two shots altogether, out of an Armalite. You can still see them in the hospital wall – some even went down through the wall, clean through. I couldn't believe it. I'm telling you, I'd never seen anything like it. It was flashes, big long flashes. Afterwards I got phone calls: a woman would ring, always at three or four o'clock in the morning, saying, 'We'll not miss you the next time.'

Lance Corporal, Royal Military Police

My father used to work in Mackies engineering firm off the Falls. On my first tour I was laid on a street corner on the Falls Road, and woe betide, who should come up but my old man on his way to work. It was the strangest bloody sensation: I'd seen the pictures on the news for years, seen soldiers on the Belfast streets ever since I was a lad in '69, but I never thought I'd actually find myself lying on the bloody street in uniform with a rifle, waiting to shoot somebody, or for somebody to shoot me, and my old man come walking up the bloody road. He looked at me, I looked at him, and he couldn't acknowledge anything: you see, somebody could have been watching, and he worked up there, so I looked away, and he looked away and just walked past. It was one of those things: we understood we couldn't say anything, couldn't look too long. I was afraid to look too long, and he was the same.

Sergeant, 1 King's Own Scottish Borderers

On the eighteen-month tour, in '76, as the medic I had to pick up a man in Ballymacarrett. He was hanging upside down on a lamp post, held up by a piece of welding rod drilled through both knees, his rib cage battered in, probably by a sledgehammer by the looks of it, and one of his eyes had been gouged out. He was alive when we got there, but died very shortly afterwards.

Sergeant, 1 King's Own Scottish Borderers

We found an ideal building for an OP. The caretaker was sweet-talked by one of the company officers, and we went in and out several times under the pretext of having a look round. Eventually we got the key, made an impression, had a new one ground down and it looked about right. We planned to occupy the location for about four days, so we organised the rations and all the special kit, put them in there, and did the briefing. At three in the morning we crept over all the back gardens so as not to be seen and got to the door, which was steel-plated. We put the key in and it didn't fit! Finally, after half an hour, we accepted the key was useless, and in the middle of this supposedly covert operation we buzzed up on the radio and sent for an armoured vehicle and had it reverse into the steel-plated door. Imagine the noise: the whole door jamb caved in, wood splinters, brickwork, breeze blocks were coming down. But in we went, got the door perched back up, naïvely hoping that no one had noticed. We stayed there for the next few days, and on the third morning we heard the caretaker down the bottom saying, 'Keep quiet, the Army are upstairs.'

Corporal, 1 King's Own Royal Border

On 10 August 1976, the anniversary of internment, one of our recce patrols was fired on by two guys who set off at a fast pace in a Ford Cortina. Luckily a mobile patrol which had just arrived at Glassmullan Camp was facing the gateway down towards Andersonstown Road, and heard the report of the contact over the radio. The gunmen's car was spotted by the section commander of the mobile vehicle, in the back of which were two privates. They were assault pioneers, and the most unlikely infantry soldiers you could ever meet – not good shots, not well trained on the rifle. The mobile patrol gave chase, the Cortina turned down Finaghy Road South, and the two lads in the back opened fire and killed the driver instantly. The Cortina unfortunately swerved into a family walking along the pavement, and killed two of the three children and injured the mother. The third child died of injuries later. The passenger got out, grabbed the Armalite inside and threatened the mobile patrol. He in turn was shot by the lads in the back of the Land Rover; he survived, and in fact our lads sustained him by giving the kiss of life. We attended to the kids before the terrorist, but unfortunately two were already dead, and as a result their auntie was one of the women who formed the peace movement.

The soldiers involved in the shooting, within three days they just couldn't go back on the streets: they were too shattered. They were never, ever put back on the streets on that tour, they just could not face it: it was a nervous breakdown. They weren't infantry, yet when we saw the Cortina afterwards the cluster of round holes in the back window was only maybe two inches across. The grouping was so good – that surprised us all.

Warrant Officer, 1 King's Own Scottish Borderers

On the anniversary of internment our company was deployed at the Falls/Springfield/Grosvenor Road junction. We had only two platoons, one spread along the side streets, one securing the junction. Each platoon was about eighteen or nineteen strong, and we were facing a crowd of about three hundred. It was four o'clock in the morning and the crowd were grown men and women, not kids: trying to take prisoners from that crowd was difficult. What stays in my mind is the sheer frustration of trying to come to grips with them. We had to fire a lot of baton rounds, I mean a lot, and yet there were questions asked as to why so many. The amount we fired was no secret, but I found it annoying that RUC chiefs were actually raising questions as to why: if they'd have seen the eighteen of us confronting that crowd of three hundred it would have been fairly obvious why. For some of the time we were literally fighting for our lives.

Private, 2 Para

I'll never forget my first journey to Belfast. We went up by troop train from North Camp, Aldershot, to Liverpool, all along the back lines. An unpleasant ride in what were virtually cattle trucks, the sort of carriages one used to expect from British Rail on a Sunday – really quite dreadful.

We were quite ruthless: we didn't want to get hurt, or our friends hurt, and we also knew who was naughty. So we intimidated known bad boys, no doubt about it. Known players in our area had a hard time. And we worked bloody hard, eighteen hours a day. Not necessarily on the street: you'd be guarding the workmen building up the barracks, making sure they didn't go anywhere they shouldn't – in those days you didn't have the IRA saying they'd top everyone in sight seen supporting the security forces; you'd be in the sangars; in the Ops Room as a runner. It was a marvellous experience, those four months, one I shall treasure all my life for the companionship.

Guardsman, 2 Coldstream Guards

My first impression on my first foot patrol was of the difference between the Protestant and Catholic areas. In a Protestant area there'd be Union Jacks hanging up, but as soon as you went into a Catholic district the housing standards changed, the people changed – even the dogs were more vicious. I think their owners must've shown them pictures of squaddies. It was true. In a Protestant area dogs would come up and wag their tails but as soon as you crossed the road into a Catholic district they'd snap your ankles off. There was a dog in the Gobnascale in Londonderry called Raggles, a little Jack Russell, and it used to chase the Land Rover down the street: we would try to kick it away, but it would literally try to jump in and bite us. Bloody amazing.

Private, 2 Para

We used to do foot and mobile patrols, and one of the Irish corporals – funnily enough he was known as Paddy – had a theory on dogs barking. He would bark back at them and nine times out of ten they shut up. One day he went down an alleyway, we could hear this dog barking, and heard him bark back. I tell you, I've never seen anybody come round a corner so fast: the biggest wolfhound I've ever seen was chasing him down the street. He'd barked and this hound had come straight over the fence after him. He was running for his life. All we could do was fall about laughing, literally. He had eyes like a racing dog's bollocks, and he was only a small stocky bloke. That knocked his theory for a ball of chalk.

Sergeant, 2 Para

I remember one instance on the '76 tour of how the media turned the good intentions of the troops into propaganda. We'd done a raid at five in the morning – nothing was said about the three Armalites we found – and next door an old man had a heart attack. So the lads went in there trying to save his life, and got an ambulance. The Irish press turned that round so as to say we'd beaten him up, killed him. He'd died from a heart attack but within twelve hours the story that we had killed him was in the English national press as well. The BBC was always shooting us down, but we didn't care, because we knew the British Army was not intelligent enough to beat them at that game. We knew whatever we did would be interpreted as the exact opposite: if you helped an old lady across the Falls Road you were trying to push her in front of a taxi – there were no ifs or buts. We were normal everyday blokes, professional blokes, doing a job, like what a priest does – it's a vocation to be a good soldier, a soldier in Northern Ireland. Nobody else could do that job – the Yanks, forget it, that's a joke; the UN, forget it, they wouldn't understand, wouldn't have the mentality. The British tom is so vastly underrated by our own people.

Corporal, 2 Para

We had to man about five sangars and the main gate of our base in Whiterock. The platoon on camp guard would take all the guarding duties. If you were working the sangars you would do two hours on with four hours off. In those four hours off you had fatigues: scrubbing the dixies, washing up, cleaning the showers, cleaning out the shop – the old charwallah's shop is probably the biggest rip-off in Northern Ireland: everything's over-priced, but then again you can't go out to buy, so he's cornered the market. Barracks were always inspected twice a week, but you'd just make sure it was kept clean and tidy because after the first week everybody was starting to get tired already. It was one of those situations where you got progressively more and more tired, and by the end of the tour you were shagged. We used to do a two-day cycle doing that. At the end of that you were pretty tired: you would only get short bursts of sleep. Then you'd go on standby.

We had what was called Red One, Red Two and Red Three. Red One was on immediate: you'd sit in the standby room, and the ruling was that the only things you could take off were your head-dress and your flak jacket, which was over the back of the chair; your equipment was on, your rifle was next to you, and you'd just sit and wait for eight-hour shifts. The Saracen would be outside, and a lot of times we had a WRAC attached to us, in case we had to go out on searches – women, things like that. On Red Two you could be in your accommodation for eight hours, but you had to be fully dressed; with Red Three you could actually get into bed and get eight hours' doss, which generally you never ever got, because when Red One went out, Red Two moved to Red One, so Red Three then had to get up, get dressed and go to Red Two. So it meant that you were generally being disturbed all the time, although Red Three did give an opportunity to get a good shower, a good scrubdown, a good leisurely scoff and three or four hours' sleep, which did everybody a lot of good.

Things would quieten down for a couple of weeks and then start up again. One lunchtime we crashed out to support the anti-tanks who'd made an arrest by one of the Republican clubs on the Whiterock Road. As the anti-tank platoon moved off to Ballymurphy they got caught by a good few rounds, so we thought we'd go in and help. We bombed up and found they were actually assaulting the flats, had virtually a platoon attack going, fighting their way through after the gunmen. We came in from the top end into the courtyard of the flats and got hit from, we thought, an open window. We could see the curtains moving as if someone was firing from behind, shot the flat to pieces, and piled up the stairs. We were all sweating and coughing and blowing, and of course the adrenalin was pumping like mad. When we got to the top flat where we reckoned the firing had come from, me and a couple of the anti-tanks covered, and the door just slowly swung open, very slowly. Immediately I took my safety catch off, the first pressure was taken, just waiting for the gunman to come out. Out walked a woman and a baby. She was literally a quarter-inch away from me and she was absolutely terrified. We could see the reason why when we got into the flat – the kitchen was in pieces, the fridge and cooker full of holes. She'd been inside the whole time.

Our policy was dominate the area to let them know we were always about. There were always two or three patrols about at any one time. The climax of the tour for me came on what started off as a routine patrol. As we went out the base, an elderly couple and a young girl were talking to the gate sentry. They were pretty shook up; they'd just been hijacked up on the Monagh roundabout by three armed youths. We were on our way to drop a letter in at Cory's wood yard. So we plodded up the road and as we came out the wood yard I saw our gate sentry run out to stop a car, which swerved and tried to run him down. It was a gold Vauxhall Viva, the description of the one that had just been hijacked, and as it came closer we could read the registration. I stepped into the road, rifle cocked, raised my hand, and the car swung across towards me, changed down and revved the engine straight for me. There were three in the car, the guy in the back had a shooter, and my first instinct was two rounds through the windscreen. As it passed me I fired a couple more into the side, and of course the rest of my section were firing because they could see the gun as well. The car swerved off the road and crashed into the fence of the special-care school opposite Cory's. The driver was down, completely out-of-date as far as we knew, but the other two were alive and probably still armed. The front passenger flipped out the car and crawled up the bank by the fencing. Then the back passenger, the guy I'd seen with the shooter, came out. He still had the shooter in his hand and I shot him twice, once in the chest and once in the head. That dropped him stone-dead.

We moved in to clear up. The driver was in a hell of a bad state. He had one round gone sideways through his upper arm, which had blown the muscle and bone of his upper arm into his chest; a bullet hole through his ear, which had missed taking his head off by a quarter of an inch; a finger missing; shrapnel in his face, little bullet wounds through his body, because the rounds had broken up as they went through the car. The guy who had crawled up the bank was still alive, so we cut his clothing off so the medics could get at him. He had an exit wound under his shoulder blade the size of a large ashtray; he was bleeding from the mouth: how he didn't die I don't know.

The two survivors were patched up in hospital, and we saw them both a year later at the court hearing. One had irreparable damage to his lungs where bullet fragments had gone through, and he could walk but slowly; the other guy's right arm was just a withered ruin. They went down for nine years apiece. The ironic thing was, we found out later that if we hadn't shot them the local IRA were going to, because they had been robbing post offices and pocketing the cash, not giving it to the cause. So we'd probably saved the PIRA a job.

Sergeant, 2 Para

We did a search, a turn-over job, on a little asbestos prefab in the Whiterock. I was a full screw then, on, say, about 120 quid a week money-wise, and we took out of a drawer there £5,000 in filthy dirty notes wrapped in elastic bands. It was from a protection racket in the Falls Road, letting the shops stay in business under threat. We used to see the slags off the street – the protection men, the boyos – they'd walk in, take packets of fags and walk out. They never put their hands near their pockets, none of them paid for anything. The money was for their ASUs – active service units of the PIRA.

Lance Corporal, Royal Military Police

As military police, we did a week's training on the law, a week moving about the streets, and then twenty-four hours based in Belfast with an infantry battalion. I ended up with the Light Infantry, who were brilliant blokes. Going out into Belfast didn't worry me too much because it was my home. That first night I'll always remember, because for me it showed the real Belfast humour. We were out checking a pub near the Divis, doing the business. One of the LI lads was lying down on the ground, I was kneeling down with the SLRs, and this tot – he was no height, he must have been ten or eleven – come walking up the hill, little lollipop stuck in his mouth. Little bloody dredger he was, and he was stood there eating his lolly looking at me, looking at the guy laying on the ground, and just simply said, 'Soldier, what you gonna do when you grow up?' Brilliant sense of humour.

Private, 2 Royal Anglian

The most memorable thing we had happen in 1977 was the district council elections. We had to protect one of the polling stations, St Thomas's secondary school on the Whiterock Road right between Ballymurphy and Turf Lodge. We got in there early, at four o'clock in the morning, and put blankets against the windows. It all started at about half past nine. We were all sat round playing cards, a couple of guys watching, when six or seven bullets flew in through the windows. Everybody scattered. They'd fired from the Turf Lodge at a patrol going past the school, so rounds were flying in all bastard directions. That calmed down, but five minutes later, in came the rounds again. They'd realised we were in there because of our reaction before. Next a big crowd came down, surrounded the building and threw petrol bombs and rocks. We were under siege, and the civilians inside who'd come to vote were extremely scared. At one point a paving stone was hurled at the plate glass in the main doors and the flying glass cut a woman to shreds. We called for an ambulance, but it couldn't get up the drive because of the crowds. I needed four people to take the woman down through these people to the ambulance. I didn't think it was dangerous; it seemed more a game. We flew out of the polling station like in a wild Western, firing off baton rounds straight into the centre of the crowd. In retrospect, it was a bloody dangerous situation, extremely scary, but at the time it just seemed very funny, and we had a really good laugh when the message came through that we had to stay until the polling station closed at five o'clock – in case in the middle of a mass riot anyone wanted to cast a vote.

Captain, 2 Royal Anglian

What struck me about our '77 tour was the change relative to 1972. I'd been out of Ireland for a few years and came back to find it was no longer the wild-arsed cowboy stuff on both sides. In '72 you were for ever charging around re-loading your magazine – certain parts of Belfast really were like cowboy towns. By 1977 the whole emphasis was on police primacy: the RUC were desperately trying to restore their normal policing role again. The main threat I recall was from command-wire bombs – there was talk of RCIEDs (radio-controlled improvised explosive devices), but we didn't come across them. There were very few cowboy shoots by the PIRA, and therefore very little chance of getting a kill. It astonished me, having just come back from the Oman where at that stage things were pretty wild-arsed as well, how strait-jacketed the Army had become. We were talking in codes because we didn't have secure radios, giving long elongated sets of orders for comparatively simple tasks; we were tying ourselves in knots, really, over-briefing and de-briefing on every single little thing, when really what we needed was more flexibility. Although the soliders were just as happy about serving in Northern Ireland as they'd been in '72, just as brave and resilient, the hierarchy was organising procedures in a way that made them lose their spontaneity.

Corporal, 45 Commando

When we took over the Turf Lodge in June 1977 the IRA knew we were coming. On one wall they'd written in letters three feet high: 'In this spot, on . . ., we killed a Royal Marine Commando', the date was left blank. We thought that was great. We all had our photos taken standing in front of it while the patrol covered us.

Sergeant, 2 Royal Green Jackets

The graffiti over there was really excellent, superb. The big one on the wall just outside the hospital on the Falls is all in the orange and white and green, with two gunmen at the top, black balaclavas on, both holding Armalites. What's the wording underneath? Oh, freedom for something, I can't remember exactly. There was another one of a guy all dressed in black with the old anti-tank weapon ready to fire, and an Army truck rolling past; the next wall along shows where he's fired, and the wagon's exploded and there're dead soldiers all over the place. They cover everything and they really are excellent drawings. Whoever did them, I mean, if they turned their hand to other subjects . . . They must have spent hours and hours non-stop painting them, and I've always assumed they could only have done them when the ghettos were no-go areas – they would have had all the time in the world then. The modern stuff isn't as good as the big ones from the seventies, but they still appear, and the blokes in off patrol always report any new ones. When and how they do them now, God only knows.

Private, 2 Royal Anglian

The feud between the Official and Provisional IRAs was spread over about a two-week period in July '77. On two nights in the Ballymurphy they really went at each other hell for leather. The unofficial order was keep off the streets and let them get on with it. So we just stayed in camp those nights and went out in the morning with the sacks almost as if calling out, 'Bring out your dead.' We found a couple of casualties in Springhill, one had been burned, the other shot, and in a strange way it was quite exhilarating. That's a sick thing to say, really, but by the time I saw those bodies I'd been out there for three months, a hell of a lot of shooting had come our way, and it was really satisfying to see those bastards gone.

Marine, 45 Commando

Turf Lodge gave us quite a hard time, but just before we left an old woman there came up and patted me on the back. She said, 'Thanks very much, son. This is the nearest we've had to peace since this trouble began in '69.' I blushed with pride.

Corporal, 3 Para

The '78 tour in West Belfast was the quietest I'd known. The only memorable incident happened about two days before we came home. We were on the doomwatch patrol, three till six, and the only thing that changes at that time of the morning in Belfast is the traffic lights. We'd bimbled around, ignoring everything that was happening, even if it was happening, because we'd only got days to do and didn't want to push our luck. About five o'clock, just as it was becoming light, we turned round a corner and there at a bus stop was a bloke lying down, obviously drunk from the position he was in, waiting for a bus. We looked him over, and he sat up: 'Aargh, I've been shot, I've been shot.' You can tell a drunk when you see one so we just carried on at two miles an hour down to the lights at the bottom of Lisburn Road. I'd just a doubt in my mind and thought we'd make sure he was okay, in case he spewed. As we got up level, the police were throwing him in the back of a grey RUC Land Rover. They said, 'He's all right. We'll put him in the cells for the rest of the night.'

We went back to Woodburn, and off to bed. About eleven o'clock in the morning the OC came in personally to wake me up: 'What's this about a man shot on the Lisburn Road at three o'clock this morning? The RUC say he's in hospital, on the critical list. You were on patrol. Apparently you passed him. Why the hell didn't you report it?' We eventually narrowed it down to the guy at the bus stop. It turned out he was a Prod barman in one of the local Prod clubs, who had been caught with his fingers in the till. He'd been taken out the back and had a .22 round whanged in the back of his head. Because he had long hair, the cops hadn't noticed either and when they went to the cells to throw him out at nine o'clock he was unconcious, the old death rattle going. It was only when he was being checked out in the hospital that the bullet hole in his neck was found. There was no exit wound: the bullet was lodged against his brain.

Corporal, Royal Military Police

I remember lifting a young guy who lived with his grandmother in the Gobnascale, a nationalist community in Londonderry. It was five o'clock in the morning and his grandmother opened the door, and said, 'Come in, boys, come in. He's upstairs just getting dressed. He'll be with you in a minute.' My job was to assist the police officer making the arrest and then take him with my brick to the police station. I hammered up the stairs, and pulled him out, half-dressed. And it sort of upset me. She was an old woman,

124

her husband was obviously dead, and her grandson was staying there to keep her company. All I got out of her was, 'This is my wee grandson,' and 'How long are you going to keep him?' and she was saying to him, 'Here, son, you'd better put a coat on. Will you be warm enough with that jumper?' She obviously didn't know what the little bastard had been up to. She was just a caring grandmother, her house had been invaded by twenty-odd bloody British soldiers and policemen who were taking her little grandson off to the nick, and she didn't know when she was going to see him again.

I didn't like things like that. I liked arresting the bloke, but I didn't like upsetting the old woman. If I'd seen her on the street prior to that, I'd have thought her just another Catholic woman who probably hated me, and wouldn't have had the time of day for her, but inside the house, when I saw the actual set-up, it was very sad, how she felt. I could see my own grandmother in her situation. I used to stay with my grandmother. That was what it was all about: just one more grandmother whose grandson was being carted off, and she didn't know why, didn't know for how long.

Rifleman, 2 Royal Green Jackets

On one occasion I was sitting in the doorway of Woolworth's in Newry, and a real beauty, long ginger hair – I mean, I was in love – came walking towards me. I was kneeling down, looking at her. I was just eyes: the IRA could've rolled convoys past and I wouldn't have noticed. She's coming towards me, stops, looks down, and says, 'What you looking at, Brit bastard?' I just said, 'I'm in love with you.' 'You look,' she says. 'They're lovely, but you ain't getting fucking none,' and walked off. The barrel melted; that killed me, it really did. They really were beautiful, but as soon as you heard that 'farking this, farking that' the spell was broken.

Corporal, Royal Military Police

We used to put a sniper screen on the bottom of the Gobnascale Hill and watch the estate. We'd stand there with batons, and women would come down from the Gobnascale to give us gip.

On one occasion they were spitting on us something rotten. I pulled my visor down but I couldn't see out of it, so I'd kept it up: didn't bother me in the slightest, because I found if you could just grin and bear it, as the Army tells you to, it got their rag up, because they knew they weren't hurting you. The spit was hanging off us and they started picking on a young WRAC girl who was stood beside me, running her down as far as her sexual attributes were concerned: the size of her breasts, the size of the gap between her legs, how she looked like she'd been fucked by a black man, those kind of really stupid but very personal comments. She was only a young girl, eighteen, and she just hadn't come up against it before, and she started crying. Now as soon as they saw someone in tears they knew they were on a winner, so I said, 'Come on, lass, get standing behind me and just don't listen to it. Stay out of the way of the spitting and all.' She moved behind, and the bloke stood beside me, who'd been looking on impassively the whole time, just clubbed the foul-mouthed old hag who'd been in front of her right across the face. Down she went like a wall collapsing. He put the truncheon back and just stood there, and I looked at the woman laying on the ground. What the hell could we do? I felt awful sorry for the WRAC girl, but obviously the other guy must have felt more sorry than I did, because he took a chance.

Sergeant, 40 Commando

My saddest moment in Northern Ireland wasn't being shot at, or bombed, or attacked by rioting crowds, but the first time I was spat at. That was the biggest shock, just being spat on, by an extremely pretty girl. If you're shot at, it's detached. They're doing it for military advantage, to create political pressure, whatever; there's no personal contact. But if someone spits at you it's hate, pure hate, and that's a very strong emotion to inflict on someone: probably the strongest emotion there is, it warps people's judgement.

Private, 1 King's Own Scottish Borderers

In 1979 my grandmother lived in the Shankill, off Moscow Street, and I used to do a tea stop up there now and again. But they got wise to it, and she came back from a holiday in Scotland to find her house had been wrecked. I was mad. I used to get very mad, wanted to take it out on them. But it was no could.

Corporal, Royal Military Police

One night on foot patrol in the Gobnascale we'd gone firm on both sides of a road when a car came and parked up behind us. His lights were on the two lads in the hedge, so I automatically moved the patrol forward out of the headlights. The guy moved his car, we moved further up the road, and he moved his car again: kept putting the blokes in the bloody headlights. I was getting a bit irate and walked over with the SLR: bang on the bonnet, a fucking big dent. Inside were a bloke and a woman, and I said, 'Look, you continually moved to put your lights on those two lads. You see that bloke there? He's a married man with two children. It's coming up to Christmas, and tomorrow he goes on leave. He's got his presents all packed to take to his two youngsters.' His wife says to the driver, 'For sure, you shouldn't have done that.' He said to me, 'What about the damage to my car?' I replied, 'That's repairable. If he'd been shot, what about those two orphans? All the presents packed, waiting to go.' The woman was in tears, and he says, 'All right, okay. I apologise.' He drove off, the woman crying her eyes out. I'd had to put the old charm on her. The story I came out with – the lad wasn't married, no two youngsters over in England waiting. But you can do it with people in Northern Ireland. Over there we look after our dogs and youngsters, all the rest of it, but we'll shoot you just as quick.

Captain, 1 King's Own Scottish Borderers

Co-operation between the Army and the RUC began to improve in about '79, when the rivalry between information agencies began to cease. The policing role was always rightfully the RUC's job, so all we'd been doing since '69, although we didn't recognise it, was holding the ring until the police could get themselves organised again. They were always going to be better at the job than we were, but the trouble was that having established a lot of expertise we weren't perhaps prepared to hand over the reins too readily.

Corporal, Royal Military Police

We used to have an RUC man attached to us to search the civilians in Derry. One day we had gone firm outside Woolworth's, the civvie searcher was stood beside me, there was a single shot, and his head disappeared, just like a balloon bursting. The skull was a mess of gore, but the rest of him, his neck and body, was quite intact. He just collapsed. Good God, the things that went through my mind then: at first the shot didn't really register, but at the same time I was waiting to feel the pain somewhere, checking myself over mentally, thinking all the time, 'Have I been hit, or haven't I?' That seemed to take a hell of a long time, and only when I realised I was still alive did it register that the bloke had been hit. He was the first person I'd actually seen shot dead. It was strange, a very strange feeling.

A few days afterwards the Old Bill boarded up the windows of the Woolworth's and marked the point of impact of the bullet through the glass on the board. All the local bastards wrote crude comments round the mark: 'Another one for the Provos', 'One-nil', all that kind of crap, because the civvie searchers were all Protestants. We never went firm there again, and on patrol we used to run past the place like the hammers of fuck. The guy's family still lived in the city, and the RUC asked me if I'd paint out the comments. So I bought a can of black spray paint, took my brick up in a Land Rover, and we pulled up in front of the store. I just got out and sprayed the boards so you couldn't see the comments or where the police had marked the bullet hole. The blokes in the street stood looking at us but no more comments were ever written up. I don't know why. Maybe it was because we had painted it out in front of them so blatantly, and maybe those blokes still had a conscience: perhaps they'd seen that we risked going back because we were hurt by it. That's what I'd like to think: I like to think that there's still some soul left in some of them.

Corporal, 1 King's Own Scottish Borderers

One of the stupidest things I've ever done was when I was in Belfast the first time. Where the Shankill joins the Clonard there was a big corrugated iron fence segregating the Protestants from the Catholics. The kids from both sides were stoning each other,

Soldiers of the Parachute Regiment taking tea in the days before the breakdown in relations between the Army and the Catholic population

Outside an East Belfast Police Station, soldiers hold back a group of women and children protesting, with jeers and V-signs, against the visit of the Prime Minister, Edward Heath, in November 1972 *(Pacemaker Press International)*

Soldiers stop protestors from the Belfast area of Andersonstown from reaching the city centre, February 1973. The marchers were protesting about sectarian killings *(Pacemaker Press International)*

Soldiers surrounded by stones thrown by rioters on the day following the fire and riots at Maze Prison, near Lisburn, October 1974 *(Pacemaker Press International)*

Soldiers of 2 Para returning to barracks from a daily routine patrol, 1973 *(Airborne Forces Museum)*

Soldiers of 1 Royal Regiment of Fusiliers, the familiar red and white hackle on their berets, enjoy some local female company *(Pacemaker Press International)*

Soldiers boarding a Lynx helicopter, with a Gazelle helicopter flying overhead. Helicopters are regularly used for border control in South Armagh

Soldier of the Ulster Defence Regiment – the youngest regiment in the British Army – equipped with radio, a few yards from the border

A 2 UDR foot patrol in beautiful South Armagh, somewhere near the almost indistinguishable border. 'Tail-end Charlie' stays constantly alert for hidden dangers

A Royal Marine crouches against a mural painted in memory of the 'H' Block hunger strikers of 1981 on the predominantly Catholic Twinbrook Estate, Belfast

A Royal Marine with a young resident of Divis Flats, in the Lower Falls, Belfast. The flats represent some of the worst living conditions in the city

The Ulster Defence Regiment, part of whose role is to protect the police, carry out a spot check in central Belfast

Northern Ireland's beautiful sandy beaches are one of the attractions the soldiers are best able to enjoy. Here members of the Queen's Lancashire Regiment cool off at Ballykinler. The mountains of Mourne are in the background *(Pacemaker Press International)*

A vehicle check point in Crossmaglen, South Armagh. Although little more than a village, it is a hotbed of terrorist activity

A suspect car on the Ballymurphy Estate, West Belfast, after a controlled explosion carried out by Ammunition Technical Officers of the Royal Army Ordnance Corps with 45 Commando as their cordon. Note the remote-controlled 'wheelbarrow' in the centre

and a grey RUC Hotspur Land Rover was parked watching the Catholic side. It was fired on by what the police thought was just a blast bomb. We were about half a mile away, and we heard the bang and then small-arms fire, about three rifles. The terrorists then fired weapons in the air to let any troops following up think they were under fire, to slow them down, and when we drove up I got tasked to check around the back of the peace line. It didn't stick in my mind at the time, but one segment of the peace line, the tin sheeting, had been ripped off – there was a small hole in the fence you could see through. On the other side was a plank of wood across some bricks, made like a little table, Coke cans with straws hanging out of them, crisp packets with stones on, so I thought the kids had been playing dolls' houses. But something didn't seem right, so I was looking around all over and I asked the company commander on the net for the search dog. He said it was getting too dark, and somebody had found a live round in an alleyway, and so my attention was taken away from the dolls' house.

The next day they found the warhead from a 20 millimetre cannon embedded in a wall behind where the Hotspur had been parked, and empty cases scattered all around the hole in the peace line. I think I missed seeing them because it had been sort of half-light, but the really stupid thing was, where I had been standing the evening before, what I thought was a dolls' house was the actual firing point they'd used. They'd put the plank across to kneel on, with the cannon through the fence. On our training we'd always been taught never to enter a terrorist firing point, because at that time they were usually booby-trapped. If you went in you'd most likely be blown away, and I'd taken my guys in there. That was the stupidest thing I've ever done. When I think about it now it fucking terrifies me.

Guardsman, 1 Coldstream Guards

When I first went to Belfast I was a young boy. I had no responsibilities, I was just a Guardsman, and so the only person I had to care about was myself. There was only one time when I was worried, when we got shot at. It was 26 January 1979, snow on the ground, four o'clock on a winter's day. We crashed out for MacRory Park to block off the Falls Road towards Andersonstown roundabout, and half way down the hill I heard this 'dt-dt-dt-dt'.

The first thing that came to my head was, 'Hmm, sounds familiar'; it was just like we were still in Northern Ireland training. Suddenly it was chaos, like out of a John Wayne movie: kids had just come out of school, there was loads of civ. pop. everywhere, and they just all dived to the floor. Fortunately our Land Rover never got hit, but a boy of eight got shot through the neck. I saw him go down but I didn't pay any particular attention, because I was more interested in following up the gunners.

We later found out, and how we never saw it I don't know, that they'd fired from the back of a pick-up truck no more than thirty-five yards up the road. They'd sand-bagged it and stuck two Armalite and Sten guns out and let rip, something like fifty-seven rounds fired. But in my eyes all the Northern Ireland training we had then geared you to believe that shots would come from a bedroom window, someone peeping round a curtain, and directly opposite on the other side of the road was a window and a bloke behind. He'd only looked out of the window because he'd heard what was happening, but in that instant I very nearly pulled the trigger – thank God I never.

Sergeant, 1 King's Own Scottish Borderers

I don't think there's a soldier who's served in Belfast who didn't feel sorry for the kids. They got the blunt end of it a lot of the time; confused, brought up to see a very biased side of life. It's a great shame, a great shame.

Private, 1 King's Own Scottish Borderers

I found the conditions people lived in really disappointing, real crap. It was awful to see the children, especially in '76 and '79; it was worse searching the houses, old back yards, alleys – the patrols would find afterbirths thrown away, with children, unborn children. I didn't believe the stories I'd heard, but in '79 we were in Divis Flats. It's six storeys high, and the lifts were always broken down, vandalised. We opened the lift doors and saw a bag lying on the floor, and we picked a dead baby with the afterbirth out of it. The whole platoon was there, and the guys just didn't feel like patrolling that day. There again, you always expected something in Divis Flats, because that was a really tough area.

Sergeant, 2 Royal Anglians

I must be the only soldier to receive any form of money from a female in the Divis Flats. This woman had had a few drinks and locked herself out of her flat. The Divis Flats have had squaddies' boots all over them, but she asked me to help her. I said the only thing I could do was put my shoulder against the door and force it. She agreed, and so I did. Once it was open she was over the moon, but before going in she went to the top of the walkway and started shouting her head off: 'Youse bastards, get youse dirty Brits out of here.' Then she said, 'Come in for a drink.' I said, 'I'd love to, but I can't,' so she got uptight: 'Is my drink not good enough for ye?' I said it wasn't that at all, and she got out her purse. The amount of dole in those days was pretty small, but she came out with a wad like Paul Getty and said, 'Here. Get yourself a drink down there if you can't have one here.' I said no thanks, and thought that was the end of the story.

But it wasn't. This female appeared at Albert Street, where we were stationed, and left the money in an envelope with the guardroom. So I informed the OC, following which the night patrol slipped the envelope back through her door. The next day she came down again, not herself but all her partners as well, and said that if we didn't take the fucking money, she'd cause a riot – and she meant it. So in the end I told the lads to hang onto it and have some cans. It was £10, which in 1975 was a lot of money. As I said, I'm the only guy I know who has ever received any form of payment in the Divis – and it wasn't for services rendered, either.

Captain, 1 King's Own Scottish Borderers

The Divis Flats complex in the Lower Falls had a population of around 6,000 people in the late 1970s, with about 40 per cent of adults unemployed. The net result was what I termed the composite twenty-four-hour cycle, whereby the man with a job got up at six or seven in the morning, went to work, returned home at five, six, seven in the evening, had tea, went to the pub, and tended to be in bed by twelve, one o'clock. Those who were unemployed would normally get up between eleven o'clock and one, go to the pub and/or the bookies, both of which were in the complex, spend the afternoon there, go back home for tea, and then return to the pub: their cycle would continue right through the night until bed at three, four or five in the morning. The overall effect within the flats was almost continuous noise of people constantly moving around, depending on which of those two particular cycles they were on, superimposed on which was the noise made by the kids. Because the population was ninety-nine per cent Catholic, with large families, the complex was teeming with children.

Architecturally Divis Flats is a concrete monstrosity, and the constant sound echoes everywhere. On each of the six levels of each block is a long balcony, like a village street, and the entrances to individual flats are recessed. When you walk along the balcony you are walking on the ceiling of the flat below, and the walls and floors are so thin that inside a flat you can hear the footfalls above you. So if you went to bed at midnight to go to work next morning, you had noise the whole night long over your bedroom.

During my time there, mothers only allowed their children to play on the balcony walkways because of problems at ground level. The complex was designed in the 1950s, and the volume of rubbish from modern prepackaged foodstuffs and disposable commodities far exceeded the capacity of the Flats' disposal shoots; they became blocked very frequently, resulting in garbage strewn everywhere and rat infestation. An additional stress factor then was that the parapets along the walkways were at that time low enough to give mothers heart attacks with worry about children falling off the tops. And the lifts seldom worked, which was a great inconvenience to old people in the Flats.

Urban violence is only an extension of those stresses and social discontents, and in addition to a small number of terrorists living within Divis Flats, there was also gang rule. The RUC never went into the complex unless we accompanied them, so routine law and order existed only when we were present. If we weren't, it was the gangland. One lad, about seventeen, eighteen, was found guilty by the local court in Divis of petty theft and told he was going to be kneecapped – that was all they said: 'You're going to be kneecapped.' About a month later he was pleading with them to do it. The pressure on him during that intervening period must have felt like the condemned cell. They took him to the bottom of the stairwell in the tower block, parted his legs, and urinated on him.

Warrenpoint and the Death of Earl Mountbatten
27 August 1979

Sergeant, 2 Para

We always knew in the Parachute Regiment that the PIRA would like one good crack at us, and they got it at Warrenpoint – killed eighteen, mostly Paras. I think they were lucky, in so much as they had a good opportunity at a target arriving at the right place at the right time. Obviously the guy who detonated the first bomb must have been experienced, to take out the rear vehicle. It was the old classic ambush technique: take the back vehicle out to cause the maximum amount of confusion, and then have a second bomb waiting for the back-up. He must have known the way the British Army worked, because when we had casualties we always swamped the area with helicopters and medics; he knew all he had to do was wait and he'd get a lot of people with the second device.

Lance Corporal, 2 Para

Our platoon was travelling down the dual carriageway from Bally-kinler Barracks to Newry in a Land Rover and two four-tonners. The platoon commander was in the Land Rover, I was in the first four-tonner, and the second four-tonner was right behind us. As soon as we heard the bang our driver pulled into the central reservation, and I jumped out the cab door on the passenger side, cocking my weapon. As I landed, I turned round and the blokes were already debussing out of the back. All I could see of the rear vehicle, well, the impression I got was just an engine block sitting in the road surrounded by hundreds of little fires. The bomb had been packed in straw inside a horsebox parked in a lay-by, and the road was littered with black, burning, smoking straw. We ran back and first thing I saw was a bloke on his hands and knees crawling amongst us, still smouldering. I threw my water bottle to another bloke to get some water on him – I was still running on to see if there was anything more. Then my memory becomes hazy. I remember going through the wreckage of the vehicle, and the ammunition started to explode, rounds and magazines going off, so we cordoned off the area and stopped the vehicles coming up from Newry on the dual carriageway. The cars were about ten feet away, and a dozen civilians lined up, arms folded, watching what was happening. One person came forward, a doctor or a fireman I think, and gave first aid to the two survivors from the four-tonner. I started directing the traffic back and over the verge, to keep the outside lane free for any back-up coming from Newry. They arrived within minutes, and I waved them through the traffic. That's the last thing I remember, because I was standing by the road next to some lodge gates, which was where the second bomb was.

Sergeant, 2 Para

I was on a routine mobile patrol in Newry when we got a very jumbled message on the net. The only words I could make out were 'contact' and 'golf course'. The only golf course was down at Warrenpoint, and what we thought was, 'Somebody's hit the Marines.' I've always maintained that those two bombs were waiting for them, because they were laid just right to take out two Land Rovers at the standard fifty-metre spacing. We rushed down along the dual carriageway to Warrenpoint in support, parked up, and I put my lads in a piece of dead ground by a big old stone wall next to a lodge house belonging to what had once been a big estate. The first person I spoke to was a Marine corporal, and I still thought it was the Marines who'd been blown. There was all the usual organised chaos, people all over the place, and he said, 'One of your trucks has been hit by a mine. We think there are about five dead.' That's when I registered it was our guys.

We started getting organised then. A section moved across to the other side of the dual carriageway to cover across Narrow Water into Southern Ireland in case an attack came from that direction. Things were starting to click into place: the trend at that time was either a shooting followed by a bomb, or a bomb followed by a shooting and/or a booby-trap. One of the lads in the gateway by the lodge house covered the hill to our rear, and I was thinking that the gateway itself would be a good place to put a pressure pad. So I shouted to the section commander, 'Get out the way: move down to the end of the wall and get up into the trees,' and literally just as I shouted the second bomb went off.

Sergeant, Army Air Corps

We arrived in the Scout at Bessbrook, and immediately were told there'd been a bombing. We flew in across the northern side of the dual carriageway, where the first bomb had gone off, dropped off a colonel from the Queen's Own Highlanders, and as we lifted up, the second bomb went off. We pulled away quickly in the updraught and circled round. There was a lot of smoke and debris. What happened was, the bombers across Narrow Water in the Republic had detonated the bomb as the colonel went through the lodge house gates. Unfortunately, all that was found of him was his flak jacket in a tree.

Sergeant, 2 Para

What sticks in my mind most wasn't so much the explosion itself, but how everything went black, and this noise: the only thing I can equate it with is thousands of gallons of water rushing, sort of roaring like a waterfall. I must have blacked out for a bit because I then clearly remember sitting in the road feeling bitterly cold – not cold like in cold weather, but like I was encased in a block of ice. It was too cold to imagine: I felt so bitterly cold, it was as though I was entombed. I was sat holding my left arm, in the road, swaying a bit. Obviously there must have been all sorts of carnage around, but none of it registered, just the bitter cold. Then I must have blacked out again. The next thing I remember was being lifted into what I thought was an ambulance, but evidently was a helicopter. I was bleeding like mad from my head and arm, and they laid me out on the helicopter seats. I was well on my way to being in shock. I can remember a medic saying, 'I've got to move your legs, to get somebody else in the chopper', and as he bent my legs, whap, I was gone – out cold.

Corporal, 2 Para

Lots of people still remember seeing on television a tom sweeping the road afterwards. Everything was put in plastic bags, and my job was to sort through them plastic bags and pick out any personal belongings. Myself and another lad spent a complete week in a Portakabin in Ballykinler going through every bag. I found the remains of a pair of denims, just the back pocket with the guy's wallet completely intact; he'd been blown to kingdom come, just vaporised. The Queen's Own Highlanders phoned up wanting to know if we'd found a tam o'shanter belonging to their CO. We found it and put it to one side. We were turning up bits of arms, parts of hands. Talk about being sickened: I used to go home at night to the barracks and my wife would say: 'I know what you've been doing, I can smell it. You just smell of death.'

Colour Sergeant, 2 Royal Anglian

Mountbatten's death that same day I think probably hit people worse than Warrenpoint, because of his standing in England and the world. We were shocked that could happen to a man like him. The murderers were so callous, the way they went about it, taking it so far with an old gentleman who'd gone through so much, plus the kids with him. And in Southern Ireland. Although we felt anger, we couldn't get aggressive, so there was nothing we could do. It was a strange old feeling.

Major, 1 King's Own Scottish Borderers

I can remember checking the people in the pubs in the Clonard, Springfield Road, on the night of Warrenpoint and Mountbatten. It was one of the quietest nights I've ever known in West Belfast. The entire Catholic community was nervous of what we might do. There was genuine apprehension – fear, I'd call it. They were too frightened to celebrate: I think they thought that if they did we'd come in and destroy the place. I went into some pretty hard bars and they were all very wary, but the reactions I could discern were an interesting mixture. Whilst most Republicans probably thought Warrenpoint was a good thing, the younger ones didn't say anything about Mountbatten, and the older men were disgusted.

Because of his links with the Second World War they identified Mountbatten with a completely different chapter of history and didn't think him a legitimate target. Even some of the most prominent older members of the Official IRA who may have served in the British Army in the Second World War thought Mountbatten was above that.

Major, 1 Para

Subsequently everybody felt they had to visit Warrenpoint, I'm sure most for the very best motives. It was an unforgettable five days, because of the enormity of what had happened. We felt, I think it must be said, a grudging admiration for the opposition. Any soldier would admit that as an operation it was very well done. But, nonetheless, we were of course very angry at the losses we had taken, which naturally the battalion had to learn to live with. It's never easy to take that number of casualties, many of them married men, but if there's a sound and understandable reason why somebody's gone down, the boys will recognise that and they will accept losses as part of their contract. When, as in a Northern Ireland-type situation, the reason isn't so clear, it becomes much more difficult for them, and the result is more frustration, more anger, and more bitterness.

Sergeant, 2 Para

I went back to Warrenpoint with two other lads who were also injured by the second bomb. An RUC man at Forkill drove us down in his car. We took photographs and we laid some flowers. I felt quite strange because the place didn't look how I'd envisaged it. It was peaceful, it was quiet; the wall which had been blown out and hit us was rebuilt. The place felt disturbing, as if things weren't right, as though I was intruding. Perhaps I was feeling guilt because I'd survived, but I don't think any of us felt quite comfortable. It was nice to get away, leave it behind us as a memory.

Lance Corporal, 2 Para

On the physical side I'm now very restricted. My hands shake – they call it clonus – and I haven't got any control over it. It's improved a lot, but when I first got out of hospital after Warrenpoint and I was in a pub talking to somebody, I'd get self-conscious about it and start shaking uncontrollably. It goes with my emotions: if I'm angry it starts shaking.

Before, I was physically very active. What I miss now is with the kids, not being able to participate in the stuff I know I would enjoy. And my wife has to do all the driving, that sort of thing; changing light bulbs, she's got to do that. Even doing up the top button of my shirt, I can't, it's very difficult with one hand. I'd honestly like to say that I didn't feel sorry for myself but I can't. I do. I think of all the other blokes and what happened to them, and what I've got and what I've still got, but it's sad the world's got to be this way. I wouldn't say life's cruel, but it is.

The Eighties

Corporal, 2 Scots Guards

The RUC were a lot more relaxed by 1980. We had to escort the RUC down the Falls Road to Springfield Road police station. As we were going in we saw a bag hanging on the gates, so we mentioned it to the policeman on the desk. He said, 'Don't worry. If it goes off we'll know it's a bomb.' About half an hour later it exploded. Then they went out to investigate it.

Corporal, 2 Scots Guards

The only time I was shot at on the '80 tour was in the last half-hour we were there. Nobody even seen it 'cos I was on my own in the sangar. The Fusilier platoon commander taking over from us was fascinated by the film from the video camera pointing out the sangar down the street, and he kept buzzing down from the Ops Room on the Tannoy, asking me about the car registration numbers he was seeing, whether I could identify people he'd spotted, who certain people were, etc. I was trying to do my job, but this fucking Fusilier was bombarding me with questions, so I thought I'd catch him out. I opened up all the windows, which we weren't meant to, picked up the clipboard with the mug shots and the dates of birth, and started sticking me head out and checking out exactly all the details he was quizzing me on. I'd just pulled me head back in when five rounds came into the sangar through the windows – I swear to this day it was a priest in a taxi, or somebody dressed up to look like a priest. And because we were just about to leave I'd had all me rounds taken off me, so I was holding the clipboard up in front of me face: it was only flimsy, but if that was going to give me protection, I was behind it.

Sergeant, 2 Royal Anglian

I went out to Derry in January 1981 expecting lots of incidents, contacts every week, like in 1977, but the situation had changed.

The IRA had become much more professional. Instead of firing off a thousand bullets they were choosing their targets very well, and the ratio of shots to kills had come down dramatically. A wild game had become far more a professional war, which was quite depressing, in the sense that although shootings were few, we felt much more tension, because if there was a shooting there was a real chance of losing somebody.

Sergeant, 1 Scots Guards

There's a lot of strain. My wife always said she couldn't take the hassle of being married to a soldier and we ended up getting divorced. She reckoned the '80/'81 tour as resident battalion changed me totally. I personally didn't feel changed at all, but she saw a change and it affected our relationship. Perhaps it was one of those things you don't see yourself unless there's somebody looking in. I suppose the pressure must've been there, otherwise she wouldn't have noticed.

Major, Royal Army Medical Corps

I'm convinced a lot of soldiers in Northern Ireland have stress they never show. It's interesting that the incidence of people with gastric problems in the Army is higher than in an equivalent sample of the civilian population in England. In addition to a psychosomatic factor, I'm sure the difference must be in some way related to their living conditions, because certainly the accommodation for the *roulement* battalions on four-month tours has never been very satisfactory, and sometimes the food tends to be wanting in nutritional terms.

Sergeant, 42 Commando

As time's gone by, I think the bases out there have improved, the facilities have improved. At Glassmullan Camp the chefs used to run a twenty-four-hour galley, because we might come in off patrol at three o'clock in the morning and need a breakfast before going straight out again. The chef would be there with a big plate of chicken, bacon, and eggs, chips, and a mug of tea; it would be,

'Cheers, mate', and away we'd go again – that quick. Sometimes the cooks would have to man the sangars, and then there might be two chefs who'd been up all night trying to feed a whole company. That's when the arguments often started: the lads would take it out on the cooks, and they'd give it back just as good: 'So you think you're hard done by?' But if the food was crap, really atrocious, because a stroppy chef was trying to put one over, then there'd be real tension. A number of times I've seen cooks dragged across the hotplate and punched in the teeth.

Captain, Army Air Corps

We had a club in the Maze, for the soldiers, the ground troops. They were tied to the base, guarding, doing Ops Room duties, working on the aircraft in shifts, and not living in very good accommodation – twelve to a room, that sort of thing – so the club was a great perk, and it was very popular with all the units. We had what was virtually a cattle market almost every night: a bus from Portadown, or Lurgan, would pull up outside the front gate, wherever, the girls would get out, and lads would decide who was going to be their escort – 'Hey you, Johnny, how about me tonight? I'll give you a good time, Johnny.' It sounds terribly uncivilised and sordid, and it was. My problem as OC was supervising, particularly the married men there. We had problems with rumours that got back to the wives in Germany, which either weren't true or were half-true. Morale and welfare were major headaches.

Lieutenant, 2 Royal Anglian

In March 1981, during the week the hunger strikes at the Maze Prison began, we were stood up on the city walls closing the gates to Londonderry and a single round came straight over my head. The interesting thing was that really it was a cowboy shoot from about four hundred yards which didn't have a chance of hitting us – too long a range, not enough firepower – and yet three foreign news teams arrived on the scene faster than our own Quick Reaction Force from Fort George. It was always said that if foreign media facilities appeared, an incident would probably occur, and I'm entirely convinced that the shot was a publicity

141

stunt, that the press had been tipped off. It left a sour taste in the mouth, particularly as I appeared on *News at Ten* that night kicking in an old lady's door: we didn't know where the shot had come from, so we started following up in the likely locations: knocked on a door, no answer, waited, kicked it in, and there was an old lady – deaf.

Captain, 2 Royal Anglian

The hunger strikes were a very, very exciting period. The scale of rioting involved hadn't been seen since the early seventies, and I don't think we'll ever see its like again. In comparison with the early years it was fairly tame, crowds in the hundreds rather than thousands, but even so, there was much more action than in the preceding several years. For example, the resident battalion we took over from in Londonderry had hardly anything to do, and before Sands' death in early May our tour had been rather boring, just occasional minor aggro from drunken yobbos on Saturday nights. So the mass demonstrations and riots were something very different, and very exciting. Basically, the riots were pitched battles, very controlled pitched battles, with control from both rioters and Army. One is tempted to describe them in terms of a game, or a sport, but that would be wrong: there was a lot of very sincere and deep emotion on their side.

Sergeant, 45 Commando

I'm sure many of us considered the hunger strikers brave men. A man who is willing to starve himself to death is showing bravery and dedication to his cause; to do that he must believe in that cause. But how much pressure was put on them from outside the Maze is open to debate. Perhaps it seemed a good idea initially to put all those people on hunger strike, but once a man had begun to fast, I firmly believe that the IRA and INLA, as they stood then, would have been very loath for him to come off hunger strike, to be seen to quit. So I would say that they were brave and dedicated, but foolhardy as well, especially once they realised that there was no way the hierarchy of the IRA and INLA were going to back down, and no way the British could give in. The government couldn't just change the rules for those people:

142

they were terrorists, and the moment we started to class them as political prisoners we would have been accepting the charge that we were running the Province wrongly. So the only people who were going to suffer were the hunger strikers themselves, and their families. For what? They didn't get the concessions they were after: their own clothing, special status as political prisoners, etc. There was no way they ever would.

Corporal, 2 Royal Anglian

In Derry Bobby Sands' death was a bit of an anti-climax. There was a hell of a lot of rioting, but the people there were waiting more for Patrick O'Hara, who was close to death as well, because he'd lived in our patch, just outside the Masonic Camp. For us, it was a very good time: there were riots every night, bricks and bottles all over the place, and some lighter moments. When O'Hara was about to die, me and my mate went round knocking on doors saying, 'He's dead, he's dead, he's gone.' All the people rushed out onto the streets to riot, and the IRA top bods had to tell them to get back in their houses. We left it for a couple of hours, then went round again: out they came once more, only to be sent back. When he actually died the IRA bods were urging them onto the streets, but they'd had enough: nobody came out.

Captain, 2 Royal Anglian

The night O'Hara died there was unbelievable damage in the centre of Londonderry. Huge crowds came down from the Bogside and the Creggan and smashed all the shop windows in. Our platoon base was attacked by a mob with petrol bombs: one of the sangars was completely gutted, the guy inside badly burned, and at one stage it looked as if the crowd would get inside the base. I was on standby at Fort George listening to the reports coming in on the net. The OC finally gave us the nod, and we careered down Rosemount Avenue in three Pigs; it was John Wayne stuff, 'The Relief of Rosemount' – all we needed was 'The Ride of the Valkyrie' blaring out.

We parked our Pigs to block off either end of the road, formed a baseline in front of the gates, and fired baton rounds to create a gap between us and them. The crowd was still throwing petrol bombs, but once we'd established that fifty-metre distance, keeping them back was straightforward. It was a terraced road, and one of the houses was ablaze. The women and children in the row were absolutely terrified, so I went up to the baseline, picked up the traditional megaphone and boomed across to the rioters: 'Can you please hold your fire. I want to move the women and children in the houses to safety.' The older men at the back of the crowd who were running the show told the yobbos to stop, and there was a general lull. We quickly got the families away, and when I got back to the baseline there was still nothing happening. So I decided to capitalise on their inactivity: I picked up the megaphone again and boomed across: 'They've gone now. You may carry on firing.' They were nonplussed: there was some jeering and a few missiles came over rather lamely but it took a lot of the steam out of them.

Sergeant, 45 Commando

We arrived in Belfast in '81, just as the fifth hunger striker, McDonnell, died. We were due to take over the Falls at 0800 on 8 July, though to reduce the likelihood of the departing battalion sustaining a casualty on their last day we actually moved in at 0530. However, the official entry in the log said 0800, and at 0801 we had a contact in the Andersonstown bus depot – one minute into the tour. When Sands had died they'd burnt the buses out in Andersonstown, so we thought it a good idea to place a couple of bricks there in case they tried again. Myself and the bricks went into the depot when it was still dark. The manager arrived at half past seven and began showing the brick commanders and myself round while the rest of the lads waited in the office. As we were looking round the back gate area a white civilian car screamed into the yard, the men inside, two depot workers, gesturing behind and shouting, 'Close the gates, close the gates.' Immediately a transit crashed in, screeched to a halt, and about a dozen young boys piled out with crates of bottle bombs. We challenged them, told them to stop, cocked our weapons. A couple ran off, but the others started throwing the bottles at us. One of the brick commanders was hit and fell to the ground, and the other corporal challenged a guy about to throw a bottle. He fired, and killed him outright. The rest of them legged it then. We didn't fire again, just one shot.

We were always told and told and told not to shoot petrol-bombers, because they didn't constitute a big enough threat. But I'm a great believer that in the heat of the moment, in that split second you flick the safety catch off and fire, if you're sure in your own mind, then as a trained man you are right to carry out that action. However much Northern Ireland training may emphasise safety, the responsibility has to be the individual soldier's, rightly or wrongly, and on that occasion I thought the corporal was quite justified. When the bottles were being thrown we didn't know whether they contained petrol, or acid, or a petrol and sugar mixture, and we had a man on the ground: we had to take some form of action, and we weren't carrying baton guns. In fact, the corporal got a GOC's commendation, and the coroner's court laid the blame for the lad's death entirely at the doorstep of the people who'd enticed these young people to attempt arson. And we later heard that IRA recruitment of eighteen-year-olds was cut substantially by that incident.

Corporal, 45 Commando

We had Hurson and the four others dying after that, plus their funerals and funeral processions. Every time one died you could stand by for a couple of thousand people, sometimes more, out on the Springfield Road attacking the bases, petrol-bombing. We were firing scores of baton rounds at night; nowadays you'd be lucky to fire four or five. Giant murals of the dead hunger strikers went up almost overnight on gable ends: 'You can kill the revolutionary but you can't kill the revolution' was one of the most famous on the Falls Road. The people there classed them as real martyrs. Myself, I thought whoever starves themselves to death for a cause must be a bit weird, but it's an Irish thing, fasting as protest. We were absolutely hated – kids, everybody. There were no foot patrols in West Belfast, too dangerous; we couldn't go on the streets except in armoured cars, and even then it was tricky. There were a lot of shootings that tour, a lot of blast bombs, a lot of petrol-bombings. It was ten weeks of frantic activity until they called off the hunger strikes in October.

Staff Sergeant, 2 Royal Green Jackets

I'll never forget driving through Toxteth in Liverpool on the way to the ferry and seeing the shop windows all covered with wire mesh, graffiti everywhere, vandalised telephone boxes, smashed-down walls, wrecked cars, and thinking, 'God, I'm only in Liverpool. What's Belfast looking like?' And by and large Belfast was far more prosperous and delightful than Liverpool. I wouldn't mind living in many parts of North and East Belfast, and even West Belfast isn't as working class as people think. The trouble has only ever come from the areas of high unemployment, because the unemployed are the easiest to recruit – the easiest to intimidate as well.

Rifleman, 2 Royal Green Jackets

I'm from Liverpool, and Belfast was just as much a shock to me as it was to somebody coming from London. The roughness and the poverty were the same, but the people were completely different to Liverpudlians. They were like chalk and cheese. I like to think, and a lot of people I've taken home say the same, that people in Liverpool are kind and friendly. Whereas over there they were cold, unfriendly, whether they wanted to be or not. Perhaps they had to be. It's just their way of life.

Corporal, 2 Royal Green Jackets

I remember the very first time I went out on patrol in Belfast. It was a very, very sunny morning and we came out of North Howard Street Mill, went up North Howard Street and then on to the Falls Road. It was a lovely November's day and the sun hit you. I stood on the corner and thought, 'This doesn't look like what I expected: people going to work, kids going to school, normal, peaceful.' It was only when I sort of turned my head slightly, when I saw the slogans and the burnt houses, that the reality suddenly hit me.

Lance Corporal, Royal Military Police

The police in Newry were very proud of the fact that they were in bandit country. The guys I shared a room with gave me all the chat, all the past incidents, in various exaggerated forms. I expected to be going down into a war zone, so on my first day on patrol in Newry I was crapping myself. But apart from a mortar attack on the police station I've never been so bored in all my life. During that attack I was scared, but the rest of the time I was bored. That was the balance: when I was bored I wanted to be scared and when I was scared I wanted to be bored.

Rifleman, 2 Royal Green Jackets

On Christmas Day '81 we went out on patrol in Santa Claus masks, mistletoe on our berets. We went into lots of nationalist pubs on routine checks. They'd all be anti, but at Christmas there was always that little bit of fun involved. They'd offer you a drink, but you'd think to yourself, 'What's in it?' They'd drink half of it, so you knew it was okay then, and if no one was looking then it was a quick one.

Major, 2 Royal Green Jackets

At Christmas we baked some cakes and took them round to the 'Save the Children' places in our patch, to the ones in the Murph, and Turf Lodge, and, I think, two cakes to the local priest in the Ballymurphy. Some of the parents didn't want the children to have any, but the children were happy to eat it. That was what it was all about.

Corporal, 2 Royal Green Jackets

On the '81/'82 tour my brick got shot at, and I thought a civvie had been hit, so I radioed back a casualty report. Back at base somebody in the phone booth was talking to their wife in Germany when a bloke from the Ops Room who'd heard my contact report came running past telling people: 'Dick's brick, one man hit', so the guy says to his wife, 'Dick's been shot.' My wife told me she had three or four of these women come round: 'Oh, haven't you heard, your husband's been shot in Ireland.' My poor wife. Our first baby was born four days before I went out to Northern Ireland, so I'd only seen my daughter for four days, and then my wife got hit with this news. She was in a shit state. I spoke to her the same evening, so she was okay, but I'd always told her that the first person who'd come would probably be the padre, or an officer from the battalion.

Myself, I'm cynical now. If it happens, it happens. As long as it don't hurt at the time I'm not too bothered. You go over to Northern Ireland and you feel confident. You say to yourself, 'How the hell can I die here? It's not pictured for me to die on a cold street with some Paddy looking down at me.'

Rifleman, 2 Royal Green Jackets

We had an excellent brick. I like to think we had an understanding, one of them things that comes once every ten years, when you get four lads who can knit together, who know what the other three were thinking, know what they're going to do, when they're going to do it. That's how it was. From the word go we all understood one another: it just went sweet. Two of us come from the same part of Liverpool, Bootle: there you have to get on to live, have to get on to be understood, so we two were both from the same shell, really. We had the same hobbies, same sports, same religion; the only difference was that I was an Evertonian and he was Liverpool. Everybody knew the understanding the four of us together had: it was like being the three musketeers, plus one.

In fact, all four of us were Catholics. And the Irish couldn't understand it. One day quite early on in the tour we were running round Ballymurphy securing the roads after a contact and a group of them gathered up and were saying to us, 'Youse British bastards, Protestant bastards.' I said, 'I'm not a Protestant. I'm Catholic.' Then I went, 'And he's a Catholic, and so is he, and him as well,' pointing to the rest of the brick. They weren't youngsters, they were grown people with kids, and they stood back shocked, flabbergasted. They couldn't understand why if we were Catholics we were doing our job, and so they started firing questions at us: 'How many decades to say the whole rosary?' 'Give us the Act of Contrition.' Granted I didn't know some of the answers, but between us we knew the lot. And after that they never really bothered us; they were always watching, but they never bothered us at all. And whereas before when we said good morning they wouldn't speak, afterwards even the hardest teenagers, the real scalliwags, would give us a 'morning' back.

Corporal, 2 Para

'Hearts and minds' – biased, I must admit it was biased. If it was a Catholic area, you didn't particularly bother with hearts and minds. If it was a Protestant area then you paid a bit more attention: you wouldn't relax any more, because obviously trouble could come at any time, but you would be a little bit more responsive to the civilians, a bit more polite. Whereas if you went to a harder area that was known to be Republican, your reactions to the civilians would be that much harder. I always told my blokes to be like a mirror: if somebody was pleasant, then be pleasant back, but don't be unwary; if somebody was bolshie, then straightaway you got bolshie back. I didn't believe in being over-polite – 'Yes, sir, no sir' – if someone was aggressive in his stance and his talk.

Captain, 2 Coldstream Guards

I felt the Catholics weren't British at all. Not because they were on a different island to us, but because they shared none of our natural attributes. To me they were more Mediterranean in their temperament: terribly volatile, a woman-dominated society. They'd have massive rows, one family against another, like something out of *Romeo and Juliet*, those sort of mad feuds and violence: it was nothing to see groups of women fighting in the middle of a housing estate. Their houses, even if brand new, were incredibly untidy, complete shit-holes really, and yet on the whole they were very intelligent. I don't know the statistics, but I reckon the standard of education in West Belfast was very high, which made our job that much more difficult. I remember going up to an Irishman and saying, 'Of course, you know that's against the law, don't you?' and he replied, 'Whose law? Against your law, yes, but it's not against mine.' Where could we start?

149

Corporal, 2 Royal Green Jackets

In my search team we had a code: if the blokes found anything interesting or wanted to attract my attention they'd ask me for the time. One particular house in the Distillery in West Belfast I was busy chatting to the WRAC searcher because as the commander, once I'd done my paperwork, I had nothing to do while the search team did their stuff. So I was being very smooth to this WRAC girl when one of the team stuck his head out of the attic and called down, 'Have you got the time?' 'Quarter past eight,' I said, and carried on chatting her up. He shouted back, 'No. Have you got the time?' 'Quarter past eight, you plonker.' I'm thinking, 'Here I am busy trying to be smooth. Why can't he shut up?' Then I remembered, so up the ladder I went to the attic. He'd pulled back some felt and turned up a silver-plated Colt 45. I thought, 'Magic. Excellent,' and as I was leaning down for a butchers with a large torch I knocked the Colt with my elbow and it fell down a hole. I shone the torch down the hole, and my heart nearly dropped out of me mouth: looking up at me was a mass of gun barrels. We smashed the wall in, and there were telescopic rifles, machine guns, shotguns, explosives, ammunition, balaclavas, gloves: you name it, it was in there. My legs were shaking. I dragged the bloke whose house it was up the ladder and confronted him with it. He just looked at me as if to say 'Huh?' but his wife was going absolutely bananas. She didn't know about the find, and when the police took him away she slapped me in the face, cut my lip. I grabbed her by the hand and took her upstairs. When she saw the weapons her face just went. She said, 'Oh, no, no. The stupid, stupid man,' went downstairs and sat in the kitchen crying her eyes out. Apparently what had happened was, one night while she was out, the IRA came round and said, 'You will help us, because if you don't . . .' so the husband, poor sod, was stuck.

The ballistics people worked on the weapons and discovered that the telescopic rifles had taken out a couple of soldiers, and the pistols matched up with various knee and head jobs. For us that was great. We'd spent a long time searching houses, and finally we'd got something: it was magic to look at a rifle and think, 'Christ, that's killed soldiers. Bloody hell, what sort of bloke pulled that trigger?'

150

Corporal, 2 Royal Green Jackets

We had three riflemen killed two days before the battalion was due to return to England in March '82. Two of our Macralon Land Rovers were ambushed in Crocus Street just after they'd left the main Springfield Road RUC station. On the morning of the incident I was to move up to 219 Springfield Road, a small fenced-off Army post. I was waiting in the vehicle when one of the lads that died came up. I said to him, of all things: 'It's a beautiful day. It's a day for people to die. You're going to die today.' He laughed, we were always saying that to each other – we got cynical about death out there.

I was in 219 playing cricket with a piece of wood and bricks in the yard when we heard the shooting. We immediately got all our kit on and ran down to the road to the scene, about six hundred yards away. The PIRA had opened up with an M60 machine gun and three rifles from a window in a house they'd taken over. Two of the lads were dead outright, head jobs; a third had got it in the stomach; a poor RAF bloke, who'd probably never ever been shot at, got hit in the neck and had his jugular cut; and one of the Coldstream Guards taking over from us was shot as well: he had all his face missing, brain and blood everywhere. It was very, very emotional for the younger guys in the battalion.

Captain, 2 Coldstream Guards

We were in the middle of our handover with the Green Jackets when they were ambushed. I was about 150 yards away on the Springfield Road. We heard this long burst of machine-gun fire, it just went on and on and on. It was a horrific, tragic scene, soldiers lying in the road. The most pathetic sight was a corporal from the Green Jackets completely in tears. That hit me more than anything else. There had been a number of little indicators beforehand that something was going to go wrong, and we missed the whole bloody lot: of course with hindsight we could see them clearly, but by God it made us angry with ourselves. There was a Dutch camera crew about that morning, definitely there to film an incident, no doubt about it. The previous night we actually patrolled past the house which had been taken over by the gunmen who were probably monitoring our patrols. If we had been really alert we would have known something was going on, even though we wouldn't have been able to put our finger on it.

Rifleman, 2 Royal Green Jackets

From being a battalion that was understanding and courteous to the people, we changed to wanting revenge, just like that. It might sound bad, but it happens throughout the Army. It was revenge we wanted, and the bosses knew, so they took almost all of us off the streets. That ambush made me very angry, because the brick that was involved had taken exactly the same route out of Springfield Road cop shop as we used to do. And I lost a good friend in that. But you have to accept it, you've just got to accept it. It's that little gamble in you that says it's either him or me.

Major, 2 Royal Green Jackets

The night after the three riflemen were killed we were trying to get two people who we thought knew something about the ambush out of a pub, and bring them in for the RUC. They wouldn't come out. All the normal, placid ways hadn't worked, so we waited outside for them. When they emerged we got one of the guys but there was a fair-sized bit of aggro, lots of stone-throwing, a pretty close situation. But one thing the Irish are, they're respecters of authority – not the terrorist, but the ordinary guy. The ordinary Paddy has a great respect for authority, and during the mêlée there were shouts of, 'Don't throw stones at him – he's the company commander.' Now as company commander you get fairly well known about the patch, and I'd had my beret grabbed off my head by the crowd. The riflemen were all for rushing in and getting it back, but I told them to forget it, and as we were just about to depart a woman from Ballymurphy came out of the crowd and said, 'Here's your beret, but do you mind if I keep the cap badge?' I said that was fine by me, and she said, 'Thanks very much. I want to put it alongside the other one.' She was the sister-in-law of two girls carrying weapons in the back of a car who were killed by a Green Jacket company in Belfast in the early seventies. She had their picture at home in a black frame with a Green Jacket cap badge and she wanted another badge to go with it. But she brought my beret back: great respecters of authority.

152

Corporal, Royal Military Police

When the Falklands blew up I was never so pleased to be in Northern Ireland in all my life. I was laughing through my back teeth. I knew that, being over there, there was no way I could get posted to the Falklands. I was nice and safe tucked up in Newry.

Private, 1 Para

We were extremely pissed off, because we were stuck patrolling bogs in Fermanagh and not down south amongst it with the rest of the regiment. All we could do was watch the TV, every newscast that came through. We were hanging on every word.

Subaltern, 2 Coldstream Guards

We certainly felt aggrieved that the first casualty of the Falklands campaign, the first hero, a cook on HMS *Hermes* who got some burns from a deep-fat fryer on the way down, made front-page headlines in the *Sun*, yet the day before a soldier from the Royal Hampshires had been blown up on the border in South Armagh, and he didn't even get a mention. The Guardsmen couldn't understand why.

Captain, 2 Coldstream Guards

During the Falklands war our patch was Divis Flats, Falls Road, parts of the Springfield Road – that area. The odd thing at the time was that while one didn't take one's eyes off the ball, the atmosphere was certainly different. When I'd first arrived in Belfast in March '82 the city seemed incredibly normal – it often struck me that I could be walking any street in the United Kingdom – and then every time one of our ships went down the Irish let us know all about it: there'd be great shouting and cheering. In fact, depending on their reaction, we could tell how the campaign was progressing, and I'll never forget on the day the surrender was announced there was not a peep out of them. We had a celebration that night – especially in front of the Irish.

Lieutenant, 2 Coldstream Guards

I remember doing a pub check on the Falls Road the lunchtime the PIRA blew up the Household Cavalry in Hyde Park in July '82. I knew nothing about it, and there it was on the television in the bar, on the one o'clock news, all these Household Cavalry lying dead. And that was the worst feeling, because none of us knew. We stood watching the news and, of course, all the Irish were looking at us watching. I must admit that it was one of the few times I felt real bitter hatred towards them.

Sergeant, 2 Royal Anglian

The lads' reactions to IRA bombings in England were very much a mixed bag of feelings, as you would get from any group of individuals. Some guys would say, 'I hate those cunts more now because they're not only doing it to us,' and some strange people thought: 'Bloody good: let them sitting at home see what it's like.' Me personally, I wasn't bothered at all; I just didn't think about it.

Lieutenant, 2 Coldstream Guards

The ironic thing was, on my R and R I got off the plane at Heathrow and took the Tube to Knightsbridge, because my girl-friend at the time worked in Harrods. As I walked out of the Tube station there was a bomb scare, and the police came up to me and said, 'Excuse me, sir, would you mind going . . .' But there again, I suppose it wasn't an irony, it was believable.

Corporal, 2 Coldstream Guards

I actually saved a bloke's life in Belfast. We were going round the Cyprus Street area, Lower Falls, and it was a very chilly night, two o'clock in the morning, pitch black. There was no street lights, and I heard moaning and shone my torch, and there was a bloke laying on the floor. He was drunk, probably come out the Cyprus Bar, and he had a big gash in his head and both legs had been broken: he'd been robbed, but it was very vicious, and he'd lost a lot of blood. We called an ambulance, and the ambulance driver told me that if someone hadn't found him within a quarter, half an hour, he'd have been dead. But luckily we got him off to hospital. We did our bit. When I was trying to help him, put a field dressing on his head, bloody big bow under his chin, all the time he was telling us to fuck off: 'Squaddies. Don't want you. Brit bastards.' His legs were splayed all over the place, and at first I thought he'd been kneecapped. He was semi-conscious: 'Brit bastards. Don't want you. Get out of my country.'

Second Lieutenant, 2 Coldstream Guards

As you go into the Clonard, there's a big monastery on the right-hand side and across from the monastery is the holy shop, where they sell big statues of the Pope, the Virgin Mary, all that. A bloke was in there and someone went after him and kneecapped both his knees while he was stood at the counter. We were QRF (Quick Reaction Force) and we got there about three minutes before the ambulance took him off to Royal Victoria Hospital. It turned my guts. You wouldn't think it until you actually see the blood oozing out the knee and the big hole and you see the kneecap. I couldn't believe how much blood there was on the floor. All the lads on the cordon were outside saying, 'Can I have a look?' I was saying, 'Go on. Five minutes.' They'd come back and another one'd go, just to have a look at what mess there was.

Corporal, 2 Royal Anglian

In Londonderry we were allowed out at nights on what we called the safe side of the water. The further east you went towards Ballykelly, Portstewart, Portrush, the more normal life became, and you could have a really good night out. Ballykelly, Limavady were lovely places. The Droppin' Well bar in Ballykelly had a weekly discotheque, and usually about sixty of our lads would be down there. That night, 6 December '82, we were boxing the Fusiliers at Ebrington Barracks so there was a three-line whip, but the Cheshires were in there 'cos they were based in Ballykelly. What happened was, a girl, a Paddy lass, took in a shoulder bag, a sports-type bag with a device inside, just dumped it and left. Of course it went off, a twenty-five- or thirty-pound bomb, and because it was in a room, a dance hall, the concussion effect of the blast took out the walls and the whole bloody hall collapsed from the top. That bomb killed seventeen, eleven of them Cheshires.

We were on call-out, and when we got down there six minutes later it was just unbelievable carnage – quite shocking: not so much because people were dead – when you look at someone who's dead they're just dead, an arm here, a leg over there; when it's dead it becomes a non-object – but because there were young girls and lads sixteen, seventeen, eighteen years old trapped in the rubble under bloody great rafters. We couldn't get at them, and we knew looking at them they were going to die. That was terrible, fucking terrible: the cow who planted that bomb should die the same way.

Warrant Officer, 2 Royal Anglian

The decent people are the ones I always remember. The whole family lived over there on the '81/'83 Londonderry tour. Absolutely beautiful country, and where there was no trouble I'd never met a friendlier, more genuine crowd of people in my life. My wife and kids loved it. We'd spend my days off on the northern coast: Dunluce Castle, Giant's Causeway, White Park Sands, all along there. And the schools were so bloody good. My kids really came out there: reading, writing and arithmetic, good old-fashioned discipline – absolutely terrific.

Corporal, 1 King's Own Scottish Borderers

When I went back to Turf Lodge in 1983 it was a completely different place. All the old flats had been done away with, new houses were being built, and the people were really getting to like the British Government. They were all friends with us, really friendly – it was quite a shock, going out and not getting any bottles thrown at you. In '78/'79/'80 you could talk to them one night in a corner and if you met them next day in the middle of the street they'd spit at you, but in '83 we'd go into the Falls Park and sit and drink with them: they'd offer us a beer, the lot. In '79 we'd tried to play with the kids, just like any normal kids in the streets, and they used to swear at us, kick our ankles. They'd been brought up to hate the British Army, but in 1983 we were sitting on the corner joking with these six kids – I let them look through my rifle, take my hat off, empty out my pockets: all good fun. That was the change; quite a change in four years. There was less trouble in Turf Lodge than anywhere else.

Private, 1 King's Own Scottish Borderers

The big thing happening in '83 when we were there were the supergrass trials. One of the supergrasses had come in and there was a big battalion operation to lift all the people he'd named. The idea was that each brick would go out with an RUC man alongside, bang on these people's doors and go in with the RUC guy there to arrest them. We were tasked to a house in one of the back streets off the Falls Road. The guy was a Sinn Fein councillor, and the address we'd been given was his mother's house. We banged on the door and nothing happened, so the platoon commander told one of the guys to kick the door in. Just as he kicked it a bloke appeared – not the bloke we wanted but a member of the household. We brought all the family into one room and had a little search around upstairs. I couldn't understand it: all their belongings were packed in cardboard boxes. The RUC guy explained that this family had just moved into the house, about a week previous. Of course we left, but two days later we did the same house again. We had a different RUC man, I told him we'd already been there, but he said we were to do what it said on the list. So again we banged on the door, fuck-all happened, and we kicked it in, again as the guy was coming down the stairs. I felt sorry for him standing there with his skinnies on and us all piling in. The same as before. He wasn't amused, but he seemed resigned. We all knew it was the wrong guy, but if the RUC said we had to go in, that was it.

Major, 2 Royal Green Jackets

On our last tour I was very heartened by the way the RUC performed. As a soldier one might say they lacked drive and forcefulness, but those qualities may not be essential in a policeman's job whereas they are to a soldier's; and, of course, they're there all the time. I was very impressed by their lack of partiality, particularly where I fitted in, in the middle management level. The sub-divisional police superintendent with whom I worked directly, his chief inspectors and inspectors were, by and large, fine, upright men. Some were very competent, some were less competent, but mostly they were straight down the middle, as opposed to one side or the other. Of course, there was always the odd chap who would say privately over a glass of beer, 'I can't stand Catholics. I can smell 'em a mile off,' but they weren't many, and I was impressed by the absence of bigotry overall.

Sergeant, 45 Commando

In 1981 we went over, did our jobs, and changed nothing. We were led by the riots and hunger strikes; our strategy for the whole tour was dictated by the political climate. Then we were doing house checks, P checks, a lot of vehicle checks, and we thought we were on top of the situation. But we weren't really. We thought we knew the people on the ground, but we didn't. In 1981 I knew of only two top IRA players in Ballymurphy; looking back, I think we'd been stopping the wrong vehicles, stopping the wrong people. On our last tour our company had Ballymurphy, the Clonard, the Beechmount, the Lower Falls and Divis, which in 1981 would have been almost three companies' worth, and I must have seen at least fifty top players. Because we weren't preoccupied with riots we had to find something else to do, and I think our terrorist recognition became much better. This time if the players walked past us we would stop them and be able to call them by their full names.

That was a major step forward, because while all appeared calm on the surface, underneath West Belfast was still turmoil. There were so many threats. The IRA have a huge arsenal of weapons: from homemade IED (identified explosive device), which is a small booby-trap device, through command wire and RCIE (remote-controlled improvised explosive) devices, to single-shot sniping, close-quarter shoots, maybe using a machine gun or pistol, RPG 7s, multi-weapon shoots, mortars: all those were high threat at some point in our tour. People say Northern Ireland's reached an acceptable level of violence, but it's only acceptable because of the Intelligence effort we can put in. So I thought it was a successful tour. We didn't achieve much, perhaps, but we did achieve something.

Sergeant, Women's Royal Army Corps Provost

Ever since I joined up I wanted to go to Northern Ireland, not just to say I'd been there, but for the experience. Everybody in the Army likes to go. But on my last tour in '85, we were driving out of Londonderry and there was a small child, couldn't have been more than five or six, at the side of the road. I saw him look up at us, and a great panic overtook him. There was a large log on the pavement, literally almost as big as he was, and I've never seen so much desperation to get it picked up to throw at us. I was destroyed. I thought, 'Why am I here?'

Captain, 1 Coldstream Guards

There is a little village consisting of about two acres of old quarters and new houses and cars and shops, where the population is mostly under twenty-five and is ninety per cent male. There are ten bombs a day exploding, a riot every three days, lots of stone-throwing, petrol bombs, murders galore, kneecappings, you name it. It is the most violent village west of Beirut. Before going to Northern Ireland each battalion spends three days in this English village, sometimes called Tin City. They live in this mock Army base which is all set up like the Northern Ireland situation. Units go out on patrol around this village and perhaps they'll do three patrols and nothing will happen, then on the fourth one they'll get shot at or bombed or they will have an incident. Everything is filmed because every square inch of the village is covered by cameras and NITAT (Northern Ireland Training and Advisory Team) monitor how everyone reacts. For each exercise we import forty men and ten women from various regiments and each is given their own house and identity. So when a member of the Army stops them and asks their name, she will say she is Mrs O'Dower from Glenalina Road. This is then checked on the computer and the whole thing tallies up.

Sometimes it is easy to forget that the cameras are working all the time. This WRAC and this soldier were in a real rooty tooty one night in the cemetery, little knowing we were all sitting there watching it on the monitor. Of course it has its lighter moments, but it's a tough three days. We make it more violent than it is in reality, but it is good preparation.

Corporal, 1 Welsh Guards

At Tin City they tried to treat you as the Irish would. So we had blokes from the Green Jackets throwing bricks, cursing you and simulating mortar attacks. Then you would be crashed out at all hours; you'd be patrolling and a bomb would go off next to you. It was a very reasonable preparation. We felt confident – frightened, but confident. But we knew where we were going would be cunning, so we were wary about that.

Major, 45 Commando

In our last tour, '86, one of the most important things we had to concentrate on in our preparation was the mental attitude of the Marines on the street. They had to soak up, be a sponge and absorb the venom and hostility that they would encounter on a daily basis. Absorb the mindless hostility and pure hatred that would come their way in some areas. There would be considerable provocation, but they would have to be above it. They must not descend to the level they were being confronted with – not mix it with them. The message was quite simple. The tightrope the Marines walk in the inner cities is very fraught. The dangers are there, real dangers.

Marine, 45 Commando

My first tour was in '86 and when we got out there we were running about like blue-arsed flies. We were looking but not seeing. They told us when we first went out there, don't walk on the pavement, don't walk anywhere near a lamppost and don't walk in the middle of the road. Where were we supposed to walk? Then it was suspicious cars that were parked awkward, beware of them. So you'd go down one street and there's about eight cars parked and you give them a wide berth. They'd come back drunk and hadn't parked them straight.

160

Corporal, 45 Commando

We were told during our training to use the soft approach, be Mr Nice Guy. But when we got there we found that it didn't work. We weren't violent as such, but it was necessary to be highly motivated with controlled aggression. We had several cases where my patrol would stop people and they would spit on us. They were used to non-reaction from Army patrols, so they got quite surprised when they got the exact opposite from us. We ran them in, because spitting is an assault.

Lance Corporal, 45 Commando

I was in West Belfast, in the Lenadoon, for the first part of the tour. Then for the last month we went to North Belfast which was the Ardoyne, the New Lodge, Tiger Bay, those sort of places; so you had the two extremes. One, the very quiet, open-plan area with no overt action and then the Ardoyne where resistance is absolutely overt to the point where they will get out of cars and fight you when you stop them at night. They'll throw bricks over walls, they'll fight you on a foot patrol. You'll stop somebody and they'll come out swinging; you knock on someone's door and you get nothing but abuse. So really we had two tours.

Captain, Army Air Corps

Whenever a new battalion starts a new tour they always want up-to-date photographs of the area they are going to patrol. So up we go. I tell you Northern Ireland is the most photographed country in the world.

Lieutenant, 1 King's Own Scottish Borderers

You could take a map and literally draw a line and say this area is Loyalist Protestant, this area Catholic. You could go to a particular area and know exactly the type of people you were going to meet and how you would deal with them and how they would deal with you. Then you would go to other areas where soldiers have not been for fifteen years and the population think

161

you have come on exercise; old ladies give you tea and it's very nice. But they do get rather frightened by soldiers with blackened faces jumping over hedges. So we had to quieten that down.

Lance Corporal, 45 Commando

We were in our first week and were on patrol in the Turf Lodge where I knew my auntie lived, because I've got a few of my family in Belfast. I was in her street with my brick and I stopped outside her house. She hadn't seen me since I was five years old. I don't know why, but she came out to the gate and stood there with her husband, and I thought, that's my auntie. I didn't recognise her and I thought she wouldn't recognise me. I wanted to talk to her but I realised that if I stopped to chat, because she was a Catholic, I would put her in jeopardy. I was just about to move off when she says to me, 'Aren't you going to talk to me then?' I was flabbergasted. I said under my breath, 'Well, do you think that I should?' She says, 'I'm sick with them. You're my bleeding blood.' So I just crouched down and talked to her out of the corner of my mouth. She was asking me about my mum and things. Then she said, 'Next time you come into this area make sure that it's dark, knock on the back door and you'll have four bacon butties waiting for you and your boys.' That was very unusual. It was hard to cope with. I phoned home that night and told my dad who told me that my aunt had phoned and that he had phoned my grandad.

My uncles, who also lived in Belfast, had come across when I got back from the Falklands, but when we got back to the house they had refused to have their picture taken with the Union Jack. They knew I might be coming over with 45 so they phoned my grandad and said, 'Is the lad going to be coming across?' My grandad, naive as he is, even though he's an ex-serviceman, said, 'Yeah, he's coming across.' They said, 'Well, tell him that as he's family, we'll make it quick, he'll not have to go through any pain.'

Sergeant, 1 Welsh Guards

In the initial stages of the tour the continuity NCO from the previous tour would walk round with us and show us some of the hoods. On the P card they'd have the hood's name, address and age and what he was arrested for in the past. Now at this time we had an excellent NCO from the permanent battalion who was a master at collating information on the PIRA. He'd find out the name of a player's dog or that he collected stamps or the name of his sister in America and the fact that her son was called Billy and had a birthday on 7 May. We'd put all this down on the P card and the next time we saw him, if it was appropriate, we'd tell him not to forget his nephew's birthday in a week's time. All this just kept him under pressure.

Marine, 45 Commando

There was two girls who must've been about fifteen, sixteen years old, quite essence looking girls as well; beautiful girls, and they really started chatting to us. It brightens up the patrol, like, so we was stood there chatting to them for about two or three minutes. We didn't realise they were stood outside their house. The next thing we heard was the front door going. One of these girls' old man comes out, drunk as a skunk, and he just grabbed hold of her by the collar and then the hair and started beating her because she was chatting to us. I just felt a bit sick like, maybe I shouldn't have said anything to her. But maybe he was doing it for the sake of the family because every single family always thinks about who's watching them. They don't want any hassle.

Marine, 45 Commando

There was this little girl, and she was identical to my niece, my sister's daughter and she was cute, about four years old. I'd perched myself in this gateway, put myself up against the wall and started talking to her. She never said a bleeding thing, she just looked at me, and then spat right in my face. To me, I was speaking to my niece, you know, because she was identical to her. That hurt.

Marine, 45 Commando

This little girl came up, she was probably about seven, and she started chatting to me. I was still looking around but I bent down

163

and I squatted against this brick wall. She said, 'Bend over, I want to whisper to you.' And I bent over and she grabbed my beret and ran away. Now, my sister's kids do things like that, no problem. So I go after her and I grabbed her and she fell over and she cracked the back of her head on the kerbstone. It didn't bleed, but obviously she was very upset. I got my beret off her and I tried to comfort her. In a situation like that, all the doors open and everybody comes out. I'm sort of the big dragon. The only thing I could do when I got back was go to the police station and get it down in the big book. Fortunately nothing ever came of it, but I felt sick about it.

Corporal, 1 Welsh Guards

Our brick was going through the Ballymurph, which is not one of the nicest places, when a Paddy came up and spoke to one of our lads in Welsh. When we translated it, we found out it meant 'Fuck the English'. It wasn't the Army they hated, it was the English.

Corporal, 45 Commando

There's a lot of humour out on the streets. For example, from a girl you'd get 'Fucking British bastards', 'Fucking Marine this and fucking Marine that' – these young girls would really be giving you shit. You'd just stand there and in a real low voice say, 'Look, I really do love it when you talk dirty to me, come round the corner and say some more, I get a real turn on.' She'd come back with more abuse and you say, 'Don't, stop it, I'll have to go away, it's too much for me.' Then you'd shout back to the boys coming behind you, 'Hey, she talks dirty to you.'

Sergeant, 1 Welsh Guards

There was a guy who was one of the main men and if anything happened in the Province we used to go up to him in this pub and say, 'You had a good night yesterday, got two of us, didn't you?' He'd smile. Or if we found a cache of explosives he used to say to us, 'We did not have a good day, did we?' It gave us some sort of hope to be on the same par as him and sometimes he would go out of his way to talk to me. He knew what my job was within the battalion and so it gave me some pride that I was doing my job properly.

It's funny really, they were all about the same age as me, but they were in the pub at ten in the morning till it shut. They were all on the dole and they never paid for the beer. But they looked old before their time. I used to look at our lads and they looked powerful, looked like soldiers, looked as if they could kill someone. But these men didn't. So you wondered how they did the killing and got away with it for years. They had to be reasonably good. I don't know if it's the right word, but I respected them. They could and did pick their time. They were better than us; very clever people. That's why it gave me a sense of achievement that no one on our tour got hit. I was proud of that, we all did our bit and all got out.

Major, 45 Commando

My principle was, if they couldn't keep a civil tongue in their head and pass the time of day, not to say anything. That is the Belfast scene today. It's the PR. I mean the opposition have got it absolutely weighed up. They'll set up a PR ambush to trap a Marine, to get him either on tape or on film doing or saying something which would discredit him, his unit, and the whole of the military. The PR is where they achieve their success. It's easy to explain to an eighteen- or nineteen-year-old about this tactic, but it's difficult for him to accept when he's out there, that he is vulnerable, and that he is the target. He is the man that they are after.

Corporal, 45 Commando

I was a brick commander in West Belfast. I used to tell my blokes, imagine your brick as your hand. Now I might be just the index finger, but without me the hand doesn't function properly and without any of you it doesn't function properly. So to work properly we've got to have all the digits there. If I try to separate my index finger from my next finger, I can only go so far. So you gotta act as a complete unit or you can't act properly at all. You've got to rely on every bloke to cover your ass, and he's got to do the same. It's hard every day to motivate the guys but the thing about the corps is, nobody likes to be classed as a wanker. If you say, 'You, son, are a wanker', that means he might as well wrap up and hand his ID card in. So, if you've got lads who are starting to get a bit slack, all you gotta say is don't be such a wanker and they get it. So they stay switched on, but it is hard sometimes. Even I get lax, but then one of them just says, 'What the fuck are you doing?' You can't relax because that's another of their weapons. They wait for the time when you are relaxed, and they're watching and waiting all the time, and as soon as you relax they hit you. Then you're fucked. So what you gotta do is, is look like you're relaxed, but don't be, and then maybe we can get one of them, which is what we want.

Major, 45 Commando

It is still a corporal's war – war may not be an appropriate word – but it's the corporal, the brick commander, who has to get his brick together in that four-man cell. They live together, train together, they eat together, and they must believe in one another. There is a dependence between them and they must know instinctively what to do and how to react.

Corporal, 45 Commando

We had a great find on our last tour. A find – that is a celebration time, great jubilation. Every man and his dog appears. Once it's dealt with, it's laid out to be photographed. It is most definitely a pat on the back for everybody.

Marine, 45 Commando

When you patrol the Divis Flats nobody comes out on the balcony, they just emerge from a doorway and you get hit with a shitty nappy or a used tampax. Anything that they think will demean you down to the lowest level; the very basest thing in life. You never see the person who throws it – but as soon as it hits you, probably a thousand voices start cheering. You never see a curtain twitch but they're all watching and they know you can't do a lot about it. You can't shoot at anyone who is throwing a nappy.

Sergeant, 1 Welsh Guards

I was walking backwards through the Divis, down the corridor bit, and the next thing this Alsatian jumped out at me. I don't like dogs at the best of times, but that dog just got at me and we slammed around and I was screaming and shouting and everyone was just watching me. What made it worse, I was shouting at them and they were laughing at me because I'd lost my temper. They'd achieved their aim. Every time I saw them after that they used to take the mick out of me, you know, 'woof woof'. I lost there, just that once.

Marine, 45 Commando

We saw a lot of the NORAID people when we were patrolling the Divis flats. They were being taken around the dirtiest areas that could be found and told how the council treats their tenants. You know, can we have some money to help us out! We later saw them taking photographs of us firing plastic bullets at the people – but they didn't seem keen to take photographs of them throwing bricks at us.

Captain, 2 Royal Anglian

The death of our company commander in South Armagh came as a great shock. It was the first time I'd ever experienced a war casualty. I got everyone working and we knew it was useless what we were trying to do, but you had to do something. In the evening I was talking to the company about what follow-up action we could take. We were all very moved by his death and at one stage I thought I was going to have to leave the room, because I felt the old lump coming into the throat. It's not just the tragedy, it's the feeling of impotence afterwards. There is nothing you can do about it in terms of retribution.

What I did find interesting was that for the next three days I was not working properly. I did what I had to do but my mind wasn't on it. I went to the memorial service out of respect to

167

Andrew. Listening to what the padre said, even as an atheist, I found it did clean the spirit somehow. I felt better after that. I was also interested to see the police reaction. The RUC lost two men in the same incident, and I think took the deaths harder. For a policeman, the sanctity of human life is so ingrained in their profession, as well as in their private life, that they felt their losses very keenly.

Rifleman, 2 Royal Green Jackets

At an IRA funeral their firing party are there wearing balaclavas and berets. But if you tried to arrest them the crowd would rip you to pieces. It frustrates you because you know that those wearing the beret have probably had a shot at someone – but you can't get at them. It's like, if you can imagine, winning the pools and the money being there and you can't touch it. You can look at it, you can photograph it, you can shout and scream, but you can't touch it.

Lieutenant, 1 Welsh Guards

There was a purpose to the Falklands, but equally there is a purpose to Northern Ireland. I mean forget all politics, as far as I'm concerned there is a definite job in so far as we're protecting that one man in blue, or in the RUC's case, green.

Sergeant, 2 Royal Green Jackets

On our tour of the hard nationalist area of West Belfast, for two policemen to patrol safely, you needed five bricks. So you had twenty men on the ground patrolling, plus another eight mounted in Land Rovers, and probably a helicopter, and the Quick Reaction Force back in the camp ready to react. This is a lot of men for two police to patrol around. Yet ten minutes away the police were patrolling on their own in clearly marked police cars.

Major, 45 Commando

The RUC have a difficult job to do, they recruit different men, they train them differently and they are policemen, they are not a pack. And whilst they are mindful of the needs of the military that supports them, they are aware, as we are, that it is a marriage of necessity, it is not a marriage of equals because there is an imbalance in the fundamental principles of the relationship.

Marine, 45 Commando

The most stressful thing was handling situations which normally a policeman would be trained for. Situations which we're not trained for. Royal Marine training is directed at confronting terrorists and if necessary killing them. We are not policemen.

Corporal, Women's Royal Army Corps Provost

It's quite a thorough body search. You have to do their hair, all through the hair, looking for anything small enough that could be concealed, such as a detonator. You also check whether they have a wig on. Now, at checkpoints there is no room for people to change, so if they have a wig on they have to take it off outside, which can be a bit embarrassing and they usually have a go at us, calling us lesbians. Then you go all round the collar. You have to be very careful when you lift the collar up before putting your hands onto it because their favourite trick is to put razor blades along the back. As you brush your fingers down it you can cut yourself to pieces. After the collar you go down the arms, under the arms, down the sides of the body, down the middle, the chest. You have to touch down the middle in case there's anything hidden inside. Then down to the hips and round the waist. If they are wearing a lot of heavy clothing, cardigans or belts, they have to remove these. With a skirt you have to go up the leg to the top of the thigh and down again, hence the reference to dykes and lesbians.

Lieutenant, 1 King's Own Scottish Borderers

An off-duty RUC man was visiting his parents and he had to drive down a long lane to visit them and there was only one way to get to them which was up a long lane and back on to the main road. He used to visit them the same day of the week every week and always travelled the same road. The terrorists got to know this routine so they lined him up. There were four gunmen involved in this shooting, two people with automatic weapons and two people with shotguns. As the RUC man came round the corner the terrorists opened fire on him from a range of about seven yards but somehow the driver managed to get away. The RUC took the car in for forensic evidence and there was one round through the fender. The RUC follow-up team found stacks of shotgun cases. We had to do the cordon for the follow-up. In that area we knew who most of the players were. The very next day one of our lads, a great six-foot-three giant of a man, went up to this player and said, 'Who does your shooting? Stevie Wonder?' And the guy turned beet red and for about two weeks they looked very uncomfortable. Then they let us know that the four blokes involved in the shooting had been punished. They'd botched up so badly and everyone was laughing at them. All the locals knew too by then, and they were really upset about that.

Lieutenant, 1 King's Own Scottish Borderers

There was a construction site and there were eight guys working, all part-time drivers for the IRA. They were all being paid but often the targets they were interested in were nearby. I used to think, why aren't the police doing anything about them. But then again, you don't know what is happening on the sneaky beaky side. We'd be at a road block and a guy with a big beard and an Irish accent would drive up. The RUC would give him a cursory check and pass him through – he'd be working for our side. It was very strange, no doubt about it.

Lieutenant, 2 Royal Anglian

We were down on a rural checkpoint near Enniskillen. The sergeant stopped this van and asked the driver if he had any identification. He said, 'Yes, I have. My name's on the van.' The sergeant said, 'No, have you got a driving licence?' He said, 'No, I haven't, but my name's on the van and it's my van!' That was the highlight of the tour.

Senior NCO, 1 Welsh Guards

We had only been there about a month and a half, and one of my staff sergeants come up to me and said, 'I'm cracking.' I said, 'What's the matter?' He said, 'I've got to get out. I want to do patrols, I want to go to another location.' He had been in Springfield Road police station for six weeks. He hadn't been outside the confines of the place. It was totally bed, work, work, bed, for six weeks. So then we started a system whereby boys could be plucked out of the job they were doing in the battalion HQ and sent to the companies, just to get out on the streets on patrol. Boredom could be a problem.

Sergeant, 45 Commando

R and R simply means getting back to my wife, because as a Marine we spend a lot of time away. If I have to do a four-month tour in Ireland then that's the way life goes. All I look forward to is to stop going in the heads and jerking off. I mean, grown men going into the bloody heads to look at their skin magazines when we have perfectly good wives at home. I don't relate this solely to Ireland but I've been going there for fifteen years and now at the end of the tour, or on R and R, all I want to do is sit in my house for a bit of quiet away from the constant banter, banter and false fucking machoism.

Corporal, 45 Commando

The best night is before your R and R, when you finish about six o'clock and go and have a couple of beers and you're on a real high, because you know you're going home and can forget it for four days. Once you come back off the R and R you can see it in the people, they're just sitting and moping about; not interested. Then it would twig that you're back, then it's all go again.

Sergeant, 45 Commando

R and R in five days – you can spend a day travelling each way, so you get three whole days at home. You come straight out of

171

an environment like West Belfast where you've probably been patrolling very hard, to go on leave. You try hard to relax, be at ease, with your wife and children, but it's very, very difficult when you're so tight. I find myself snapping at people and by and large I don't enjoy R and Rs. I don't believe it's long enough. There's even talk of cutting it. Why can't they give you a week, for Christ's sake? The lads out there are working their guts off, why can't they just say, right, you can have the week? At least you'd get five days at home.

Marine, 45 Commando

At the end of the tour you are probably doing the same amount of running about but you begin to see things more. You know where to run and where to waltz, what's important and where to look for it.

Corporal, 45 Commando

On a four-month tour it's work, followed by work, followed by work, followed by work. That's it. You don't go anywhere, you can't leave your base location unless you're at work, so basically Northern Ireland is the pits. You have done a tour of duty, of which I suppose ninety per cent is sheer boredom followed by about ten per cent of rush around.

Sergeant, 45 Commando

We get there. Day one, bang: everyone's out on the street, great, paperwork's coming in, photographs, things are happening. Right, we're going home. Kit's packed, gone. Back home. Forget it. I mean I can't remember knack all about four months last year. You just switch off, it's just another four months out of your life.

South Armagh

Major, 1 Para

South Armagh is unique, it's really an area of its own in terms of the factors which bear on it. It's very beautiful indeed. It's perhaps a little like some areas of Derbyshire or Yorkshire: rolling hills, stone walls, little farm buildings, and when it isn't raining, which isn't often, it's very attractive indeed. The people keep themselves to themselves. I don't think a lot of them give a damn who governs them, provided whoever governs them stays out of the way. I don't think they're very keen on paying taxes or acknowledging authority of any particular nature, whether it be North or South. Very Irish. They enjoy their independence. Of course South Armagh basically is a hard Republican area and the people living there are nearly all Republicans.

The border is totally indistinguishable: just wanders over fields. It's very easy to cross it by mistake, because nothing marks it whatsoever, except on a metal rail where you've got a yellow paint line across the rail, but in the countryside it might be a small stream, it might be a dry stone wall between two fields. It looks the same on both sides.

It's a totally different problem operating down there than it is in the streets of Belfast. Totally different. In the urban area you're working in close confines; your ranges, for example, are probably not more than two or three hundred yards. There are always a lot of people around because you're working in a built-up area. You don't go out probably more than three, four, five hours at a time; it's very close and tight. Reinforcements are always to hand. You can basically drive a military vehicle with, not complete impunity, but getting on that way. In the countryside, particularly in South Armagh, the population is very dispersed and therefore you've got large areas of nothing. Fields, hillsides and the odd wood. You don't have reinforcements easily to hand and driving is a crazy thing to do because you'll get blown up. So either you walk or you fly by helicopter. You've got the consideration of the border, always the border, which is the sanctuary for the terrorist, whereas in Belfast and other urban areas his immediate sanctuary has to be within the town itself. So you might be able to find it and if you can find it you can do something about it. On the border you can do nothing because his sanctuary is off limits to you. I think it's a more dangerous scene of operations than the town. He can hurt you and run across the border and, equally, he can hurt you without even being on your side of the border. If he's got a bomb just outside, he either detonates it by radio or by landline from the other side and there's nothing you can do against it. You have to be very careful to incorporate the Republic's security forces into any operation you may do, if they can be of value to you, which very often they can be.

It's very much more a game of lethal chess down there than operating in the streets of Belfast or Derry or wherever. Much slower, much more deliberate and, in terms of intensity, actual frequency of incidents, much less. But in terms of concentration and adrenalin, equally high, if not higher, because you will spend long periods, a long wait and then something will just happen out of the blue, and you've probably got fifteen or thirty seconds to make something of it, or not.

Warrant Officer, Ulster Defence Regiment

Working on the border can be very infuriating. Time and again you find yourself not able to cross the frontier post, or you find that one half of the field that you're standing in with fifty cows is in the North and you're okay, but if you're in the bottom end of the field, you're standing in the Republic of Ireland.

One side of the street at Jonesborough, which is about ten miles east of Crossmaglen, runs into the South, and the other side runs into the North, and there is a white line down the middle to indicate this. We had a cordon on our side round this house that was sitting on the border and being used as a bomb factory. At the same time the Republican Irish Army, the Irish Army itself, as opposed to the IRA, was supposed, along with the Gardai, to be sealing certain roads in the areas in the South. But as dawn broke it became obvious that there wasn't anybody there on the Republican side, because as the teams moved down to search this house, we were opened up on from the other side of the border. As we didn't have any follow-up on the Southern side, the IRA were able to sit and shoot at us, then just get in their car and drive off. We therefore found ourselves in an extremely unreal situation, all because of this simple white line in the middle of the road.

174

Captain, 1 King's Own Scottish Borderers

It's very noticeable the difference between the city and the country. I mean in South Armagh there are many wealthy people and lovely houses. The whole area is delightful, with new houses. If the circumstances were different, I could retire there most happily. It's a far higher standard of living than anywhere else that I've seen in Britain, and certainly higher than living in Scotland. Light years ahead. They get ninety per cent grants for building and rebuilding. So if they've got the old shed that had been the farmhouse, they just keep it there and they build a hundred thousand pounds' worth of house for ten grand. So they're on the pig's back. Lots of money, but there has always been lots of money in Ireland.

Guardsman, 2 Coldstream Guards

I thought South Armagh would be bleak, I knew it would be horrible countryside. In the Army the country's always horrible. Never been anywhere that wasn't. Brecon, Wales, Scotland, everywhere we go it's horrible, so I knew it wasn't going to be nice in South Armagh. So when we got out there, I wasn't really surprised by any of it. To a civilian, on holiday, passing through the countryside in a car, it's nice, yeah. But actually marching through marshes and those spiky bushes, brambles, things like that, it's different: tabbing miles on end, day after day, like.

Captain, 1 Para

Crossmaglen's a one-horse town, there's bugger all there. It's not like Belfast, where there are all the back alleys and ginnels. You know, walk up Newry Street, Newry Road, Dundalk Road, walk round the school and that's it – there's absolutely nothing!

Corporal, 1 Para

We were strolling around Crossmaglen. In the middle of the patrol was a pig – you know, an animal pig! And it followed us around the town. It was walking around with the patrol. We couldn't get rid of it, so we just kept the pig with us. When we were getting down in the doorways this pig was stopping by the side of us – sniff, sniff – one of the blokes was using the pig for cover!

Once we had a little Jack Russell called Ruffles. He came into our place to be part of our situation; we had him for ages and ages, he was dedicated to soldiers. The Green Jackets and the Guards were arguing who got it first but it came in to be with us. If the Paddys ever saw that dog going round they knew that the patrol was around somewhere. The dog was always there. We used to keep it with us because it used to run through the gaps in the hedges and had there been anything there, like a trip wire, it would have set it off. So we kept him there as a work dog. Handy that! We used to take him out in the chopper with us.

Major, 1 King's Own Scottish Borderers

Having been in Belfast one heard of security forces casualties and instances in Crossmaglen. I came to it with the impression that it was steeped in hard-line terrorism and a citadel. If you look at it geographically, it sits majestically within a stone's throw of the border on that sort of South Armagh salient. It has six key roads that feed into the heart of Crossmaglen village itself, which is the square, and four of those roads lead directly to the border: either west, south or south-east, and two lead deep into the other heartland of South Armagh itself. It is geographically a key place and as far as South Armagh PIRA are concerned, it has always been a place where they have practised and launched the latest techniques of terrorism against the security forces. So this was uppermost, almost, in my mind when I went there. Daunting, and unfortunately the Army never plays it down. The Army adds to the folklore, almost as if we should keep on generating it and increasing the tension. The chronology of incidents that have happened in and around Crossmaglen Square, which is just a blasted heath, are commemorated, certainly within the Army base itself and I'm sure in the hearts of every Provo in South Armagh.

Corporal, 1 King's Own Scottish Borderers

Crossmaglen is a little place, very quiet, sort of, for a border town. I don't know why the fuck it's British because I don't think any Prods live there. Those who do live there don't like you. I think the main thing that strikes you when you go to Crossmaglen is the little Ops Room upstairs. In there they've got a list of the people that's been killed in the area and that is quite phenomenal. Then they've got photographs of different incidents. Everything is so well laid out. In the briefing room they've got two big models, one of the surrounding countryside and one of the village itself, and you could pick out anything, like a house – the detail is immaculate. Once you see that and you see all the photographs it makes you realise how sinister the place is. I mean, over the years watching on the TV and reading all the different books about it, Crossmaglen's always the big mention. So when you go out there, when you actually move out onto it, there's a sense about the place. It's a very frightened community and I think they're intimidated by the IRA who have a very strong hold on the whole place, so anywhere we used to go we would be watched. The IRA who operate in that area are, I would say, probably the best that they've got, so you're up against a very determined enemy. Everything you do down there's got to be well thought out.

Captain, 1 King's Own Scottish Borderers

Because South Armagh used to be the flagship of IRA activity, it feels obliged to keep on staging things there because if they don't, then the big boys up in Belfast start putting pressure on them saying, 'Why haven't you done something?' Things generally happen there fairly frequently. My first impression of Crossmaglen was that it was quiet, an old little town. The only way I could differentiate it from a Scottish border town was the shops, like B. R. O'Grady, and the street signs as well. Also, when you walk out, even though you've psyched yourself up for it, you suddenly realise that people don't really want to talk to you, and even if they want to talk to you, they can't unless they're unobserved. Even though part of me wanted to believe that they might want to talk, I psyched myself by saying a Paddy's a Paddy; there's no such thing as a good one or a bad one. They're just all Paddys. We're Jocks and we're here to do a job and they can either like us or lump us.

177

Sergeant, 2 Para

When I was first up at Bessbrook it was a fenced-off field, a swamp. The pilots used to land on two elevated piles of railway sleepers on scaffolding. You used to get out, throw your bergen, and climb down. So did your pilot. You didn't get observers in those days, just a pilot. A year later the place was concreted and they'd got pads. Now it's like an international heliport: you could land a Hurricane.

Corporal, 2 Para

I was just eighteen when I went out there. We moved into Bessbrook. At that time we had two locations, Bessbrook Mill which was company HQ, and Bessbrook Infant School which was a laugh because when we first got there all the dinner tables were infants' tables, the chairs were infants' chairs, and the toilets were little tiny, low toilets. And some of our blokes were six feet six!

When we cleared the route from Bessbrook to Crossmaglen for support company, one of the problems we had on the way in was that somebody had changed all the road signs round. So you reached a road sign that read 'Crossmaglen 15 miles' and the next one would say 'Crossmaglen 1 mile' and the one after that would say 'Crossmaglen 5 miles'. Somebody had been out swapping them all round just to make life confusing.

Our road-clearing technique then probably wasn't down to the fine art it is now. We didn't have the equipment. It was mainly a couple of guys with mine prodders poking them into piles of stones and into bushes in the hope that they were going to come up with something – primitive compared with the equipment we've got available now.

Sergeant, 2 Para

Bessbrook wasn't what it is now: it was an old, dingy, no-good, burnt out real stinking horrible base. We had the first two floors because that was all that was built up; so we had the Engineers put on the third floor because we wanted to be isolated and on our own. That was of our own choosing. All they could provide us with was a light strung across the top, some old beds and a couple of gas heaters. We were there to teach guys how to do their Ops. Teaching guys who are not even in the same frame of mind as you. And teaching 'on-the-job training'. It's the hardest life because regardless of the weather, if your task's important, you stay there, behind a rock, behind a bush, wherever, you stay there. To do that, you've got to be a complete robot, switch off and identify with the task. Ignore your surroundings and just die for the job. We live in it and we like it. We would take out patrol commanders to come and live with us for four days and explain the routine, how you got in, how you got out, how you made the decision, why you picked that spot – it's all to do with observation, cameras or whatever.

The guy in charge came down to see our accommodation because he'd asked for us to go and help with the area. He was appalled at the conditions. We weren't too bothered, we were quite happy with this place, but he was really appalled. He asked us about rations, all the typical things. We complained about a few things and I'll never forget, four days later he came down in a chopper in the middle of the flaming night with this great big cardboard box full of these self-heating cans that the Navy get, soups and stews. We'd heard about them and we'd mentioned them, and now he'd got them. God knows who he sent to get them off the Navy. It must have come from England. If the truth be known we never used them because they were too bloody heavy, but the thought was there – very considerate. Then over a period of a week the inside of the place started to change, a couple of toilets and three or four washbasins were put in, and the whole thing became an individual complex, just like that. It's not what you know, it's who you know!

Captain, 1 Para

We went round, did the old patrols night and day. Fairly routine, mundane, nothing ever really happened. You were tired at the end of the day; so you'd take up a position in a field with your twelve-man patrol, post sentries or look-outs, go to sleep – and when you wake up your head's in a cow-pat and you've gone through the crust.

Chaplain, 2 Para

There were moments that enlivened the boredom. Our quarter-master was an avid bird fancier and when we were in Bessbrook he got his staff to knock up a pen in the yard and he arrived with half a dozen bantams and ducks. He put the bantams in the pen, except the cockerel which would need to go into another room to settle down. In this room he had ducks swimming around in a zinc bath which disturbed this bloody cockerel, who started crowing. He couldn't silence it, short of wringing its neck, so he picked it up and took it outside. The sentries got this treat of seeing their quartermaster in pyjamas and dressing gown with a cockerel under his arm at three o'clock in the morning, trying to silence it. Then to make it worse someone released his bantams and these things were then flapping up and down Bessbrook High Street with the entire quartermaster's staff chasing them, trying to throw smocks over them!

Captain, 1 Para

Winthrop, a subaltern in Northern Ireland, led us to a great breakthrough in arms discoveries. One day, a bit like Archimedes, he sat down and thought: 'How is it that people picking up arms caches can recognise where to look from some veiled speech? Caches must, therefore, always be near a prominent feature, viz: 'Go to a field, look to a break in a wall, arms cache fifty metres to the right.' So he employed what we now call the Winthrop theory for searching out dangerous kit. On patrols you apply the same sort of thing: steering clear of a gap in a hedge, say, or a white post down the road – you could be seen from a hill and as soon as you go past there could be a bomb. You think of these things and try to blend with the background as much as possible. How successful one is or isn't I'm not sure can ever be measured.

Sergeant, 1 King's Own Scottish Borderers

The farmers down there are more anti – not what's happening, but to what's happening to the farm itself. I mean, down in South Armagh on my last tour, we were patrolling and we used to go straight through their fences, break their fences. We had no option, we couldn't use the obvious route, because that could expose us to danger.

Sergeant, 2 Royal Green Jackets

When we go out for patrol we take normal twenty-four-hour ration packs, small boxes plus whatever else we could get from the cookhouse. A lot of guys take chocolate. With the rations is a Hexi stove but a lot of blokes have small gas burners, though I find in the cold they're not very good. It's a sad fact in today's Army that if a guy's going somewhere cold he has to spend a lot of his money on his own personal comfort: Norwegian shirts and longjohns, because the Army longjohns are pathetic things. Guys buy their own thermal underclothes and stuff like that; their own socks. A lot use their own boots as well. But we have to wear our beret because the SAS are running around in all sorts of kit so you have to be identified.

If six of us were going out into the cuds, usually for a day or two, we'd take three sleeping bags because there was always three people up. We don't use a bed roll, put it straight on the ground. I experimented while I was out there on different ways of keeping warm, because the sleeping bag is so bulky. I went out and only took a sleeping bag liner and an Army blanket; that is not recommended. Now I put the sleeping bag in a Gortex bag which is totally waterproof. You put your sleeping bag inside it. They're very good. I took one of them out with an Army blanket. I'm a confirmed sleeping bag carrier. If it means getting rid of a little bit of rations or a bit of kit to make space for the bag, I do it. I've had times when I've been wet in a sleeping bag but warm and that's lovely. It's when you have to do that dreaded unzip to get out. You think, 'Why am I here, I'd like to be in bed somewhere.'

Private, 1 King's Own Scottish Borderers

It was a sixteen-hour day, and we always seemed to be soaked. We'd sleep in this bullet-proof hut where there was no room for our gear. The majority of the time we left it outside because you could nae get that and all the bodies in the hut. But we kept our weapons, bullet-proof vests, tin helmets inside, and maybe a book, or a small tape recorder, and a torch to read the book.

When it rained our kit got wet. I mean our kit was wet anyway so it didn't really matter. We never changed our clothes, but we always shaved – that's personal discipline really. I mean you'd get up, go outside, fucking freezing and you're trying to wash your face breaking the ice. When we first got to Bessbrook, we only went in to dump some of the kit and immediately went straight out to the chopper. We didn't even get into a normal bed for the first ten days. We had fresh rations, but you'd find that they didn't last long. We made a rota for making the scoff. Whoever's up at the time on stag or just coming off stag, you'd make the scoff for the rest of the guys. I like stews, I did a lot of stews and curries. Fills you up more and it looks better on the plate. I mind one time, for the last three days we were living on just shredded wheat for breakfast, dinner and tea, and we had no milk, no sugar and no fags!

Once when we were out on a patrol we came across some barbed wire. Our section commander, who was a second lieutenant, said, 'Well, I'll go first.' He climbed up on the barbed wire and jumped off and fucking went into this cesspit. He was in shit up to his chest. Of course we couldn't do anything but laugh. We dunked him in the river on the way back. Couldn't have that sleeping in the room.

Sergeant, 2 Para

I've gone into farms and said to the old girl, 'I've come to have a chat with your son.' 'Sean's up the top field, you don't have to go on up there, he'll be down in five minutes. Have a cup of tea, have some cakes, have some bread.' We wanted to talk to Sean who was a normal, everyday, hard-working, happy-go-lucky, nineteen-year-old bloke who doesn't want anything to do with war. His problems are getting his crops in, his tractor going, can he get a bit of petrol off the boyos, and that's it. He hasn't got time to fuck about with wars and crap like that, wars interfere with his work, his whole life is the farm. He came down and said, 'Ah, Jesus, boys, good morning, but I'm not talking to you because there might be people watching me!'

Private, 1 King's Own Scottish Borderers

On one of the searches there was myself and a corporal. He picked up something on his detector; so he asked for a shovel, and right enough there was a wire in the ground. We know in our guts it's for real, so I moved in to cover, into this hedge. Harry pulled the wire and of course as it lifted up it broke the earth and stopped right at the end of my feet. I just turned puke pale. I shovelled the earth away and there was a big metal plate underneath. When I lifted that up there was a rubber tyre and two pairs of pans taped together which were filled with explosive. The reason it didn't go off was because as Harry pulled it, it had uncoupled the explosives.

Guardsman, 2 Coldstream Guards

I was tired throughout the whole tour. I was based in Keady, and the day was divided up into four six-hour parts: on sangars; on sentry guarding the barracks; on QRF (Quick Reaction Force) 1, or stand-by QRF 2; on rest. You used to go on at eight o'clock and if you were on rest first, you couldn't really get your sleep because everyone was busy in the morning, so you were pretty shattered and then you might be on QRF 1 next. You'd have to put on all your kit, all your webbing, and sit in the QRF room ready to go in thirty seconds. You have to go to meals in your full kit, and to the toilet. Then you might be on six-hour sangars, observing the outwards, protecting the base – that's really boring. We didn't have a toilet there. There's three sangars and you used to do every one twice, you'd swap round every hour, and if you were quick you could go to the toilet. When you were in the sangar you had to wear a steel helmet and you'd have to stand, you couldn't sit down. If you were on at two o'clock in the morning till eight o'clock, it seemed terrible. Nothing happened. You weren't allowed to read or write letters, you were just observing constantly, on your own, bored out of your mind.

I'd spend the time thinking of the good times I'd have when I got back. Because you're guaranteed three weeks' leave when you returned. But early on in the tour it seemed ages away, I was really depressed at times. I'm a bit of a lad really, I'm always a bit of a joker, and now I wasn't joking. So people used to say, 'Cheer up,' but everyone's the same, everyone knows everyone's pissed off. So I used to knock off my anger in the squash court.

You had one day off during the whole tour, one full day off and that day I went to Bangor. That was nice. We used to go there in these CPVs (covert personnel vehicles). With these vans coming out of the base with windows boarded up it was obvious we were in there so I was a bit scared. When we got there we looked like soldiers and everyone knew we were soldiers, but Bangor was a different atmosphere altogether. People were nice to us, we never got filthy looks like we did in Keady.

I was always low. I used to write letters whenever I could and phone home.

Lieutenant, 1 King's Own Scottish Borderers

We got a call from a permanent OP in the hills that an illegal VCP had been set up so we charged up there. It was just getting dark, sort of half-light. I couldn't quite make out what this bloke was doing, but he was definitely stopping cars in the road. So I piled over the wall and shouted, 'Army. Halt or I'll fire.' I thought: 'This is my moment of glory. The Military Cross coming up.' But he was stopping traffic to let the cows cross the road!

Corporal, 2 Para

We rated the North Louth ASU (active service units) well in 1976 because they'd attacked one of our OPs. They'd sussed it out through various mistakes that we'd made and shot at it and bombed it, luckily after we'd moved out about eight hours before. That was a good attack. About ten people took part in it. Because of attacks like that no VCPs were allowed in the border area. But we got clearance from the brigadier to go down and set one up to see if we could attract fire, and find out where it was coming from. So we went down and within about ten minutes we got a couple of rounds. Fairly close shooting as well, passing within a couple of feet of the old Land Rover, so we skidaddled out. About ten days later we went back but this time we put out three sniper crews to cover that area. We rode down in the two Land Rovers to do the old VCP and he's watched it. He's watched how we'd done it before and we did the same again. The first Land Rover pulls into his left and blocks off the road. We pull into the church driveway, and reverse out across the road and block the other side. But twenty pounds of explosive go off as we drive into this gateway! Front wheel's gone, driver's out the back and we've gone down with a dummy that's had its head blown off in the passenger seat. Then, 'wham, wham', about eight or nine rounds come at us. Watching in front of a house was this bloke with a fisherman's hat. We're all scurrying all over the place, but we still haven't picked up where the shooting is coming from. We contact the sniper party, and one of them reckoned he'd seen something, so they'd put down a couple of rounds and said they'd got a kill. We found out later the guy who we saw with the fisherman's hat, four hundred metres away, had tipped the wink to a guy who was hiding behind the church, who couldn't see us, and he pressed the button. Very, very good. The same night we went up this great big hill of gorse and found two dead cows that the snipers had shot!

We targeted one of these North Louth ASU guys. We got information coming across from the South as well as our own. He was seen in this scrapyard right on the border. We put in two OPs, and watched for a couple of days. We see the guy is definitely in there and we send a message back to base and wait. To relieve the boredom we leave guys to watch the scrapyard while we do some VCPs on the back roads. About three o'clock in the morning we see this brand new Peugeot, of which there's not a lot around, and decide to stop him. In the back seat he's got about twenty chickens, opens up the boot and there's six piglets. Only the Irish could do this. He didn't want us to open the boot but we thought we might have a kidnapping or something going on and the chickens were a cover. His old man owns two farms in this area and the pigs are some sort of illegal trade. Don't ask me what the EEC rules are between North and South but he's on a winner, so he offers us a pig. So we get back to our OP and tie it up and feed it biscuits for a day. Then we get the call that they've seen the guy we want in the scrapyard and he's got a beard.

We move in slowly, then we charge down through this house into the scrapyard. Out they came, not one guy with a beard, but six of them! I'm saying, 'Which one? Which one?' I haven't got a clue which one it is because the photograph that we have is a blow-up that looks like a bag of sugar. So now it's like something out of *Blazing Saddles*, we're running around this scrapyard, they're trying to hide, we're trying to grab them. Eventually, we got all of them plastic-cuffed under a car. But we had to wait for Pete, the colour sergeant who can identify them, but he's fallen into a swamp on the way down! Eventually he staggers in covered in slimy shit and the other lads are panting behind him. So I said, 'Which one is it?' He goes, 'Oh fuck. I don't know.' Now you've got a ridiculous situation, because the whole yard is erupting. The woman at this farmhouse, she's screaming, the dogs are giving it max, Pete's standing there, not knowing – then he says, 'That's him.' So we cut this guy off the fender and leave the others chained up while we make our getaway – we could hear the Wessex coming. But it turns out we've picked the scrapyard owner's son so now his mother's screaming and kicking us. But Pete's adamant that this is the guy so we drag him off. On the way through we pass my OP and pick up the bergens and the old pig. If you had this on film you wouldn't believe it because you had this great, tough, hairy Paratrooper with all his kit dragging this young lad up the hill and his mother clinging on to him, a right frail old dear, and I've got this pig on a lead. Imagine the old loadmaster sat in the chopper: he kicks the door open, doing his business, looks down and sees this bloody group of Paras with this woman throwing punches and kicking and this pig leaping around going spare because of the old rotors – absolute chaos. So we throw the bergens on, the woman's screaming and she's hanging on, so Pete, very gentlemanly, decks her. We jump in with the pig and the guy and take off.

It's only six minutes to Bessbrook, and a couple of minutes from approach the 'loady' flicks the door open in readiness for our exit, the chopper banks, the pig panics, slips his lead. I make a grab at him, miss, and he goes hurtling out! The young guy with the beard, who has obviously never been in a helicopter, thinks he's next – it was outrageous. You wouldn't believe it if it was on telly. We were raging because we'd lost the pig. And the bloke was the wrong one and released that afternoon.

Major, 1 Royal Green Jackets

In Northern Ireland they have a Territorial Army but they are not involved with security forces, they're not in the UDR. One was a customs inspector whom I got to know. He told me that an awful lot of smuggling goes on along the whole of the border. Well, when I didn't find any terrorists within the first two weeks I came to the conclusion I should pursue the pig smugglers, because they had a thing down there called Dizzy Pigs. I'm not sure who pays what, but within the EEC there are various subsidies for pigs. In the North I think they're paid when a pig is slightly smaller and weighs less and in the South they're paid when the pig is slightly bigger and weighs a little bit more. So it was the same pig that travelled across the border. Then in one of the places you get a subsidy when it's finally slaughtered and converted to bacon; so people were making a lot of profit on pigs going backwards and forwards. The Ministry of Agriculture rules require you to have a special licence to move pigs because of disease, so we stopped lorry loads of pigs going across the border without a licence. When we had three or four we would then ring up and the customs man would come and do the business. I was told when we left that we'd certainly made the Exchequer about 1.4 million pounds in dues. It was quite funny because the smuggling in my patch dropped off significantly when one day we stopped two hundred lorries with illegal agricultural fuel in them. Towards the end we got it down to twenty or thirty a day. About three or four days before we left, one local chap said, 'Ah, Major, you'll be gone in a week and the next regiment won't worry about this, so we'll carry on in our own way.'

Senior NCO, 2 Royal Anglian

Smuggling is so rife in South Armagh. There's a lot of rich people live down there and a lot of money is made in smuggling, it's unbelievable. I'm not talking pence. I called at a small dwelling, I wouldn't call it a farm, cottage with land really, and in the outbuildings were twelve, fourteen gross of Guinness, half a dozen crates of spirits at least and so many barrels. They had a bill for £1,280. We had this RUC sergeant with us and he worked it out and apparently the profit from that was colossal, it was unbelievable. But I mean, why the hell should they work for the Army for a mere pittance of £100 backhander and risk everything, when they can make twice as much money by chipping in £100 into the IRA funds and having freedom across the border?

Captain, 1 King's Own Scottish Borderers

At a VCP I began talking to a local who didn't really want to talk to me but we were searching his tanker at the time. I said, 'I put it to you, that what you would like to see least is us withdraw from here.' He said, 'What do you mean?' I said, 'Well, I reckon that you've got a very nice set-up here, I know you smuggle fuel. I've seen your tanker on regular occasions and you're probably involved with all the other smuggling along the border. You must make a fortune. I reckon if we gave the Gardai a few phone calls now and again you'd probably make less of a fortune, but it wouldn't stop you doing it. You'd move to another area of the border.' He said, 'So?' I said, 'Well, it occurs to me that it's handy for you to have the police so involved with law and order that they haven't got time to get the customs people down here to investigate the smuggling.' He said, 'You're not wrong. I'm not in the IRA. I'm not the slightest bit interested in political change, integration for Northern Ireland. I'm quite happy. If we became one Ireland, I'd lose the border, I'd lose my livelihood.' I said, 'It's all a charade then.' He said, 'Up to a point. Of course we get pressurised from people and we have to put on incidents.' I said, 'Just make sure I'm not one of them.' That's when you can see the barriers coming across the eyes. Who knows what he could be doing tomorrow.

Corporal, 1 King's Own Scottish Borderers

Out of every thirty days we'd do ten days on an OP; the other twenty we'd be doing guards around the camp, or patrols, which took you all over Armagh. One minute you'd be in Bessbrook, the next you'd be in Forkill. But I think the OPs were the dread. Nobody liked doing them. On the OPs you knew who the baddies were, you just had to keep your eye on them, and with the kit we had it was excellent. But these guys knew we were watching them: they're not stupid. I don't know why they make those jokes up about the Irish. I think they're about the brainiest guys I've met yet. Really clued up. These guys know that we know them so there's no way you'll find anything on them. We have all the information about them, whether they've been in jail, or if they are INLA, PIRA, Official IRA. One of them will be walking past you and you know that he is probably the bloke who has killed three soldiers, but you can't do anything.

Sergeant, 1 King's Own Scottish Borderers

On the medical side, unusual things happened. I mean, you only expect frostbite and trench foot in the First World War but we got it in Northern Ireland. In South Armagh quite a lot of it, especially with the recce platoons, which led to a lot of sleepless nights because of painful feet. Professional soldiers are sensible enough to get it treated as soon as they can, but that is not always possible. For instance, in the recce platoon you can be lying in a 'hide' maybe for six or seven days, laying perfectly still, and in that time your feet'll sweat and then they'll freeze. But the job they do is so important, or so dangerous, that they can't move, so they have to stay still. You think about what the SAS do, but this is a normal infantryman doing his job.

Sergeant, 2 Para

We were at this OP and it was very close to a family, right tight on the border. This guy was heavily involved and they wanted some photographic evidence that there was something going on at this particular address. So we went in by night. We'd just come from six months in Berlin where they'd asked for all the single men to volunteer to make up this special patrol, for a six-month covering period. So the dress we had was what we'd cobbled together to look semi-military, but something to keep us warm and dry. I used to wear wellies, really baggy trousers and a Royal Navy flight deck jacket which had the big peak and hood on it, lovely and warm. Bob had a donkey jacket, and Andy had a set of American jungle fatigues. We went really close to this job, against all tactics for OPs. Ideally you should stay in a position so as to see anyone approaching you; well, we couldn't get it, we could not get a decent view. So we established our OP in a dip between two hills – I mean, tactically totally useless, totally unsound, but it was right for the task. We thought that if we relied on cunning and stealth and camouflage then we probably might get away with it. We dug in through the night, filling sandbags and constructing a hole, a very small hole, which would give us some protection. It was sparse but it wasn't too bad. It was acceptable. We thought, 'We've got a chance here.' So we set up all the big long lenses, and we had a lovely view. We were almost on the same level as the people we were watching. No problem with a frontal attack but if we'd been attacked from the flank or the rear there'd have been no escape for us, we'd have had to sit there and fight.

We went through this bitter cold night and just before first light we thought we'd have a brew, make a cup of coffee; we were fucking frozen. We thought if we keep it low, we'll be okay. So we set up this gas stove, it only gives a little tiny blue glow. Now, with it being so cold, the gas sort of froze, so that when we went to light the stove nothing happened. 'Christ,' we thought, 'bloody empty.' So we discard it and sat it down on some sand. Got another gas bottle out of the bottom of the sleeping bag where we kept it warm. Screwed it on, lit it, lovely. Temperature goes up and the next thing we know all this butane gas is hissing out the top of the other can! Fuck! Rammed it in and let it empty itself into the sand. No problems. Had the brew, lit a cigarette, which we shouldn't have done, but bollocks to it. Keep it down, sort of one between us. Struck the match, lit the fag, throw it into the sand, and the next thing you know it just went 'vroom'! The whole fucking thing was enveloped in a ball of orange flame, eyebrows singed. I mean this thing was like a fucking beacon for miles around. It blew the tarpaulin off and everything. All this gas had gone into the sand and it just fucking exploded. We really thought we'd been compromised. Then on top of that a dog, a Jack Russell, came in. We fed it a couple of biscuits and hoped it would fuck off. Next thing you know, this guy stuck his head in and he was confronted by us three. Bob, who was from Londonderry anyway, said, 'Just sit the fuck still.' This guy, I mean you could see him shit his pants. What he saw was me in a Royal Navy blue flying jacket, Bob in combat jacket, Andy in American jungle fatigues, unshaven. He must have thought he'd come across the IRA Ops Room.

Guardsman, 1 Coldstream Guards

The incident that made me the most angry was when we got ambushed on the Dublin road in South Armagh. This was in the '72/'73 tour. We'd just got off the helicopter and were doing a routine check down the Dublin road when we got shot at. I was on the other side of the road to where the ambush had taken place and it was only when somebody shouted 'Get down!' that I found out what was happening. There were cars and lorries stopping or crashing into the back of each other, so I ran straight across the road into a ditch, I was carrying an LMG (light machine gun) at the time and I cocked it. The fire seemed to be coming from the direction of three houses at the top of the hill. Two more or less brand new Spanish-type villas and there was a derelict in the middle. I just opened up on the derelict hoping and praying it was the right one. They were returning fire. All this rubbish that you get taught about the IRA, that they let a couple of rounds off and run, well, bullshit. We was there for about two or three minutes having a fire fight with them. It was really tense stuff, the adrenalin was going. We then got the order to stop firing. We ran up but by the time we'd got there, the border being a hundred metres behind the house, they'd gone. We all went back down to the road and were looking in all these cars to see if everybody was all right. This big articulated lorry had obviously seen what was going on and heard the shots and had stopped dead. This woman drove into the back of him and another car into the back of her and pushed the car into the lorry and she was trapped. She was screaming in agony. She had a little kid in the back in a child's seat and he was screaming too. That made me really angry: the innocent kids, women, the old people. It really made me want to get hold of a few and put them up against a wall and shoot the bastards. It really made me mad.

Sergeant, 2 Para

When you prepare an ambush you put the boys in, check all the business and you give 'Ambush Set'. That means nobody moves unless a war happens. In front, you've got a killing area. Each man has, say, sixty yards, that is his killing area. There we were: cold, wet, laying in a ditch, when two blokes walked into the ambush. We positively identified weapons and we had to open fire.

Unfortunately, it was our young lieutenant and his signaller. He'd walked down the road and come back up the wrong side. They were both killed.

Private, 1 Para

There used to be a tramp in Crossmaglen. I think he got topped in the end. I felt sorry for him, as one feels sorry for an injured animal. He was a drunk. He used to crawl up the street like a dog outside the front gate, and occasionally we'd bring him in for a brew, or let him sleep under the sangar, not that we were supposed to.

Lieutenant, 1 Para

In Crossmaglen they had a market on a Saturday. Lots of people about, you know, it's Saturday morning in a village, so I felt perfectly safe about going into the square. I sort of vaguely went through the process of looking at cars, pretending we were alert to our surroundings, assure the locals, give them visible signs that we are paying attention to what's going on and what's about. I walked up to this car and started to look in it, suddenly the whole thing went up, exploded, and I was covered in fire. I was up shit creek without a paddle. I was screaming, floundering around and I couldn't see a way out. I thought, 'What's going on? What's going on? Oh my God, I'm going to die.' I started heading down the square like a bloody great fireball. One of my platoon had recovered very quickly and shouted to me, I homed into his voice and I ran in his direction. I couldn't see because I was almost blind. I knew my hands, my legs and my head and all the rest of me were on fire but I kept running till I got to him. Whether I rolled myself or whether he rolled me – I don't know – whatever happened, I rolled. By now my eyes began to go; the last thing I saw were my hands, huge blisters were forming and just bursting – the stench was pretty awful. I was lying there smelling myself frying. The guy who I'd run to had whipped off his smock and smothered the flames. It felt strange being underneath that. By then others were around me so I took a deep breath and calmed down and thought, 'It's okay, I'm all right. I'll be okay.' I believe I started asking questions as to how everyone else was, but I can only guess, because I would imagine that severe shock had set in, so whatever I may think is probably a dream of what I thought happened. Once the toms had the situation under control – and I had a guy talking to me – I don't think I ever panicked after that. I always remember the medic coming up and talking to me and saying something about morphine. I had a hole in my chest and the back of my head, and that was pretty sore. Then the helicopter came and I remember them putting me in a stretcher, and because it was a Scout my feet and head were out of the helicopter so I caught this very cool breeze which was very soothing. At Bessbrook they transferred me to a Wessex. But by then I was as blind as a bat and I thought I was going to be blind for ever. Because there were no recognisable features on my face, the doctor on the Wessex said, 'Well, who are you?' I said, 'You bloody well ought to know who I am. I took you round the square at Crossmaglen two weeks ago!' By all accounts the doctor performed a miracle because in my swollen body he managed to find a vein and pumped two litres of drip into me. After that it's difficult to say, because it was the longest and shortest day of my life.

Private, 1 Para

We were coming in from the school to the square and the other section were coming down the bottom of the square and just as we crossed at the top this car exploded. Instead of getting down and looking around, we all went galloping across the square. There was a load of big, black smoke coming off the motor. When we got there one of the section, who must have been in shock, was just sitting there having a fag. Another was bimbling about. But the lieutenant, I couldn't believe it, he was on fire – from head to foot, totally smothered in fire, just running across, and really screaming. We ran and pulled him down and started putting him out. Paddy did it with a flak jacket on his face, but we told him to stop because a flak jacket's made of a sort of plastic material, and it had started melting on his face. I got my smock off and wrapped it round his legs and someone was using their beret. He was screaming all the time. I couldn't believe that smell, it was terrible. I was sick on him. Looking at him, his face was a mess, like an ashtray. He was black, his nose seemed to have gone, his lips had gone, and his eyes were closed, his hair and his flak jacket had gone. I remember he had his underpants on, and his putties and boots, and his weapon had melted. But for me there was no way he was going to die. The platoon sergeant was calling the camp, asking for a chopper and a medic. I remember the medic sticking these saline drips into him: he looked more in control than our bunch. I just kept telling the lieutenant he was going to be all right. I'd just got a medical note before we went out there, and I remember it saying, 'In the case of injury, reassure, reassure.' That was coming through straight into my head. I was shocked that he didn't pass out, because he must have been in some pain – but he was awake all the time. I've seen him once since then, but I don't think he recognised me. It's not the sort of thing you say, 'Hello, sir, I put you out once!'

When we got back to the camp they gave us a cup of tea. Then they took us straight out on a confidence patrol – straight back out. We weren't talking much – we were just quiet. Then when we got back in, we didn't stop talking. I slept like a log that night. But I can also remember most of that day seeing the company commander directly after the blast. You know in those black and white cartoon films, where there's an explosion, and there's a bloke standing there with shredded clothes on and his hair all smoking – it was like that. He had a Pye set in his hand and he was talking into it, but it had melted.

Corporal, 1 Para

Apart from being a medic, I was also the battalion photographer. I was in the dark room when there was an almighty fucking bang, and the whole place shook, and I knew that was my cue. That's when I get scared. Even though you're trained, that's when you get scared. Because that's the time when you are being tested for real, you're being tested under everybody else's gaze. I scrambled upstairs, grabbed my pistol, my bergen and a stretcher. We had this sort of monitoring set which covered most of the square. I could see this little black blob in the centre of the screen, which was not moving; I realised it was a bloke. I wanted to get down there as fast as possible. A sergeant came in as I was charging out and said, 'Where are you going?' I told him but of course he couldn't let me go, he had to get his alert platoon together, and then we could go. He stuck me in the middle, and we were to patrol down in case it had been set up, one bomb and then another.

As my adrenalin started pumping I started walking a bit faster and passed the patrol. I got level with the sergeant and we both started walking faster until we ended up doing a basic run, and in fact we sprinted into the square, leaving the patrol behind. When I got to him bits of kit were still left on him, and he was smouldering away, not burning, but a lot of his kit had burnt into him. The first thing that struck me was his cotton underpants, they were singed, but they were complete. His boots were on but the socks at the top had melted. His hair was smouldering, the thick part of the collar that was part of his flak jacket had burnt into his neck. He was there with his flak jacket, just bits of plastic, hanging down. Underneath, he had a normal shirt, but I think even that had disintegrated with the rest of it. I did not think he had long with us. I quickly turned him over, and he howled a bit; but all I was worried about was his fucking airways. I stuck an airway in, or I tried to, and he just rejected it. He was moaning and howling, and I was talking to him. He was on about not telling his mother, that was all he seemed to be bothered about. That was reassuring to me. I tried an airway again, but that just made him want to be sick; he wouldn't take it. He obviously felt he wanted to keep talking but I wanted to get this airway in because I would be able to hear his breathing better. But he wouldn't accept it, so I kept talking to him. Then from out of the blue a fucking helicopter arrived. By that time I'd got my drip things into him. We got him onto the stretcher, but nobody had undone the doors. I just went up and ejected the doors. It was immaterial to me if it broke the fuckers, we just wanted to get him in. He kept saying, 'Don't tell me mum, don't tell me mum.' He must have been in a hell of a lot of pain, but he didn't show it. Then we took off. He should have had a drip in, but it was going to cause discomfort and hassle because I'd have had to be pulling kit away, so I left it, relying on the speed of the helicopter to get him to Bessbrook. I got down beside him and was talking to him. He was fairly coherent and he understood what I was saying. All the time inside the helicopter the smell of burnt flesh was appalling – the pilot was nearly puking.

When we got him to Bessbrook we didn't hang around. There was my mate Dave with the battalion doctor. I tried to tell him something but he was in a hurry to get to work on the injured man. My adrenalin had been running so high up till then and now I had to hand over the responsibility to someone else. My thoughts also went out to the company commander who'd also been injured in the explosion. He'd remained cool throughout the incident. When I was talking to him he looked all right, a bit pale, but when he turned round I realised that he'd been badly burned, all his back, the back of his hands and his legs. That was weird. I tried to get him to go on the helicopter but he refused – he knew that someone had to remain to control the situation.

Sergeant, 1 Para

I was waiting at Bessbrook when we had a call about an incoming casualty. I think they said forty to sixty per cent burns. We couldn't believe it. Our doctor got his kit out and the rest of the crew were getting to the helipad. I thought, 'Ice. Got to get ice.' The doctor said, 'Where are you going?' and I said, 'Cookhouse.

Ice.' He said, 'Ice?' I said, 'Airways, swelling.' You pack the ice onto the throat and neck to try and reduce swelling to stop the airways blocking up. I went to the cookhouse and said, 'I've got a casualty, give me all the ice you've got.' I wasn't stationed there, the cook didn't know me, but he was brilliant, he gave me a big bin liner full. It was ridiculous the amount of ice I had. As the Scout arrived we just ran forward and the lads got the stretcher off. I ran towards the Wessex which was winding up, and tossed in my bag of ice. Then I jumped in to be in the chopper to lift the stretcher on. I thought the medic on the Scout was going to get on, but he didn't. Suddenly, we were off. That was the first time I saw the casualty and oh dear, what a mess. He was black and his face had gone. I remember distinctly his Northern Ireland watch. The plastic strap had all melted away but the watch was impaled into his flesh.

The doctor was busy checking his airways and I was thinking about IVI (intravenous injection) by this time. I'd seen him put an IVI in before and he was a bag of nerves, and I thought, 'Oh please don't fuck up, don't mess this one up.' I cut away the jumper and smock, trying to find his vein. The doctor found it, first go. That was remarkable in a Wessex that's just taken off: shaking and jumping about. Cool as a cucumber. He also put some pain-relieving drug into the IVI. I got down alongside him and his face was dripping plasma. He was in a lot of pain, but the doctor had already given him as much pain relief as possible. He probably had more pain on his bottom half where the skin was still intact. But I was getting worried about his airways. I just kept talking to him, but he was begging for pain relief. I kept thinking, 'Let's get him there fast,' because I didn't expect him to live. The journey seemed for ever. But we got him to Belfast and I had to leave him there. I never thought I'd ever see him back in the Parachute Regiment – but he is.

Captain, Army Air Corps

One of the jobs we had was a Special Dispatch service every couple of days. We'd send a helicopter to Lisburn to pick up the mail and a postman and then go round the Province dropping him off and collecting. One pilot dumped his postman and headed back for Armagh but lost his way. Now, the border is very, very crooked. You do not fly across the border, border incursion is frowned upon, so he panicked a bit and called on the radio: 'This is me, I'm lost. Can you help?' Another helicopter up on the North coast replied, 'I can hear you, what can you see?' 'I can see a big mass of water.' 'Okay, turn right.' So he turns right, then a little warning light came on to indicate his fuel filter was being blocked. But ahead he saw a barracks: what he didn't realise was that it was the Irish Army barracks at Monaghan. They wouldn't let him land, and parked their armoured cars in the square and drove round. So he ended up parking on the grass in front of the officers' mess. Out came their CO: 'What are you doing here then, Sarg?' 'Well, it's like this . . .' They took it in good spirit.

An Irish Army helicopter pilot came in to sort out the problem. The sergeant said to the Irish pilot, 'I'm in the shit now. I shouldn't have landed here, but I was pushed.' 'Oh,' said the Irish pilot, 'I spend more nights in the field in Northern Ireland than I do in me own home, don't worry about it.' Just before he took off one of their officers said, 'Hey, Sarg, we have a disco every Friday night. If you want to come down with your mates, you're welcome! And Sarg, if I was you, I'd go straight up now because the boyos are at their windows waiting for you!'

Captain, Army Air Corps

One of the Para battalions had taken over from 42 Commando just before Christmas. The services had laid on entertainment for the troops. Being South Armagh, you can only take people really to the main areas, like Bessbrook and Crossmaglen. They'd done a show – strippers and a comedian. According to the guys, it was fantastic. Then we thought, 'What about the lads in the OPs sitting up in the hill looking down on the road?' We thought that was a bit unfair, those poor buggers up in the hills have seen nothing. So we called the operators at the OPs and said, 'Whatever you do, get all your guys out and we'll bring you a surprise.' We flew up there and opened the side of the Lynx and the girls, in all their gear, or without all their gear, stood there for the boys to applaud, clap, or do what they liked. The girls just stood inside the aircraft waving at the boys!

Chaplain, 2 Para

I was flying back from Crossmaglen in '76, with a lad who'd fallen off a wall and broken his leg. We had this lad with his leg in inflatable splints in the front of the chopper and me in the back when we developed gearbox failure not far from Crossmaglen and came down. We got away with hitting the ground and the pilot put out a mayday call. The Quick Reaction Force had already been committed elsewhere. So we had to wait until they scrambled together enough men to fly out to us for protection. So there we sat: a pilot in uniform, soldier with a broken leg in uniform, and me in civvies with a dog collar, a couple of miles outside Crossmaglen, with the pilot's pistol the only protection. I thought, 'What happens to a chaplain in this position?' It was such an unlikely set of circumstances, but what do you do? I'm told the casualty said the Lord's Prayer four times on the way down!

Corporal, 45 Commando

We were a totally independent Royal Marine detachment: a lieutenant, a sergeant, and two sections. We worked eighteen days on shore and eighteen days at sea for the protection of the border, the imaginary border that runs down Carlingford Lough, a salt water lough which enters the Newry Canal at the narrowest point where the Paras got killed at Warrenpoint. When we went to board a vessel we'd use the fog horn and call to them that we were putting a boarding party on their vessel. I mean that's how the Marines started off their lives: as boarding soldiers. The Navy's soldiers. These ships almost never slow down for you. They just drop the ladder over the side, you grab hold of it and climb aboard. Sometimes they play with you then, and it gets quite hairy when it's rough and you're trying to get on board and they're not co-operating.

Captain, 45 Commando

I was up in Newry with half of my detachment, the other half were on one of the patrol vessels. A radar contact indicated a crossing from the South to the North at Warrenpoint. You pick up a lot of rubbish on the screen, but you check out everything.

A unit went down to investigate, couldn't find anything, got back and there was another contact. So they went down again. As they approached, they shut the engines off and saw a boat crossing with five men in it. They let the boat get well into Northern waters, very close to Warrenpoint, and just before it sort of slipped behind a tanker they challenged it. All hell broke loose. The blokes in the boat had fire support on the Southern shore, because at Warrenpoint it's bloody narrow, about 800 metres. These opened up but a Marine fired back. The boat immediately swung round to head back for Southern waters but the Marine put a round through it. The guys in the boat then stood up with their hands up. It was a case actually of six men arresting five. When I arrived, there were five terrorists lying on the ground. They'd got explosives, weapons, and they were obviously coming in to either plant something in Warrenpoint or to blow up one of the vessels. We were very excited because the operation had been going for a long time at that stage and there had been no real successes. Now, two weeks before we were going home, we'd got this big success. The recce party from the next lot had already arrived to visit us. I didn't feel at all envious of the people who were taking over from us because they would have a barren, totally barren four and a half months.

We were later involved in the trial. It was the first time I'd had to go to court and they went down, two for eighteen years, two for sixteen, and one for fifteen. When I saw them at Warrenpoint, they were young blokes, frightened, scared, two of the blokes had wet themselves with fear. When I saw them in court a year later, they were arrogant and they were hard. They had the support of their families and at all the times any of our guys were giving evidence, there were threatening gestures being made. The prosecution handled it very well; if you tell the truth, it's very difficult to find fault with it. When it came to the point about did anybody stamp on hands, the answer was, yes, they did. They were told to lie down, face down, if they moved they were going to get hurt. One of them moved and he got his hand stamped on and I would support anyone doing that far better than blow his head off.

Major, 1 King's Own Scottish Borderers

In 1985 we were involved in an extremely bold attack by the PIRA in the heart of Crossmaglen. It occurred when I had consciously,

199

through a pre-planned operation, put just about all of my company out of the base in another area within the Crossmaglen TAOR (tactical area of responsibility). We had been out lock, stock and barrel, except for base security, for a full day prior to the attack. We came back in to grab some lunch and sixty minutes before the normal patrol programme in and around the town recommenced, the IRA struck. They moved a truck with two Brownings on the back, concealed under a wooden frame covered in black bin liners, up to the Dundalk Road, which is literally two minutes from the border, and shot at a Wessex and then made their escape back down the same road.

That was a bold attack and clearly they knew exactly where my soldiers were, except for, I would suggest, the covert ones. They knew the majority of my patrolling force had been out and were now back in. They have a lot of people working and living in Crossmaglen who were providing them with all this information. So they were pretty well briefed before they set up the attack. Very bold and, of course, they risked a lot. They produced premium weapons, high visibility weapons, in an attempt to shoot down a high visibility target, a helicopter, a Wessex.

Corporal, 1 King's Own Scottish Borderers

Old Paddy from the old days of the nail bomb and the petrol bomb, he'd now come up to 1985 in this attack. He had a van and he sawed the roof off it, put four mortars inside, put wriggly cardboard stuff on top and fucking resprayed it. Brilliant, no two ways about it.

Senior NCO, 1 King's Own Scottish Borderers

The Wessex loadmaster was hanging out, on a strap. He looked up and he said, 'They're mortaring.' He'd actually seen the mortars coming in and shouted to the pilot who sent the contact report straightaway. I think he probably sent that contact report before the actual first mortar hit the deck.

Major, 1 King's Own Scottish Borderers

I was sitting in my office at three o'clock in the afternoon and I heard these three mega-fucking explosions and I thought, 'This is happening to you, boy.' I rushed straight out and through a narrow corridor into a pokey little anteroom that was full of debris. I noticed that an old beer can was lying on the floor; it had come out of the rafters somewhere. I rushed out into the yard and the place was full of dust and smoke and haze. There was an Alsatian dog running up and down and I thought, 'Shit, that's the search dog. What's it doing?' I rushed into the Ops Room and hit the mortar alarm. Then rushed out to the back, couldn't see any bodies in the square, then came back into the Ops Room. The company sergeant major who'd been out on the square was there. I didn't realise at that stage that he'd been slashed quite badly with a piece of shrapnel so I said, 'Sergeant Major, get out there and just fucking well make sure there are no casualties. If there are, make sure there are no unexploded bombs. Get them into the fucking sangars and make sure the area's clear.' We had patrols on the ground who were coming in with reports that no one could find the base plate. I said, 'Look, there must be a fucking great flat-bed truck with stacks of mortar tubes on the back, or something.' Then all of a sudden a Gazelle helicopter came overhead, with the sergeant major of The Prince of Wales's Own company and I said, 'Can you find the base plate?' After a while, between him and a patrol on the ground, they discovered there was something at the back of a house off the Dundalk Road. So I said, 'Right, land and pick me up.'

We'd disobeyed all the rules for mortar clearance drills; wait this amount of time, do this, do that. We just went. By that stage I had got my platoon commanders together and I said, 'Right, get out now. Get out now. I'm going up in the chopper and I'll tell you where to go.' So I whizzed around in the Gazelle and clearly identified where the base plate was; tasked all my troops, told them where to put the white tape, where to stop movement and all the rest of it. Then landed again and we then went into the full procedure. But there was no fleeing terrorists; no cars, no trucks, nothing. They'd gone.

Major, 1 King's Own Scottish Borderers

You start to think towards the end, 'Christ, am I actually going to get my company out of this place without a serious injury or a death?' Death is the hardest thing to justify. The separation and the heartbreak and the worry you can talk around, and write off in terms of duty. I'm an infantryman, that's what I'm here for, but death is hard to justify. In that counter-terrorist war I feel no sort of moral weakness in terms of taking my soldiers anywhere and expecting that they or I might die. But when you get to within two or three weeks of the end of a tour in Crossmaglen you begin to think, wouldn't it be nice if we all sort of got on a helicopter. To the Jocks, to get the company back and not a single casualty, not a single death, that is a good tour. They don't like to see a fellow Jock killed.

Captain, 1 King's Own Scottish Borderers

There's this Scottish–Irish thing. In Crossmaglen they've got their local GA club right beside the camp. I don't know what that stands for, but most towns have got one. It's a social club. On a Saturday night they'd be playing sort of Celtic folk music and we'd know half the songs. It felt a bit weird standing outside listening to that. People coming past and you're saying that's nice music, and they look at you as though you've got two heads. As a piper I used to practise regularly on the helipad. You could hear it all over the town. I'm a Catholic myself, but I used to play one of the Orange tunes, 'The Sash'. I'd only play it to wind the locals up. I mean, I played a lot of Irish tunes, folk songs. Patrols used to hear it when they were coming in and they used to say it sounded nice. The day we left, the company commander and about twelve men marched out with me and I was just piping away. We marched out the front gate, which turned a lot of heads. I stood in front of the main sangar and played a selection while they patrolled round the square, and I finished off with 'The Sash'. People were walking past. They didn't like it at all. They didn't like it because they knew what it was. It was a big two fingers up at them, because we didn't lose anyone in Crossmaglen. I think it was just a nice little parting gesture to them. Two hours later we were lifted out by helicopter.

202

Bombs and Bomb Disposal

Staff-Sergeant, Royal Army Ordnance Corps

In the early days bomb disposal was very much with crossed fingers. We were all feeling our way. The kit we had was exactly the same kit as we had in Hong Kong and consisted more or less of a Stanley knife and a pair of wire cutters. I remember I carried all my kit in the left-hand flak jacket pocket. Fortunately, in the early days they were feeling their way too. The bulk of the devices were comparatively primitive. Their idea of a micro-switch was a piece of dowel with two pieces of metal and it was fed through a box: you undid the box and the two pieces of metal made contact – quite effective.

All through my first tour the devices were of two types. There were simple explosive devices, about four ounces or thereabouts, designed to frighten people and destroy commercial property, and incendiary devices, mainly passed through letter boxes. A lot of them were made by the same chap, he had a production line going. They were built about the clothes peg relay system, using solder wire wrapped round a clothes peg. This chap was quite good, but once we'd spotted them and dealt with two or three, we knew exactly what we were dealing with in each case. And, as is ever the case, the bulk of our tasks were false alarms.

Captain, RAOC

Some ATOs (Ammunition Technical Officers) are naturally good at bomb disposal, but not all of them by any means, because not everybody is naturally good at it completely. They may have a great deal of manual dexterity, or the right technological background, or they may be very good in the field as commanders, but it takes an odd, difficult-to-define mixture of qualities to find someone who's going to make a really good operator.

An ATO has got to be able to command the situation. He's going into a situation where people are already rather tense; they've found what they think is a bomb, and certainly, thinking in Northern Ireland terms, they know what that means, and they know what to expect. So when the ATO comes on the scene they think they're getting an expert. Of course, it could be the guy's first job. He's done a lot of training, but suddenly everybody is looking at him to take the lead, and to say what to do next, and there are usually a lot of very experienced people on the street: RUC men who've seen it all before, firemen, and troops on the ground who've maybe had several tours there before. Therefore it does take somebody who can naturally take command of that situation and give everybody confidence in him, and the kind of decisions he's taking. Secondly, perhaps, the ability to think logically through a situation which may be constantly developing because you're getting new information all the time. You arrive at the scene of the incident absolutely cold, and you've got to find out what's going on from asking questions of people. You've got to be able to draw logical conclusions very coolly, and decide what to do next. You've got to be able to make decisions whilst you're talking and looking confident, while actually you may have absolutely no idea! So there's a little bit of the actor required in some respects, not too much, because you naturally want somebody who does know what he's doing, and can draw logical conclusions, and then take the right course of action.

There is a tremendous amount of lateral thinking going on with bombs. The most difficult thing about the situation in Northern Ireland is not particularly the technology of bombs, or the technology of bomb disposal, but the tactical situation one finds oneself confronting known as the 'come-on', where the situation is set up to draw the security forces into some kind of trap. So there you are, thinking, 'This is a "come-on". What if I look completely stupid? What will I be expected to do? Then if they give me a bit of credit for that, if they think I've already thought of it, they'll go for the double-bluff.' One is constantly thinking in terms of bluff, double-bluff, and counter-bluff. That can make life very difficult.

Captain, RAOC

There's always a number one operator and a number two: that's the team. The number two basically handles, puts together and deploys equipment, like the wheelbarrow. The number one is more of a thinker.

When I was in Belfast in '72 I found that the number ones

always went out with the same number twos. The same people were always paired together. We did change round: Fred would be number one and Bill number two and the next day Bill would be number one and Fred would be number two. Those two always wanted to go out together and it got to the stage where it would almost be unhealthily superstitious. People were not prepared to break their luck by going out with somebody else because they'd always been out with a particular person. It is understandable, but I thought it was unhealthy because if, through no fault of anybody else's, illness, injury, or what-have-you, that pattern was broken, then somebody might be completely thrown. People were intensely on edge in those days, particularly in Belfast: we'd had some unpleasant experiences that year. Two ATOs were killed at the same job, in the same car, when they thought they'd finished the job. And that was in a small section – pretty bad for morale. So the officer commanding elected to go out and do the next job himself, and he was killed doing it. People were tense, so it was possible for silly superstition to thrive. It was understandable, but unhealthy.

The great problem was . . . well, there were a great many problems, but one of them was car bombs. We actively deployed ways of dealing with them, and developed our robot vehicle: the wheelbarrow. We had to develop rapidly from the original wheelbarrow, which was a machine that could only go forward and not come back – wouldn't even switch off; it had to hit something or hit the target before it would stop. You guided it with two ropes: you pulled the left rope or the right rope to make it go left and right. It had a hook on the front which would spring up underneath the axle of a car and then you could put a tow rope onto an armoured vehicle, and tow the car away from the target, in the hope that if the bomb was going to go off, getting it twenty yards away from a building would mean less damage would be done. That's all that the original wheelbarrow was. However, we very quickly developed a more usable apparatus which could break a car window and drop a disruptive charge inside it to open it up. Fitting weapons and television cameras on it and using remote control followed on naturally and very quickly. That invention has really saved many lives.

In one early incident, a team had been sent down to have a look at a suspected car bomb. They fixed a charge to the front, which was to be dropped inside the car, pressed the button to make it go backwards, and it dropped the charge instead. The three of them just stood there, only yards away, with this charge on the ground, looking at it, and thinking: 'That shouldn't be there.' Then it went and blew them in different directions across the street. I got a message over the radio saying, 'Three of your men have been blown up.' I went rushing down to the scene where two guys had been hauled off to hospital and the other, a WO1, a splendid man, was at the police station. I found him in the superintendent's office with a very large whiskey. He couldn't actually hear what I was saying very clearly because his ear drums had been perforated, and although he was a very cool man, he was obviously shaken. I said, 'You should be in hospital. Off you go, I'll finish this job.' He felt he had to finish the job, because if he didn't, he might never do it again. I stood back and let him do it: he finished the job and he was fine. He then went to hospital. He was discharged within a day and he never had any problems thereafter. In fact he became one of the best EOD (explosive ordnance disposal) operators in this country.

One of the other technicians who had been blown up in the incident also had his eardrums perforated. He came out of hospital a week later, we had a good look at him and let him go out as number two on a number of occasions. He was anxious to get back on the streets but I was a little doubtful about it. Eventually I let him go out as number one because a job came in that sounded small – a doddle – and I thought it wouldn't give him any problems. It turned out to be a real viper. He came back in, he'd done the job and his adrenalin was pumping so much he couldn't talk; he was elated, over the top in a big way – it was very clear to us that he'd lost his nerve. He'd actually lost his nerve, but done the job. That was the most extraordinary breakthrough. He had lost his nerve, gone through with it, and he'd done it, completed it. We sent him home, but with dignity. He hadn't failed, and that, to my mind, is bravery. He'd lost his bottle but he'd insisted on going and doing the job.

Major, RAOC

Physical manifestations of fear are very difficult to disguise. You may be a good actor, but fear grips you, and it brings out certain physical reactions which you can't hide. Shortness of breath, when it becomes difficult to actually get through a sentence of more than three words because your adrenalin is pumping so much, and you're sweating, and your hands are shaking. I've seen that in others, working as their number two, very experienced people too.

Corporal, 1 Para

When you get an explosion it can burn at four miles a second. There's a tremendous rush of air, warm air, and dust which hits the body and feeds its way down, at that speed, into the lungs – there's always a channel opening to the lungs. It causes a slight bellow in the lungs, they expand minutely, and then the lungs protect themselves by secreting fluid which is a form of pneumonia. When that happens blokes have to be screened within twenty-four hours. I didn't know about this at first, but when the blokes were coming in sick with chronic chest complaints I soon realised. You see, the blokes didn't always realise they had been hurt internally because it's only a millisecond's aggravation. You feel the blast and the heat and that sort of thing and you think you've got away with it. It's not till later that you find you haven't.

Subaltern, RAOC

This car was on a roundabout with the doors open, a gift, according to the story. All I had to do was get this bag out of the back. I was a bit critical of the story that I'd been given and I sent a wheelbarrow up to the car. Just as it got there the wind blew the door shut! Sod's law – it had been open for an hour. I thought, someone somewhere doesn't want me to get his bomb out. I couldn't believe it. At first I thought my number two had done it and I kicked his ass. He said, 'It wasn't me.' Anyway, the wheelbarrow was set for hooking this thing out but I had to bring it back to change the configuration and as it came back it threw a track, and although we tried to put the track back it wasn't going to have it, there was something wong with the alignment of the wheels. So I got my other wheelbarrow out, configured that up and sent it off up the street where it just died. It died there. I thought, 'There's somebody working against us. This can't be happening.' We got this wheelbarrow back and tried to repair it but it was dead. Meantime all the traffic's held up on that road. I was then forced into doing a manual. I wasn't terribly convinced there was anything other than a suspicious plastic bag in the back of the car and, God knows, I'd done a few of them.

My soak time was up so I felt it safe to start. I tried three times to hook it out, but the plastic bag kept ripping. It was one of these very, very flimsy supermarket ones. I weighed up the pros and cons and decided that if it was booby-trapped it had had a good bouncing about with the hook and line, and it hadn't gone off, so I picked it up in my hands and put it on the road outside. I reckoned that if I did it quickly, I could get it outside and make it available to a weapon, if I needed to. As I put the bag on the ground it rolled over and this huge sausage-like thing rolled out. It was a clock battery with a detonator plugged into it! So there it was sitting in front of me – a bomb. At that stage nobody had come across explosives of that shape in Northern Ireland before.

My initial plan hadn't involved this suspicious object so I didn't have any weapons with me. I had to return, pick up a weapon and go back to the bomb. I wasn't too slow about that. Once I got back to the ICP (incident control point) and told the colonel what was there, I had no other option but to go back to it with a weapon. There comes a time in every operator's life when he has to take his heart in his mouth and his bottle in his hand and go and do it. I walked back up to the bomb and put my weapon down beside it. A long walk. Back behind cover we fired the weapon by remote control using a firing cable. There had been two people in the car with this bomb in the seat behind them. I assumed that they were going to place the bomb, flick the switch and run away. That's the normal IRA *modus operandi*. They would have a timer and power unit with a switch they could throw which sets the thing running. But it was not an IRA bomb but an INLA one. They are insane and this thing was – I later found out – running! What sane terrorist would have a running bomb in the back of his car? The INLA.

Senior NCO, RAOC

I had a suitcase found in Londonderry. I couldn't get the wheelbarrow anywhere near it as it was in undergrowth next to a wall. I decided that circumstances dictated the use of the shotgun. I had used a shotgun quite often. I didn't think it could be much of a bomb because you get a feel about these things. When people don't want to leave their houses you know there's not a lot there.

The locals know what's there very often. If they've all gone then you've got a big one. They hadn't gone so I had a wang at this thing with the shotgun. On the fifth shot, bloody twenty-five pounds of explosives detonated. I was only thirty metres from it – that was a bit of a frightener.

The biggest fright was on the same tour, at a supermarket. There had been about six attempts on this guy's premises and as luck would have it, the police had to deal with the inner cordon at the time and the military were on the outer cordon. When I got there I was assured by the police that everybody'd been evacuated. You can't go round checking yourself, you take their word for it. I was dealing with this car which had about two or three hundred pounds in the boot, and I'd been at it for about three hours, really concentrating. We neutralised it and I was rooting around in the boot when somebody tapped me on the shoulder. It was the supermarket owner and he said, 'When you going to be finished?' He'd been sitting up in his living room watching me and not only had he not been evacuated, he'd refused to be evacuated. I nearly had brown trousers!

Captain, Royal Military Police

One of my section sergeants had a car bomb and he and the ATO had done the business and were ready to blow this car. They were convinced that the area was clear of people. They were just getting wound up to pop the cork on this blasted car and a drunk fell out of a doorway. So there was a pregnant pause, the sergeant went forward and grabbed this bloody guy and said, 'What the hell are you doing here? Don't you realise there's a car bomb?' This drunk says, 'Ah, sure I do. I bloody alerted you!' There always seems to be a duty drunk. You get the cordon up and he materialises from nowhere, you can guarantee it.

Senior NCO, RAOC

There's this poor guy delivering Mother's Pride bread down the road when he's held up by a terrorist standing there with a shotgun who says, 'We're taking you in the vehicle.' They open up the back, pile all their stuff in and the younger of the two terrorists gets in the back with all the bits and pieces and starts putting a

209

bomb together. The other jumps in front with the gun and makes the guy drive, under threat, to the marked VCP (vehicle checkpoint). The idea was, when they got there, the terrorist in the front would tap on the partition in the cab to indicate that they had arrived. The one in the back would then set the bomb, jump out, and they would run across the border. The alarm would be raised, the place evacuated, then destroyed, and nobody would be hurt and the job would be done.

When they reach the VCP the bloke in the front taps on the partition, and jumps out the cab and runs across the field. Now for the bloke in the back, who has set the bomb, this is a pretty bad time to find out that there's no handle on the inside of a Mother's Pride van! We were just bringing up the Carl Gustav to blow the doors open when we heard this desperate thumping coming from inside the van. We opened the doors and there was this lad sitting there as white as a sheet. He hadn't had the common sense to take the bits apart, so the clock was still running and there was about seven minutes left. I kept him in the vehicle with his legs wrapped round one of the bins while I gaily pulled out bundles of explosive. He was in some state. He was put in the back of the Saracen and interviewed by the local constabulary. He got nineteen years, which was quite appropriate for his age.

Captain, RAOC

We were called out to an incident just round the corner from Girdwood Park Camp. The fire brigade were there putting out a fire in a car, which had previously been reported stolen. Its owner had gone missing. When we arrived the car was down on its axles at the back, suggesting for all the world as if he was in the boot, and the car had been set alight to destroy the evidence.

A cordon had been set up so the job was really to blow open the boot, as carefully as one might, and see what was in there, whether it was a body, whether it was a bomb, or whether it was a booby-trapped body. One thing with a boot is that when you blow it open with a detonating cord, it can come up and then slam closed again. So I had to find ways of preventing that happening. This car had a roof rack so I thought it would be very clever to run a hook and line through the roof rack and down to the boot so that when I blew the boot open the hook and line would keep the boot door open. What I hadn't reckoned with was that the fire in the car had burnt through all the supports that were keeping this roof rack in place. I pressed the button and the boot flew open, the chap pulled the line, and the roof rack came off! So the boot came up and went down again – which is just what I jolly well wanted to avoid. My number two fell about laughing.

All that apart, it certainly wasn't at all an amusing job. I opened the boot, confident that it had now been opened anyway, and there indeed was the body of the owner. When you see somebody in that situation, who's been told to lie in the boot of his car, and then shot through the head, you tend not to see people at their best moment, you see them in the position in which they die a fairly horrible death.

I then had to poke around and make sure that it wasn't concealing anything. This was my first body and my first job! It was mighty unpleasant – a grotesque introduction to bomb disposal. I then had to come back to my incident control point and say to this sixteen-year-old boy, 'Will you come with me and tell me if this is your father?' Think of the memories he'll have to live with.

I examined the rest of the car, the fire hadn't got to the boot as the bulkhead had stopped it getting through, but the rest of the car was burnt out, and I thought, 'There's nothing left in here,' and declared it clear. The police moved in five minutes later and one came back to me and said, 'Did you know about the second body?' I said, 'What second body?' I went down and looked at what I had thought was the black and charred remains of the back seat: I thought it was some unburnt padding sticking out. But when I looked more closely I realised . . . I actually saw it was another body on the back seat.

The following day I was called for and told that they wanted to see me at the mortuary. So I pitched up there and a couple of chaps came out in white aprons with blood all over them and I thought, 'Yes, this must be the mortuary.' I went in and the post mortem was in progress. The pathologist wanted to know what various marks on the body were: would they have been caused by the boot opening, breaking glass, or had he actually been attacked and tortured before he was killed? He also wanted me to confirm that the odd marks on his back were caused by the boot opening, because he had this vivid red criss-cross pattern on his back which had come from his string vest when I had blown the cortex to open the boot. Then I suddenly thought, in the middle of this interview, 'Is he telling me that I killed this man?' I realised that that wasn't the case at all, but it was a nasty moment. I attended the trial for that murder ten years later, in 1982.

The next body job was again at night. Shots had been heard, and when I got there I saw well enough that there was a body in the car. But cars gave people so many problems in Belfast in those days – they still do – but at the time, people were paranoid about cars: nobody would open a car door, apart from an ATO. I got it open with a hook and line. I then had to get hold of this recently dead body and put a line round the arm, and then drag him out – flop, horribly, on the pavement. I was conscious that his relatives were within fifty yards of where I was and seeing or discussing the way that I was dealing with the person whom they loved.

Senior NCO, RAOC

It was about ten years ago I was operating in Belfast. The IRA used to make a homemade explosive called co-op; it was so called because the first had been used in a Co-op store. They would set up 'disruption day' in Belfast. They'd steal twenty or thirty vehicles and say there's a bomb in every one. But of course there'd be a bomb in a couple and there'd be nothing in the others. But it just brought the city to a standstill. I was tasked to deal with a Ford Transit van on the Malone Road, which was closed off. While the world is waiting I'm trying to get the back door of the van opened. Eventually I had to open it with a hook and line. As I approached this van, my glasses and my helmet were getting very steamed up. I looked in the back and it was full of bags of co-op. I thought, 'Well, I'm buggered. I've found the biggest bloody bomb ever.' But when I got closer to it, it was a bundle of sausages. It wasn't a bomb at all. It was bloody sausages: Mattesons' best pork sausages!

Sergeant, 2 Para

I've been sniped at and not seen where it's come from. It frightens the Christ out of you, to be sure it does. I don't mind being shot at because then it's down to you, at grass roots level, to your soldiering ability. If you were shot at, you weren't being professional enough. Okay, it may be a sniper firing across a couple of fields, but you should have been aware of that and covered your eventualities. But the bomber, he's just a yellow bastard, because there's no way can you counter a bomb. It's there, and it's waiting for you. You're going to walk into it: end of story. So I think if you get shot at, then you're on equal terms, because you're trained as a soldier to do all your various drills and things like that, but there is no reaction to a bomb – what can you do?

This one guy, we used to call him the little rooster. He was about four foot ten, big-chested little bugger for his size. Very small, but very strong. I've still got a photograph of him. He'd won a lottery to get into our patrol company. He'd only been with us a month when his patrol went into a house that was supposed to be clear. But a bomb had been prepared and dug into the ground. Very cunning, very clever. It had a huge amount of nitrate fertilizer put together with about twenty pounds of commercial explosives. They'd buried it underneath the floorboards with one of those baby alarms, you know, the intercom thing. This young lad was putting a brew on, he was sat in the middle of the floor and everybody else was in sleeping bags all round the edge of the room. He'd just called 'Brew's ready' when *bang*, this fucking device went off. It was only twenty pounds of commercial, the rest didn't detonate, but he was sitting right on top of it. Straight up through the shagging roof he went. Fucking gone. There was nobody else injured except one corporal who got his heel fractured. This poor little sod who was sat on top of it finished up wedged into a tree, his legs in bits and pieces, with a tin of chicken spread still clutched in his hands.

Major, 1 King's Own Scottish Borderers

I suppose the death of our colour-sergeant will always be with me. In December 1972 a patrol had done a routine walk through some gardens and found the tail end of a 3.5 rocket; in those days we were finding so much stuff that the RMP did a weekly run in the Land Rover, and we'd throw all this rubbish in the back. It was brought back to battalion headquarters. It still had two wires on the back: that particular rocket was electrically fired, and we were delighted with the find because we had found a launcher in the same road some months before. Over a period of about four hours it was handled by the patrol, their company commander, the commanding officer, myself, and several others.

The colour-sergeant was going off the following day to be an instructor at Sandhurst. He picked it up, and happened to turn to one of the photographers, and said, 'Oh, take a photograph of me holding this as a souvenir.' As he held up this 3.5 it exploded. It was booby-trapped, and blew him to pieces. His wife had just taken out a life insurance and paid one premium.

Corporal, 2 Scots Guards

We heard on the radio about this explosion. When we arrived there was this smouldering heap of rubble, and they were dragging a few bodies out, some unconscious. A whole crowd of Catholics had come around from the Clonard, Springfield Road side, and they were shouting and laughing and saying, 'Ah, we'll get the rest of you next time.' Laughing at the boys who'd been blown up. Sickening. When you're bringing bodies out just blown up, you expect at least a little bit of sympathy, but not a shred. Not a shred. They did the same thing again at 219 Springfield Road. Planted a bomb just outside the building where the cookhouse was and they could see the cook was working in there. It blew inwards and took him straight out. They knew the building was manned and that's it. They don't get mentioned much but cooks are in as much danger as anybody else. Probably not to the same extent now, because the bases are much more fortified. In those days places were open and they had blind sides.

Senior NCO, RAOC

The really bad one I suppose was in Strabane. Strabane is really the pits of the world. It's the most bombed area of Northern Ireland, it really is. It's the worst place you've ever seen in your life. The people are so hostile there. I went there one day after someone had left a suspicious bag which the police thought had a device in it. As I was walking, there was a bunch of bloody yobs behind me and because there weren't enough police on patrol they started prodding me. I ran, I couldn't do anything else. I went back later to the device and as I was walking down I could hear these jeers, 'Die you bastard' and 'I hope you get fucking blown up'. Very sociable people.

Corporal, Women's Royal Army

I was a hundred yards down the road from the Strabane checkpoint when there was this enormous explosion. I was sitting in this pre-fabricated building and the walls and the roof were shaken. I didn't jump. I went very, very cold and I started to sweat. It was a strange feeling, but that is always my reaction every time a bomb goes off.

Senior NCO, RAOC

One Sunday morning we went to an explosion down at a place called Garrison. We got there and there was a dead woman. They had positioned the bomb outside her bedroom wall and it had come straight across and crushed her in her bed. She was laying there very dead and we were foraging around but we couldn't find the seat of the explosion. There was a little lean-to which was the kitchen so we thought it could have been a gas cylinder bomb explosion. One of the coppers who was with us heard us say this, so as we were driving back to get some help from the forensic laboratories it came over the radio that the bomb disposal experts had said it wasn't a bomb but a gas explosion. Of course when we went back the second time they found the huge seat of the explosion. There was this dead lady still in her bed, forensic staff still working and everyone else, including her daughter outside accusing us of trying to cover up the murder by the IRA bastards. The local MP was there and questions were raised in the House of Commons over it. It was a Protestant woman killed. The ironic thing is, she didn't own the house, a bloke had let it out to her, a UDR bloke who'd left because of threats made to him. The IRA targeted the house but didn't realise the bloke had gone, so they stuck one there, and killed the old dear.

Senior NCO, RAOC

The very last job I did, my hand-over job, we had this bloke who had been topped in Belfast a couple of days previously. They'd left him just this side of one of the minor border crossings in South Armagh. He was literally lying on the side of the road face down, a couple of yards from the border. Of course there was all the

Southern Irish TV, BBC: they were all there. You couldn't tell them to go away because they wanted pictures. You know, they've got their job to do. We knew that what we were going to do would not look good. In case the body was booby-trapped we had to put a hook on him and pull. He didn't fall to bits, but he left some of his head behind. They just stood there in a sort of stunned silence really, you know, they couldn't really believe what they were seeing – but what else could we do?

Sergeant, 2 Para

We were in South Armagh and we were running round doing a recce for an OP that we were going to put in on a house that was being targeted, when there was a great big whoomph, an explosion – not a big explosion, a fairly low-powered one at the rear of the house. It was about two in the morning so we diddles around and there's a van with the doors open, a stiff dead and a bit of another, with their clothes blown off them. So we stake the area out and leave it till the morning. Come the morning, it's like the cavalry; there was four choppers with engineer's kit, an engineer crew, the bomb disposal blokes and all their bits and pieces. They suss out the van is definitely a non-goer. It had been blown up, an own goal, with a milk churn. The ATO gets his little compass and tells us where to look for bits of the body. We get the old plastic bags out and start looking. The head of one is completely missing but we got most of him and we got about three-quarters of the other. We were looking for an arm and a leg: it took ages. We didn't find the arm, but we found the hand and a shoe but we didn't find anything with it. Probably just disintegrated. We bring it all back and he says, 'That'll do. I'm happy with that.' It's fairly morbid. We're looking at lumps of meat, like. We had this guy with us from Manchester, a little dry sod. He says to the ATO, 'Excuse me, sir. I can't understand this.' 'Can't understand what?' says the ATO. 'Why would anybody want to plant a bomb in the nude?' Classic. We all creased up laughing, like.

Sergeant, RAOC

It was an INLA job, quite reasonable for INLA. They actually put a beer keg under the bridge on a Friday night, and phoned to say there was a bomb. As it was one of the areas we didn't go into by road, the next morning we went up in the helicopter and we could see the beer keg and on the way back we got a report of an explosion. I asked the pilot to go back and we saw that the roof had been blown off a nearby bungalow. In fact the beer keg was a hoax. INLA had kidnapped the guy who lived in the bungalow and taken him over the border. They then fitted a bell-push to his front door and wired it up to explosives behind the door. What they were hoping was that the security forces, having seen the beer keg, would evacuate the area and a policeman or soldier would go up and use the bell-push and set the bomb off. Well, as it happened, the guy who lived in this house was an alcoholic, always in drunken stupors, and his next door neighbour, hearing that there was a bomb by the bridge, went down to ring his doorbell and warn him, and off it went: the poor old bloody neighbour, doing a good turn, was killed.

Senior NCO, RAOC

One particular device had blown up a civvie. He was unlucky. The device was in a culvert. An unmarked Army car was coming down the road leading the traffic when a bloke behind it overtook. The observer for the IRA saw the Army car at the front and told his mate to take out the first car, but by the time the bloke who was doing the firing saw the first car it wasn't the Army car. The car they hit was a civilian's Ford Cortina. It was blown 130 yards and burned for four hours. The driver was dead, obviously, but we were not prepared to go and get his body because we were convinced that we were being set up. He ran a factory in Crossmaglen, nothing very big, it made something very trivial, but all the people in Crossmaglen who were working for him were out of work; he had gone.

Corporal, 1 Para

We'd come through the training together. We'd come through the NITAT (Northern Ireland Training and Advisory Team) and we went to Northern Ireland together. Then he went to A Company and I went to B Company. But we kept meeting up, like. He was gonna spend two weeks at my house and I was gonna spend two weeks at his – you get a month off after Ireland. So we sorted that out. However, he'd sort of, how shall I put it, let us down once because he said he was coming on leave with us, but he didn't. Me mam went up the wall. So I phoned me mam up and told her that he was definitely coming on leave this time and sorted everything out for the first two weeks. Then I was on a thing called ARF, Airborne Reaction Force, you just sit in this little hut, and you wait. Then this Wessex come in with a stretcher. It was obviously a dead body so we pulled the stretcher off and put it into a Gazelle. Then I turned around and there was a plastic bag with bits and pieces of body in. So that went in the Gazelle. Two minutes later I found out it was him.

Captain, Royal Army Medical Corps

We had one soldier who was on patrol in Crossmaglen when his platoon commander was injured. I saw him later that afternoon to check that there were no blast injuries to the chest, ears, and again the following morning to ensure that nothing had developed. He was evacuated to Bessbrook from Crossmaglen on the Monday complaining of one problem after another. I couldn't find any serious injury, anything wrong, any illness. I was naive enough to believe that he was malingering. For the next few days he kept coming to me with one story after another and it was evident that he didn't want to play ball, he didn't want to go out again. I felt there was nothing I could do with him. So I sent a message to his colour sergeant in Crossmaglen stating that he didn't want to play soldiers and would he look after him, give him reasonable duties, perhaps in the command room or sit him in front of the television. He sat in front of the box and meals were provided for him – that was it. Obviously this young lad felt that this was not the life for a soldier. He was getting really pissed off with it so he eventually volunteered to go back to the front and go on patrols. He came to see me before he went out and explained that he knew he was going to die if he went back onto the streets. But he couldn't go on sitting in front of the television. He was on patrol outside the school in Crossmaglen four days before we were due to return to the UK when he was killed by a culvert bomb. He was the only soldier killed on that tour. I had to go out and pick up his remains and put him in a bag. I felt guilty; it had been my responsibility. I wrote to his parents and told them.

Also injured in that explosion was a dog that the battalion had adopted. Dogs and kiddies mean a lot to them. The dog was brought to me to be sorted out and given first aid. As we'd only three or four days before going back to the UK the soldiers desperately wanted this dog treated and brought back to Cross-maglen. The Army Air Corps are not allowed to fly civilian dogs but they understood how the lads felt about it so they brought it up to me. They then flew it on to a veterinary unit where they did surgery on the dog and sent it back. We didn't get the dog back before we left but at least the soldiers knew that the dog was being looked after there. It was some consolation to them. To the best of my knowledge it survived.

Staff-Sergeant, RAOC

The watchkeeper rang me up one night, one Friday evening just when I was going out with a young lady. He said, 'Can you go down to Belleek, County Fermanagh? There's been a negligent discharge' – or an ND as we call them – 'with a 40mm grenade launcher.' I said, 'Oh, what now, can't it wait till the morning?' He said, 'No, can you get here?' I said, 'Where is it?' and he replied, 'It's laying in the middle of a pub in Belleek.' These squaddies were on foot patrol and they were hard targeting around this bar. They used to really annoy the hotel owner. One guy had done all the posing bit, in front of a mirror, on one of the outside doors, stepped back and fallen arse over bollocks down this big long row of steps. On his way down he'd fired a 40mm grenade launcher off. The grenade had gone in through the window, hit heavy drapes and landed at the feet of a party of journalists who were dining at the time, but it hadn't gone off. So I flew down and met the hotel owner and I apologised for what had happened. He said, 'For Christ's sake can you refrain from doing any damage, because we've got a wedding reception in there tomorrow.' But a grenade is dangerous, you should really blow it where it is because it's armed and it's extremely sensitive. I went in, picked it up and put it on a sandbag, then pulled the sandbag out on a hook and line. Got it into the middle of the lawn, blew it up, and made a big hole in his lawn. I thought, 'Christ, what a wonderful job I've done, saved all that damage, must be in line for a bottle of Blackbush.' But the bloody owner came over and created shit because I'd made a hole in the middle of his lawn. He wanted to know who to send the bill to for repairing his lawn. I didn't even get a drink out of the bastard.

Senior NCO, RAOC

In an English court you actually sit outside until you're called. In the Irish court you sit at the back from the beginning and watch the entire case unfold before you until you're actually called to give evidence. Some of the more interesting cases in Northern Ireland are where there are claims for civil damage. You get people claiming that their house was damaged from a bomb that went off three miles away. It's quite a thriving industry. There was a bomb that went off in 1971 and a chicken farmer, years later, 1975 or '76 claimed that the bomb stopped his hens laying eggs, and he lived eleven miles away! We all fell about laughing – what a wanker, you know. But nobody could stand up in court and prove it wasn't so. They brought a meteorologist to comment about the cloud base that day; they brought a chicken expert from America; they brought in another bloke to give evidence on the rock sub-strata to see whether the detonation wave could have been transmitted that way. The case must've cost thousands. It went on for the best part of twelve months, because they kept adjourning and bringing more experts in. It was incredible.

Subaltern, RAOC

I wouldn't mind going back to Northern Ireland, to be honest, because it is, professionally, a very rewarding job. It does have its moments but now there is a great deal of inactivity. Not like in the early 1970s when I know one bloke had 190 calls in four and a half months. When you're trained to do a job you want to do it but of course in bomb disposal you only get to do those jobs that the enemy sets you. If he decides to take a couple of weeks off, you know, you can't take the time off, you have to be ready to do it. So it's a bit of a challenge to keep yourself motivated and your soldiers motivated. So although I wouldn't ever say I was bored, I wouldn't say that is the right word, there is a lot of inactivity which you have to fill with meaningful occupation. So you do a lot of continuation training and practice, and practise deploying very quickly. We also play volleyball, and go out on

220

runs. We have a video, we have a stereo, the TV, magazines, plus a computer. Guys were quite keen on computer games. Especially the ones where you're actually the fighter pilot in a jet and you can have great duels in the sky. Great fun. So there's ways you can occupy your time until the next call out.

Marine, 42 Commando

When I was away from Ireland I'd always dive when there was a loud noise. People would look at me as if I was crazy – I didn't even realise I was doing it. Another thing I did for ages, and it took me six to nine months to get out of the habit, every time I saw a parked car I'd read off the registration number. Sometimes I still do it now, and if I see a package or box by the side of a road, or something stuck in a hedgerow, I still have to check myself: 'Hang on, this is England.'

Ulster Defence Regiment

Sergeant, UDR

A lot of people across the border in England see the UDR as a block, but there is quite a big difference between full-time and part-time UDR service. I joined as a part-timer in the early seventies. We came in at night after we finished work and we were on duty from seven o'clock until six the following morning; then it was back to work again. We obviously weren't able to do that every day. But in those days we were fairly young, and single, so we would do maybe seventeen or eighteen duties a month, and certainly every weekend. Now we are limited to doing twelve duties of eight hours a month unless there are exceptional circumstances. The full-time UDR soldier is on duty twenty-four hours a day. He does his border trips, guard duties, and all his normal patrolling. For him, there isn't such a thing as a weekend off. He may get a Tuesday, or a Thursday; he may be off on a Sunday, but it's a 7-day-a-week, 24-hour-a-day job.

Colonel, UDR

To me, the UDR has been the opportunity for local people to provide adequate security for the country in which they're prepared to live; and I believe that in the end, local people have failed themselves miserably. It has been a fact of life that we've had to provide our own security in this province at least for the last sixty-five years, if not longer. So there was always that element of the citizen army. I believe those who serve in the UDR are of the bravest that can be found, and I believe they're the best in society, and their motivation is certainly second to none.

Major, UDR

I'm married with two sons, aged eleven and nine, and they have lived through my part-time service so they are also very much part of the whole business of the UDR. I'm usually in the office until 17.30, I then come home, have a quick bite to eat, and two or three nights in the week I go to the company where I'm either behind my desk catching up on admin., interviews, orders, or commanding troops on the ground. I've got a company strength of 163, which includes HQ staff and four part-time platoons, and a permanent cadre to guard the location for sixteen hours a day. The part-time soldiers guard the company base by night, seven days a week, three hundred and sixty-five days a year. Sadly, because of the unemployment situation, quite a few of my younger soldiers don't have jobs, but because they are single and young, they are quite happy to come in night after night and put the hours in, and it's financially attractive for them. They're very good soldiers. I've seen the average age of the soldiers coming down now to under twenty-five, whereas at the beginning we did have a certain amount of the 'Dad's Army' image, because there were some fairly senior characters.

Sergeant, UDR

As far as the part-timers were concerned, when I first joined, we were dressed in sort of olive-grey combat dress which, in my mind, classified us as second-rate soldiers. All the rest of the regular Army troops over here were running around in camouflage trousers. All we were getting was this surplus kit, the big heavy boots, and .303 rifles. We felt we were only there to guard the bases, we were like gatekeepers. The regular Army did all the major stuff. But we've progressed so much since the early seventies. We now work closely with other regular battalions who come in for four and a half months. Our average private soldier has a high degree of knowledge of the area and its people, simply because he's had years and years of experience in the situation.

Sergeant, UDR

The terrorist is very well identified. We are on sixty per cent first-name terms with the main terrorists in this area and they are, likewise, with us.

Major, 1 King's Own Scottish Borderers

I had to work quite closely with the UDR on the very last tour that we did. I was under command of a UDR battalion in Ballykelly. The advantage of the UDR is, of course, that an Irishman can pick out a goodie or a baddie. They know what to look for because there are certain indicators that they've grown up with and they can see them intuitively. Now, we go over looking for our own indicators of the sort of people they are, and they're different in Ireland, which is why you end up with bank managers being thought of as terrorists, and pulled out of their cars. That's because, to a Scotsman, they don't give the right signs that say he's a bank manager. Our soldiers aren't good at picking up these indicators, but the Irish are. In a line of cars, they're cleverer at picking out the people who are worth searching. My soldiers often felt that the UDR were too lax at road checks and quite often didn't check somebody's driving licence, they just waved them through. But again, I believe it's because they were sharper. They knew more. They had a feeling for when to make an effort and when not to.

Colour-Sergeant, UDR

I joined the regiment on 26 March 1970, and was the third one to be enlisted in our battalion. I'm an Englishman and I'd been in the regular Army before that. I joined as a full-time warrant officer. The thing that always struck me was the first night A Company formed in Armagh. The previous night the biggest part of the company were ex-B Specials, and the next night they were in Army uniform. I remember four hundred and thirty-odd men paraded that night. That was one company. Today my company is seventy-odd.

Colonel, UDR

When the regiment was raised we had a high proportion of Catholics, but I understand totally why few join now. It's not for want of trying as far as the regiment is concerned. It is difficult for a Catholic to serve because they know eyes are on them, and their families.

Colonel, UDR

Those that are serving, and the thirty-five-odd thousand who have served, are all targets.

Officer, UDR

In March 1973 I had a farmer in my company murdered in his own home at Garrison, County Fermanagh. They pumped twenty-two bullets into his head, then conveniently disappeared over the border. Subsequent to that six soldiers in the UDR company from that area came to me and said that their families would like to move, adding quite categorically that no IRA man was going to force them out of the Ulster Defence Regiment. So we guarded them until alternative accommodation was found, and then with tractors, trailers, and Land Rovers moved them lock, stock and barrel overnight. Most of those people are still serving.

I invited many pressmen to take up that story, briefed them quite adequately, and not one was prepared to make news out of it, with the result that those people lost everything that they had. They'd had to move out of their farms, their homes, make new acquaintances, new friends inland, and they never got any recognition for that. You hear nowadays of people who are supposed to have been intimidated receiving up to £20,000 – those people received not one penny.

Female Sergeant, UDR

I used to rabbit on about the fact that women terrorists were getting away with it. I kept saying, 'Why don't they have women in the UDR?' I kept on about it. Then one day my husband, who was in the UDR, brought home a form for me to join up. This was August 1973. They weren't really prepared for women recruits. The doctor who was doing the medical was asking me questions from a prepared form, and he asked me had my testicles descended. I said, 'Beg your pardon?' and he went, 'Sorry, wrong form.' So that was it. I was accepted. But I had to wait until 25 September when five other women joined. When I took the Oath of Allegiance to the Queen, I was more nervous than I was on my wedding day. I got so emotional about it, I actually gave my maiden name.

My husband was on permanent cadre during the day and at night the roles were reversed. I went on night patrols for the first two years. In those days you never knew what was going to happen, whether you were going to get stoned going through Newry or get shots fired at you in other places. The first few patrols that I went on, the men really resented our presence. They gave us all the dirty jobs; car and lorry searches. Then they'd take us slogging to break us down. I said to the lasses, 'They're not going to break us. They'll crawl before we do.' About the third night, as we were going back at the end of the patrol, one of the boys said, 'I got to hand it to you. Youse can bloody work. How do you fancy fish and chips?' Then I knew we were accepted. But it was a strange life, I'd be at home one day feeding the baby and washing the clothes, and the next day I'd be flying around the skies of South Armagh. One day we flew into Crossmaglen for an operational task. We were then taken out in a Saracen armoured car and it was exciting. You felt you were invulnerable, it didn't happen to you. It happened to everybody else, other soldiers got killed, but you didn't die. That did not last long.

There was a need for first-aid training for Greenfinches because soldiers were getting shot and injured and first aid was not very good. I worked in the same office as our regular Army signals instructor. He was in the Irish Guards. His wife, Jean, although she had two children, joined the Greenfinches. She had a fantastic sense of humour and worked very hard and was really keen to learn. I remember we won the first ever inter-battalion competition for girls. Jean ran out to tell her cadre she'd won and they were crying with excitement. She asked to have her time extended because she loved the work of the UDR. As she was making my daughter's bridesmaid's dress we went round to see her one evening. The night before, one of our boys had been killed, so I said, 'You're not out tonight are you, Jean?' and she said, 'Yes.' And I said, 'Nervous?' and she said, 'Yes. I'd be a liar if I didn't say I was frightened. But somebody's got to stop them. I'll be out there tonight – frightened – but I'll be out there.' That night she was killed by a high-velocity bullet through the base of her skull. The soldier driving was also hit, but his life was saved by the other Greenfinch who gave him first aid. With Jean's death, all of a sudden we became vulnerable. We realised we could be killed because a bullet doesn't discriminate. Our company commander was so angry. He said to us, 'That's it. You girls aren't going on the ground again.' I said, 'Now wait a minute, sir. Come on, I've enough trouble with the girls. They're frightened. Your fear will go right through them.' 'They're girls,' he said. 'I'll bury a man, it's accepted. But not a girl. I can't hack that. You're not going out.' I could understand how he felt; it took a couple of weeks before he let us back on the ground.

Two years after Jean was killed another Greenfinch, Margaret, was singled out by the terrorists and killed at home. Margaret knew it could happen and had left her will in her drawer. She had a little girl and although she was unmarried, the father and her were good friends. She was killed in her caravan. The terrorists riddled it with bullets all on one side. The baby was lying in bed with her and the rounds went right through Margaret and Kermit the Frog, who was in the baby's arms. The baby slept right through the shooting. When they picked up the baby she was still asleep; they thought she was dead. The rest of the Greenfinches in her company were really very upset, and we went up to console the mother. That afternoon the coffin had arrived, and her father came out and said to me, 'Sergeant, before anybody else sees her, I think you should, because you were her sergeant.' To this day, I'll never forget it. She had been so full of life and vibrance, and now, there she was, lying in this coffin, not a mark on her, in this pink nightie. She looked so pretty, so peaceful, and so bloody dead.

A few years later I heard on the news that her father had been killed by terrorists. When I got to the family house there was the little girl who not only had had her mother murdered by the terrorists, but now the only man she really knew as a father was dead too. His sons were very bitter because they'd lost their sister and now their father. When we got to the scene, his wife desperately wanted to go to him but the body hadn't been re-covered. A police officer took me to one side and said, 'We can't let her near that body. It could be booby-trapped. Will you explain it?' I spoke with her but she didn't take it in – she was too numb, and said, 'Will you come with me and bring back the body?' I took her hand and said, 'Out there at this precise moment they can't do any more harm to your husband, but they may have booby-trapped him.' I went over to the police sergeant and said, 'You get that body out by twelve o'clock or you're in trouble.' And he went, 'I promise, I promise.' At twelve o'clock we went back and just as we got up to where the body had been, the hearse passed us. It was the biggest relief of my life. If they had not recovered it, I was going to go up to it. I knew they'd stop me anyway, but at least I had to pretend for that woman's sanity.

Female Corporal, UDR

My brother-in-law's death, he was killed by the IRA, does weigh heavily on me. I was there a few minutes after it happened and saw him there and saw the results of it. He was an only child of a very old couple who lived just across the road. He was a terrific fella, he helped both sides. I read the statement of the man who killed him, it was so callous and so cold. They asked him what he felt about leaving a woman with two young children: 'That's part of life' was all he could say. The police arrested him and put him away in the Maze. Then he broke out again and has killed about five or six members of the security forces in Fermanagh. To make matters worse, I was at school with him. We used to employ the man who did the targeting for him on our farm. All the time he was working for us he was collecting information. So it makes you bitter; it makes you feel, who do you trust?

Female Sergeant, UDR

In the early days, when I first joined, it was difficult for the family, because they were young. The youngest was two years old, and it was difficult getting baby-sitters. Many a time I paid my night's pay to a baby-sitter, so I was working for nothing. But now the family are grown up, I am full time. When I first started I was on £2.35 a day, which was taxed. Now we are paid the same as the regular Army. But I would do this work even if I wasn't paid; I'm devoted to it. I love Ireland and I wouldn't dream of going elsewhere.

Captain, UDR

I remember as a child of three being taken down by my father, who was a policeman, to a spot where an RUC sergeant had been killed by a booby-trap in 1956. Now, thirty years later, I take my own children to that spot. Terrorism has been here a long time. The people of 1956 are the godfathers of today's fighters. They haven't changed all that much. In East Tyrone terrorism is a family business – and you'll find that security forces is a family business. So if your father was in it, you probably join. My local teacher, who recruits, he said, 'Come on, you're of age, time you got the uniform on.'

Major, UDR

I'd been out only a minute on my first patrol, I was still at school, when we were caught in an ambush, and I was shot, shot in the hand. Quite an experience! I came up through the ranks and got a full-time commission in '76. I shall be in until I'm aged fifty-five, so I would class myself as a professional anti-terrorist fighter because I have been at it a long time. Also, the opposition you are up against are one of the most professional groups in the Western world. They are very committed. But even at school, I disliked bullies and I see the IRA as bullies. They have a history, though – I mean three hundred years ago the Brits had convoys between Dublin and Londonderry that had to pass through Dungannon and they had to have a battalion of men there then.

I grew up with Catholics who have joined the IRA. I have a healthy respect for them and they for me. I'd love to get at them and they'd love to get at me – it's a game of guile, you have to be crafty. You must never be seen to be weak.

Corporal, UDR

When I'm recruiting I don't apologise for using the word loyalist, no matter whether they're Roman Catholics, Protestants, or what. I always tell them when they join that they have to be a loyalist. Loyalist is considered a dirty word now. It's not. If you join the Ulster Defence Regiment you're here to defend Ulster against its enemies. You have to be a loyalist, loyal to the Queen.

Female Sergeant, UDR

Recently we had a corporal who lived in a very Protestant area, who was intimidated because his wife was a Catholic. We had to move them and their children in the middle of the night. They were picked up with all their belongings and moved within two hours. Their home, where they have had their marriage and brought up their children, was just completely wiped out. That's a sickening form of violence. When it is directed against a soldier it is something that we grow to accept, but when it goes against a family then that's a different ball game.

I work in the Intelligence side. In the last few years we have started what we call 'Risk Assessment', which involves looking after our soldiers who find themselves intimidated. This can come from the Republican side, or mixed marriages. Occasions also arise when we're really nobody's friend, for example if we are put in a situation where we are in confrontation with Protestants, or seen to be helping the government with whatever displeases someone, then we become the enemy. We have then got a problem at home, because most of us live in Protestant areas, which means, even there, we're not safe.

Private, UDR

Joining the UDR in 1973 certainly put a strain on my wife. At the start she was just worried about me going out at night and coming in in the mornings. Then in the middle of my time I was involved in a few incidents and people came looking for me. I had the wife and a youngster in the house by this time, so we had to move. I was angry about having to move because I'd just started to buy our house, which was just round the corner from my wife's mother, who looked after it when I wasn't there. But I never questioned the decision – I just had to go.

Sergeant, UDR

Our cottage is on the side of the road. When teenagers go past they shout slogans at us, and defy us to come out, and call us Protestant bastards. They fire shots in the air, and challenge us at two, three, four o'clock in the morning. They throw bottles against the doors and the front of the house.

Female Corporal, UDR

I was prepared to join full-time UDR, but to do so I had to leave home because my parents lived on the border. I do visit them but usually in one of my other sisters' houses. They weren't happy with me joining because my brother-in-law, who had been a policeman, had been killed, and my brother had been blown up but luckily survived. There are other difficulties as well, for instance if you go out to a hotel and meet people, they want to know what you do and you can't tell them. Then if you get to know them better you can't keep telling them some story, but you don't really know who they are or what they may be involved in. You could be set up to meet these people. We don't live in the barracks, being UDR we have to live out. You have to find your own accommodation in the right area. Then you have to go in and out through that same door all the time. So I have to change out of my uniform before I go home.

Private, UDR

I was just walking towards the garage when a car stopped in front of me. Three boys got out, one stood at a pillar of the garage as a lookout and the other two went across the forecourt towards the office, with guns out. The boy who was doing the lookout must have recognised me because as I looked to see what he was doing, he ran away. So I went and stood where he had been standing, and took his job. When the first lad came out of the garage he thought he saw his lookout and gave the all clear, and the other one came out carrying the tray from the till. I pulled out my gun and ID card and challenged them. They threw the tray of money in the air and ran back inside the garage. There were pound notes and fivers everywhere. Just then a car drove into the garage. I told the driver what had happened, and asked him to get help. He went away and the next moment a Land Rover came over the brow of the hill. So I thought, 'Dead on, here's the police.' I slipped the gun back into my pocket and held up my ID card when the Land Rover was twenty-five metres away. The police all jumped out, hid behind a wall, and started shooting at me! One particular fellow fired eleven rounds at me. I dived over a wall but I still got shot. I was hit twice in the leg and once in the side. I spent six weeks in Musgrave Park Hospital. It was the policeman's first incident. They came up to see me in hospital and apologised. It was just one of those things.

Some time after that I was duty driver and I had to go home for something. I borrowed my mate's car and as I was driving up the road these two blokes ran out of a house, they had guns in their hands, and there was a motorbike outside. So I decided to stop and have a quick look. They heard me brake and took off. One ran through the estate and the other down the main road. I went after the first one who had turned back shouting that he had a gun and was going to shoot me. I caught him and reversed the car back round again and rang a doorbell and asked the old dear to ring the police. The Land Rover arrived and it turned out to be the same one as before, the same blokes as the night I was shot. They took the man away. He was eventually sentenced to ninety-nine years for offences. His last words to me were, 'I'll get you.'

Sergeant, UDR

I suppose it was partly my own fault for using the same route too often. I was going on duty and was late as well. I was driving over the top of a hill when they opened up and hit me in both legs. I realised that my right leg was dead so I had to use the injured left leg to drive. I tried to get to a fellow who I knew was in the old B Specials, but I didn't get far. The car packed up so I was just sitting there waiting for a patrol to come along to help me. About a dozen other cars went past first, but they all drove on, even though I had the flashers going and was leaning out the door. They were probably afraid to stop in case it was a hold-up, or something like that. I was in hospital for seven weeks – and many times I thought, 'Why me?' I've never done any harm to anyone. Many of my friends are Catholics.

I'd like to know who did it. I'm thirty-eight now, and I can never use my right leg again, which means I cannot return to my work as a bricklayer. My wife has shown great strength through all this – my brother was killed in the RUC – it makes me feel bitter. But we will keep going. People have to live on.

Sergeant, UDR

There's parts of my farm I've never been on because I farm right up against Armagh and against a nationalist estate. It's three acres that I wouldn't go to. Two years ago the IRA came for me. They mistook me for my brother. I was carrying a shotgun and I really think it was that which put them off. The Special Branch picked up a young chap a few days after, and he told them about it. After that I had the SAS in for ten days. One of them lived in the house, and the others slept in the barn for a time. For thirteen months I had different units of the Army in and out. For all that time I never milked the cows on my own. I either had the SAS or some Special Branch police with me or our own UDR.

Colonel, UDR

If your employer is not sympathetic to the situation, or if you're in the regiment and he doesn't want to know, he can make life tough. He can make you leave your job. If he is sympathetic, then his own life is on the line, because the terrorist is using employers in Northern Ireland, who work with the security forces, as legitimate targets.

Sergeant, UDR

I have a manhole with a twisted lid on it. I could get it replaced but if anybody steps on it you can hear it. My family know where to walk, they step over it. But if somebody else steps on it, we know they're coming to the door.

Sergeant, UDR

An Englishman I met said that whenever he reads his paper or watches his television all he sees is blood on the roads and funerals. Well, I can understand that. You see I had a son of seventeen who went to put away my car one night, but it had a bomb in it for me. He used to garage the car at night. He was seventeen and due to join the RUC. One of the Roman Catholics that came to the house said, 'We are ashamed, desperately ashamed.' On the same day the IRA killed a close friend of mine who was in the UDR. He was fifty-seven. We buried that man and my boy the same day. That deeply affected us all.

Sergeant, UDR

We are a citizen army and we are living in the community and we either know or strongly suspect who is involved in an incident. We have been very angry at times. It's hard not to be when you know as intimately as we've known so many of the men who have been killed. There was a captain very early on, who was shot just outside the city of Londonderry, as he came home from duty. We attended his funeral, and his daughter was so overcome with grief she had to be restrained from throwing herself into the grave. It was a most heartbreaking experience, yet no act of retribution was taken.

Captain, UDR

We have had people who have attracted some adverse publicity. But I think that should be set against the great number of people who have served with this regiment. I think that the latest figure is something like 35,000, and out of those I think you will find that there's been about a dozen people who've been involved in murders and so forth. As a founder member of the UDR I regret that there should have been even a dozen cases.

Colour-Sergeant, UDR

The first OC of my company was killed in a crash in Belfast. His successor was blown up in Armagh where he was the chairman of Armagh Council. He had his car booby-trapped while he was at a council meeting. It got to the stage where I would not go and see another body laid out. I would go to the house, pay my condolences, attend the funeral, but I could not bring myself to see the body. I got so depressed because there were so many of them. I'd known the last one for years. He died a British soldier, he led a British way of life. He served in the RAF before the UDR. He loved both Catholic and Protestant alike. On the day that he was laid out, the local Catholic teacher brought the school children in. Every one of those little tots was going up to his wife saying, 'Sorry for your troubles', 'Sorry for your troubles', 'Sorry for your troubles'.

234

Female Corporal, UDR

Heather and I had been at primary and secondary school together and we were working in a couple of pubs but we used to meet every lunchtime. One day there was a UDR recruiting van outside, so as a joke we went in and filled up the forms. We thought no more about it until three months later we got the word to go for a medical. The two of us joined together as part-timers. We enjoyed our time together.

I had just come off stag (duty) one morning at 1000 hours and Heather and I passed each other on the road. We had planned to go out that night with all the other Greenfinches in the company. Their unit was short of one person and Heather had asked me if I would do a double shift and go with them. I said I couldn't as I had been on stag all night. She asked me to go to a shop and get her an outfit for the evening. By the time I got it and arrived home, the word had come over the news that a Greenfinch had been blown up. I knew it was Heather. A UDR man was killed as well. She was killed instantly. It changed my life completely. She was only twenty. Before that, Heather and myself used to go to a lot of car rallies and travel a lot with Catholic and Protestant fellas, but when Heather was killed I saw a different light. I just couldn't understand how people could be so biased. What was the difference between Catholic and Protestant? The day she was killed I blamed everyone in my home town for knowing about it and I blamed every Catholic in the town. It is only now, two years later, that I've come to my senses again, and I don't think everybody is exactly the same. It's the one bunch that is doing it. It changed my life completely.

The actual hurting side is gone, but in my mind Heather is always there. If I'm in trouble or if I have a problem, I go out to Heather's grave and sit for ages talking to myself; the comfort of knowing she's there helps. It was an awful blow to me. Neither of us ever took much drink, but a month after she was killed I drank a lot. That carried on for about six months. Finally I went to see my doctor who brought me to my senses. Now I don't drink at all.

I've lost all sense of fear. I don't fear any more. When I'm out I keep my eyes open, but it doesn't really matter who's watching me, I don't really care. All you can do with the present troubles in Northern Ireland is to keep watching around, but as far as fear is concerned I don't have any. I lost my sense of fear when I lost

Heather. Before Heather was killed I was having a bit of bother with the public. There used to be a lot of hassling. They used to come at night and knock at the door, things like that. When she was killed I had no bother whatsoever. I think they knew when they took Heather that they took a certain part of me as well. They probably knew I'd had enough torture and hurt so they would leave it there.

About two months before she was killed her brother-in-law was also blown up – her sister's husband, they'd just got married. This happened in March and Heather was killed in July 1984. So in a short space of time they nearly wiped out a family. The night he was killed it was the first time Heather and I ever discussed anything about death. We suddenly realised how easy a target you can be in the UDR. The two of us sat that night and talked about what we would do, what we would wear. She wanted Number 2 dress if she ever got killed. I took it down to the morgue the next day. All she had was a small cut above her right eye. The blast, the actual blast had killed her.

Major, UDR

One of my soldiers had just been murdered and the day after he'd been shot I had to take the commanding officer along to meet his family. We went into the house and I didn't know all the members of the family who were sitting in the lounge. The heat was on and it was like a turkish bath. All the women were sitting crying. There was no conversation and we had to have the ritual cup of tea. I couldn't find any words which would either relieve the tension or make the commanding officer feel a little bit more comfortable. We sat there for an hour supposedly sympathising but it really was absolute hell. We left and the family were much too upset to even get up from their chairs or even understand why we were there. We tried to speak but nothing registered at all. The only man who was able to bring some semblance of normality into that grieving household was the clergyman. After the funeral he was able to comfort the family to a much greater extent than all the relatives and all the other members of the family who arrived at the house before the funeral.

Captain, UDR

I think we have a great capacity to love, and not in the frivolous sense, and we have a great capacity to destroy. We have these two sides to our character and it's not peculiar to any one part of the race. It's probably, to some extent, the reason why religion has survived in Ireland longer than it has survived on the mainland.

Captain, UDR

There was a young policeman killed some years ago who was visiting his wife in hospital; that was hard to accept. It makes you angry as much as it makes you sad. But it also makes me sad when I see young Republicans killed. Not that I have any respect for their cause, but it seems such a waste of life when you see somebody as young as sixteen or seventeen, no matter what persuasion they are, being killed. I just wonder how any cause can be worth it. A bit hard to put it into words, but I think it's the utter futility of it. The waste.

Major, UDR

I have seen stress over the years, especially with some of the older men who were not able to combine the pressures of a civilian job with the long hours and the stress caused by military duties. I see less of that in the younger soldiers, obviously because they're more resilient. Sadly, I know a number of the older soldiers who have retired on reaching the upper age limit of fifty-five and have only had a short time to enjoy their retirement, because they actually died. It saddens me because I think that maybe I'm shortening my own life to some extent. But at the end of the day, I always sustain myself with the fact that if the job wasn't worth doing, then I wouldn't do it.

Sergeant, UDR

You get over to the UK, as we tend to call it, get to Warcop where we train with the British Army, and sit in a pub with three or four guys who are on the same course, and every time a door

237

opens you look round, it's just a natural reaction. It made us laugh because even the barman started to do it. You're always aware of where you are. In a shopping precinct you tend to look at the cars and what the drivers are up to. I frequently go across to Coventry where my wife's family are, and in the pub there, people come across and say, 'You're a member of the Ulster Defence Association, here's some money to take back to Northern Ireland.' They don't realise there's a difference between the UDA and the UDR. Mind you, some places do, because I would go as far to say parts of Coventry are somewhat like Turf Lodge. There are strong Republican enclaves and there are Irish bars that I would not dare to go into with a Belfast accent, or looking like a soldier.

Warrant Officer, UDR

Every two years we get a new commanding officer and RSM (regimental sergeant major) in the battalion and we have to readjust to their way of thinking. They come fresh from their regiment and it's always someone we haven't had before, who will have his own ideas. This can be frustrating, because one man can really be dead keen on something and you live with that, and the next guy comes along and he's really not so worried about that. There are advantages to this system because you can get fresh, good ideas. I mean, very few people like change because they get set in their ways, but sometimes it can be for the good.

One problem for us in the UDR is that in the officers' and sergeants' mess we do not have our own customs. In all the years we've been a regiment, it seems a shame that we don't have our own. In our mess we take on the regimental customs of the incoming RSM.

Sergeant, UDR

If the troubles were happening in Birmingham or Manchester the guys who are in the Territorial Army would possibly be mobilised to do the same sort of civil defence that we are attempting. But there's no other regiment in the world who's gone for the number of years that we have and had to take the sort of political pressure, and the casualties.

Sergeant, UDR

My wife has got used to it, she's quite tough really. I think it's made my eighteen-year-old very bitter because he's seen what's happened to us. You see, we don't really live a normal life. My children can never walk into Armagh, they always have to be cautious. The IRA have had a go at me once so there is every possibility that I'll be killed if I stay here. I accept that – but if we give in, we surrender.

Colour-Sergeant, UDR

I can't see any change in the near future and I think it's a sad state of affairs when youngsters can't live the normal life that I lived. They're restricted in where they can go, what areas they can visit, and they're in a situation where they can't talk about what their mother and father do for a living, and that is very sad.

Major, UDR

The last Sunday in November we have a memorial service to the men lost in the Province. We bought a big stone about five or six years ago and there was about twenty names on it then. It was a centrepiece. Over the years the names have built up – that's very alarming to watch. At the same time we bought two smaller stones to go with it. We put the two stones up and there was a single name on one, and the other was blank. That's bad for morale for the men, and their families. We're waiting for the next death to balance it out. That's a sad fact of life.

Colonel, UDR

There is a remarkable amount of support for the security forces in country areas. A lot of people daren't admit it, in our part of the world, but behind the scenes there are many people who come to me with useful information and advice. I, in turn, can offer them advice, on a need-to-know basis, of course. I believe that is the whole secret of society in Northern Ireland today. I've been very encouraged with the attitudes that are being expressed at this moment in time, particularly from the Catholic community. Inroads are being made every day at a local level.

Sergeant, UDR

I wouldn't leave, no way. I'd rather go out laying in a box. It's no good running away. We've too much to lose.

Captain, UDR

We had a company sergeant major who was a Roman Catholic who lived in a local village. As he didn't have a car, he had a habit of thumbing a lift to the barracks three miles away. I overheard a discussion between two very right-wing Unionists who were also serving in the UDR at the time. They were discussing the CSM and how, if he continued hitching, he was likely to get himself killed. It was later agreed between them that the only solution to the problem was to take it in turns to pick him up and take him back. I thought at the time: 'There's some hope for Northern Ireland yet.'

Major, Army Air Corps

I've got a friend who's commanding one of the battalions out there. He says you can tell me as much as you like about corruption in the UDR, but you will never detract from the vast number of men that work themselves year in, year out, daytime jobs, night-time work, and they do it because they want to improve Ireland. It makes you feel very humble, really.

Conclusions

Sergeant, 2 Para

All of Ireland is cold, tired, piss-wet through, and knackered; that is Ireland summed up.

Lieutenant, 1 King's Own Scottish Borderers

From the moment I went there to the minute I left, I thought it was great. I'm sure any young platoon commander would say the same. It's good money as well. You don't drink, you don't go out, you patrol all the time. You're just not spending money. I got back with a couple of thousand pounds.

Sergeant, 2 Royal Green Jackets

Northern Ireland these days is all things to all men. It provides an outlet for Army training, it's exciting and challenging for the officers, it's good for the young soldiers, but for the older men like me, who've seen it more than once, it's just more of one's life being taken away. One obviously does one's duty, stays aware and alert to the situation, but one certainly doesn't go out there thinking this time we've got an answer. One's far too long in the tooth for that.

Corporal, 1 Welsh Guards

I totally, really enjoy Northern Ireland. If I was killed in Ireland, I'd do so without regret. I enjoyed everything that I did. I took an interest in the area, a continued interest. I've still got all my terrorist recognition leaflets, all my maps; I took a camera over there, I suppose I've got about four thousand photographs. I'm ready to go again.

Rifleman, 2 Royal Green Jackets

I'm always talking about Northern Ireland. I love it, it's my bread and butter. If I was asked to go to Northern Ireland tomorrow, I'd go. I would consult the wife, I'd say to them that I am going and then tell the wife. I wouldn't tell her they asked me to go, I'd say I've got to go. I love it over there. Everybody, all my family and friends, know how I feel about Ireland. I've no remorse, no hatred for Ireland.

Guardsman, 1 Coldstream Guards

The first time you get back to England you think you've done it all; you think everybody's going to treat you like a war hero, but you've done nothing spectacular. In fact, a lot of people think you shouldn't be there. When we got back to base the boss said to us, 'You're nothing special. Get your kit: drill time.' That's when I realised I'd only done what hundreds of thousands of soldiers had done already.

Corporal, 3 Para

Northern Ireland is a good experience for somebody who's young and just come out of the depot. It puts them into reality, puts everything into perspective. The majority of recruits go to Ireland, do a little bit, come back and they're a bit more mature. Instead of having a fight in Aldershot on a Saturday night they have a real fight out there, and when they've done it, they don't have to prove themselves. Ireland is not for everybody, I know that, but it is an experience I wouldn't have missed. I wouldn't join the Army just to go there, but it is something I'm glad I did.

Sergeant, 2 Para

You get nineteen-year-old lads going to Ireland and in those four months they gain ten years, ten years I'd say.

Conclusions

Sergeant, 1 Scots Guards

For a young lad, immature, after his four-month stint, you can class him as an adult. But us older guys who've been there five or six times, we've had enough of it. I sit in my stupid little bunk and think, I've got a nice house at home, a wife, I could be doing something better with than what I am here, and I've got kids.

Captain, 2 Royal Anglian

My wife used to tell me that I was very quiet when I came back, subdued, I think that is probably because although you are surrounded by umpteen soldiers you are on your own over there and you tend to have your own thoughts. When you come back, perhaps the wife is shopping, the kids are playing and dad's looking around trying to get back into the swing of family life again. Being back at home is a big change. Time stands still for the soldier during those four months and you seem to think that it stands still for the family as well. But it doesn't: their life goes on.

Sergeant, 45 Commando

There is a lot of depression out there. In four months we are on a level, and to get a high is unusual, maybe one or two a tour. We're Pavlov's dogs really, trained to go by the whistle; when we go to Ireland every man gets shown his little kennel and a little spot for his kit, and gets into his routine. The depression comes if he phones his wife and she's getting pissed off. The reason why we often say 'fucking Northern Ireland' is because we know the repercussions. It's not us, it's our wives.

Sergeant Major, 2 Coldstream Guards

I've certainly got to the point where I resent going out there, and my wife resents it, and my mother resents it. It's had knock-on effects with my family. My mother won't buy Irish butter, she won't buy Irish linen. She's reacted very strongly: anything with 'Made in Ireland' on it she won't touch. She's not bigoted, she's not a racialist, she's a normal, middle-line conservative, but if I bought her a lace tablecloth made in Ireland she would take it as a very gross insult. She hates me going over there.

Guardsman, 1 Coldstream Guards

When I look at my Northern Ireland medal now, I think I bloody deserved it. I've got my photographs and the memories, but my medal is the only thing I really look at and think, 'Me, that is.' To a civilian it's just another shiny queen, but I shall always be proud of it. My mum and dad, girlfriend, they're proud of me, but they don't really understand what I've been through. Nor will I ever be able to communicate it to them, and that's a shame, because I'd love to and I can't – that's half the frustration. We're the only people that understand what we've been through, and when civilians say, 'Oh, not another war story', that really gets me down.

Sergeant, 45 Commando

I've just got remarried. My wife is twelve years younger than I, and in '84 we had occasion to go down to 42 Commando's camp at Bickleigh. I took her to the Northern Ireland memorial, which was erected in the early seventies; around it they've planted a tree with a little brass plaque for every guy killed. We walked down the path to the granite monument and I said, 'Well, what do you think?' She just looked at me: 'Shall we go back to the mess for a drink?' She was not interested. Northern Ireland hadn't affected her at all, and it's the same for any civvie. I stood there looking at the names which meant all those years, and thought, 'Why are these plaques here? What have those men achieved?'

Corporal, 40 Commando

It's a cheap war, let's face it; we're getting practical experience, which can only be good for any armed force; the logistics side is easy to handle; plus, if you look on the bad side, it doesn't even cost much to fly bodies back home.

Sergeant, 45 Commando

To me, it's a sickening conflict, because you can't identify the enemy. A soldier likes to be briefed that the enemy is a certain type of person, wearing a certain type of equipment, which he can identify and destroy if that is his mission. Over there you're in a corner of what's supposed to be Britain and you can't tell one from another. It goes against the grain to be thrown into an environment where people of your own race are trying to kill you. We've adapted and geared ourselves to counter-revolutionary operations now, and we're very sophisticated at it, but that doesn't alter the fact that we're fighting an enemy within, an enemy we can't identify. As soldiers we don't like to be stood on a street corner in Britain. People say Northern Ireland's a good training ground, but to me it's sad when conflict within the boundaries of your own country provides training. I really can't understand all the bravado and gung-ho people show when we've got a Northern Ireland tour coming up.

Corporal, 40 Commando

In the early and mid 1970s Northern Ireland was good news. You know, the little joke: not much of a war, but it's the only one we've got. People say now it's just a police action, but if you get shot it hurts just as much in a police action as it does in a battle.

Sergeant, 45 Commando

Frankly, it's an Intelligence war now. I think that's the nature of the conflict. I don't think it's worth beating about the bush: people resent us calling it a war. But it is a war. When all is said and done we are trying to defeat a terrorist organisation and they are trying to kill us.

Major, 2 Royal Green Jackets

I think as time goes by our job gets more and more difficult. There is less and less chance for us as soldiers to take initiatives because the police are directing operations and we are in support. Fifteen years ago, perhaps wrongly, if a soldier suspected something was going on he kicked down a door and sorted it out. We can't do that now. So it just gets more difficult, but I don't see that as any reason to stop. We're doing the right thing.

Lance Corporal, 1 Welsh Guards

What we do over there is worthwhile because it stops . . . well, it doesn't stop but it cuts down the violence and the terrorist activity. Our presence out there makes some side feel safer but I'm not sure which side.

Colour-Sergeant, 1 Welsh Guards

Northern Ireland gives you a broader outlook on life, the whole Army does really. But it also brings home the stupidity of the place. It's a waste of time, because we're protecting one from the other, but it's such a stupid waste of the people there. One person against another, for so-called beliefs which are long gone. It's no longer religion, it's all IRA terrorism. If only a few more people would stand up and start reporting terrorists to the proper authorities we could get it over with in a couple of months.

Major, 1 King's Own Scottish Borderers

Soldiers are aware of the IRA principally as people who are likely to try and kill them. We don't have any difficulty in trying to sell to them who the baddies are; terrorists are the baddies by virtue of the fact that they try to kill soldiers.

Corporal, 1 Welsh Guards

At times, I can see the IRA's point of view. If I'd been born in the Falls Road I know I'd be in the IRA. They want a free Ireland. They see the British Army as oppressors, and back home if I was a Welsh Nationalist and Wales wasn't part of Britain and English troops came in, I'd throw bricks, stones and petrol bombs. Most times out there I was dedicated to my job, stopping these terrorists, and that's why I enjoyed it so much. But other days I could see that those IRA guys are really dedicated to their cause, prepared to die for it, and I respect them for that.

Warrant Officer, Royal Army Ordnance Corps

Myself, I see them as a bunch of bloody hooligans, quite frankly, with a strong criminal element. Far be it from me to comment on the political situation, but you only have to see the type of people who get lifted: they are equivalent to bloody football hooligans. They're Northern Ireland's version of Chelsea supporters.

Colour-Sergeant, 2 Para

In all honesty, had I been born Irish and Catholic I would probably have been involved, because in the early days I do feel that the Republicans had just cause for extremism. These days there may be a few Republicans left with deep-rooted ideals, but as far as I'm concerned their campaign carries on now mainly because the children there have grown up with violence. The sixteen- to eighteen-year-old kids were brought up during the savage days, the early and mid seventies. A little girl came up to me in Newry in 1979 – she must have been about five or six – she sort of smiled under a runny nose and I said, 'Hello, sweetheart.' She said, 'Can't talk to you. Soldiers eat little girls.' Wicked – how can you pervert a child's mind to believe that?

Corporal, 40 Commando

If I'd been born there I'd probably be doing the same as them. I'd be out on the streets, but I don't think I'd be doing it the same way. I'd be looking for the legitimate target, the soldiers. The main thing that most of our lads hate about the IRA is the way they pick women and kids as targets. There ain't no heroes in the IRA, no matter what their propaganda says: if they can shoot you in the back and get away with it, they will. We have a set code of honour. The actual gunman who takes us on one to one we've probably got quite a lot of respect for because he's got the bottle. But if it comes to a stand-up fight, they won't risk it. They can confront us any time: that's why we are there.

Northern Ireland: Soldiers Talking

Officer, Ulster Defence Regiment

They have the upper hand all the time, the element of surprise, whereas all the time we are looking to see if we can catch them out. It doesn't require a great number of people to keep this campaign going. Nor does it require a great deal of intelligence. It only requires an incident in any one area. It's terribly difficult, we all speak the one language, we all look the same, we cannot really overcome that element of surprise. I suppose if it wasn't a political situation, the border issue for example, they would find some other excuse to keep on. It's not something that's been going on just for seventeen years. I mean, it's been happening since Wolfe Tone was defeated at the Battle of Vinegar Hill in 1798, and probably before that.

Corporal, 42 Commando

Before we go over there they start giving us the history of Ireland, what happened in the 1600s, Oliver Cromwell, and all that. We all know why we're there, so why don't they just start from the political stress in '69, when it all started? I don't think anything before that's of interest to a young eighteen-year-old. Why go on about it? I can't see what happened in Dublin sixty years ago is relevant to what's going on in Belfast now.

Sergeant, 45 Commando

We try to instruct the lads as to why the troubles are the way they are, but really we haven't got the time to go deeply enough into the subject to weigh up the pros and cons. I've read a few books on Ireland, both staunch Republican views and staunch Loyalist views and, let's face it, at the end of the day Irish Nationalists believe in a united Ireland and we've just got to live with it.

Sergeant, 40 Commando

I think the people, away from the nausea and the troubles, are terrific on both sides of the community. If there was no trouble over there, if it was all quietened down either one way or the other, to be honest, I wouldn't mind living there, because they are terrific people.

Sergeant, 45 Commando

It really is tragic that since 1969 Northern Ireland has degenerated into what it is now. The generation coming through now is the poisoned generation from the early days of the troubles. Some of your two- or three-year-olds in 1969 are now your hardened terrorists. All he's known throughout his life is hatred and bitterness and conflict. That's a damnation on society.

Captain, 40 Commando

The people of Northern Ireland are living through an intolerable situation, and like all of us they have become hardened to violence. While I would never advocate censorship of the press and television, I hold the media largely responsible for the familiarity with violence we all have. I do not approve of the showing of dead bodies on the news or current affairs programmes. What is the purpose other than to shock, and of course repeated exposure means that people are no longer shocked. It's not the sort of thing I want my children to see, not because I don't want them to see how terrifying it is, but because if they see violence continually it becomes less terrifying. One only has to look at the history of media coverage of Northern Ireland, how from at the start a shot being fired was front-page headlines to the fact that today killings there barely make the second page. And, of course, both factions in the Province have responded to this, and know they must commit even more violent and devastating acts to get the same media attention.

Major, 2 Royal Green Jackets

If I could wave a magic wand and put one thing right in Northern Ireland I would raze the Divis Flats to the ground and rehouse the unfortunate people who live there. It's a sordid place, an insult to any human being to be invited to live there. The only reason I can see for leaving them up is to put the architect who designed them in there for the rest of his life. Dreadful: I'm not surprised that people who live there bear a grudge. Much of the pressure to demolish the Divis Flats is hardcore Republican, but to my mind that doesn't matter. It's a sordid place to ask human beings to live.

Corporal, 40 Commando

People in England only see the newsworthy bits about Northern Ireland – a bombing or a shooting – and they get the impression that's how it is all the time. And it's not. It's ninety-nine per cent boredom. That's been said about wars from Day One.

Sergeant, 42 Commando

How alive do you feel when you're in the darkness in South Armagh? When you're all switched on and alert, you smell things, get that sixth sense, and when you come back into camp you feel high. How many times out there do we have that feeling? Minutes, only minutes in any four-month tour.

Sergeant, 3 Para

I'd sooner go back to the Falklands tomorrow morning than Northern Ireland. I suppose I was more likely to be killed in the Falklands because of the amount of ammunition fired, but I feel safer in a conventional war than walking about the streets of Belfast like a figure eleven target. In the Falklands many times my life was in my own hands, but in Northern Ireland I'm afraid it isn't, no matter how good your skills are, because without a doubt they're the best terrorists in the world, without a shadow of a doubt. You can be talking to him one minute, and the next minute he can be shooting you.

Corporal, 40 Commando

The IRA have had eighteen years' practice; I would rate them as probably the most professional terrorists in the world. You've got to have respect for their abilities. You can't go over there and class them all as a bunch of clowns: you're dead if you do, you come back in a black box. But I've no respect for them as people. I've been a few times to the memorial for dead terrorists in Milltown cemetery just off the Turf Lodge in Andersonstown. They've got a big blue marble slab with gold lettering on; I feel no remorse reading about all those officers and explosives experts blowing themselves up.

Major, 1 King's Own Scottish Borderers

Tactically I think they're stuck because the men of violence are so caught up in it now that they can't be stopped, even commanded. Their campaign seems localised, not really co-ordinated in perhaps the way it should be. They can still create an incident pretty well whenever they wish, and that will continue, but in the future I see the rest of the community getting on with life in the normal way.

Officer, Ulster Defence Regiment

I don't think the answer's very far away now. For the first time in my service career, and I've worn a King's and Queen's uniform for forty years, I do think the Anglo-Irish Agreement may hold a solution. Certain aspects require modification, and it will take a while to get organised, but I think the agreement will go forward. The answer's coming.

Private, Ulster Defence Regiment

There are so many people making money out of the troubles, so many people. A large percentage of the population is employed in security work and if it stopped tomorrow what would these people do? They'd be redundant. I'm only part-time UDR, I also work in the camp as a civilian.

Sergeant, 42 Commando

There's rebellion in every generation in Ireland. I think if Ireland was united the people in South Armagh would still be rebellious to that government. They think it's romance, the bold rebel. It goes on and on, and they believe it: the highwayman.

Sergeant, 45 Commando

I would like to see a solution, for the people we've known who have died, because maybe then they'd have died for something worthwhile. I would like to see us achieve a solution. I believe we've spent long enough there, gained enough experience and Intelligence to sort it all out.

Lieutenant, 2 Royal Anglian

I would like to see more being done to get people into decent jobs, provide people with a decent standard of living. Money will solve this problem, because a terrorist can't flourish in a place where a man's got a decent life and can see a decent future: a man will protect his own future. Everything in life is answerable with money.

Corporal, 42 Commando

They don't need soldiers in Northern Ireland. They need peace-keepers, policemen, civilians who are nice to people twenty-four hours a day; diplomats, whatever. But not soldiers; I mean, they gave me thousands and thousands of pounds' worth of training to get me to this stage and I'm wasted on a street in Belfast.

Corporal, Royal Military Police

I get the idea that many soldiers go to Northern Ireland with big expectations and come back disappointed because they haven't fired a shot. It's a bit like going to Spain and coming back without a suntan.

Sergeant Major, 2 Royal Green Jackets

People in Britain are always saying pull the troops out. To me that's inconceivable. I don't think the general public understand what it would mean, I don't think they understand the precedent it would set. I can't even imagine why anyone would think that nothing would happen. It would be civil war, it would be appalling, even worse than it is now.

Major, 1 King's Own Scottish Borderers

Terrorist organisations can function perfectly happily with or without the support of the community, and because they have become more isolated from their constituency they will continue as fanatics rather than as expressions of any great groundswells of public support. They don't really care about local opinion in Ireland because they're not going to win any propaganda battles there, but they do care what the Americans think. So it doesn't matter what they do locally as long as they get their international coverage correct.

Lieutenant, 2 Royal Green Jackets

If anyone says to me we're not getting any further forward in Northern Ireland I give them a measure from my own experience. In 1973 in Londonderry there were five battalions and independent companies; a terrific amount of troops. In Londonderry today, there is one battalion and probably no more than a hundred men on the streets at any one time. People say to me, Americans in particular, 'How long is Northern Ireland going on for?' I say it's finished. You get more crime in large American towns in a day than you get in a week in Northern Ireland. You don't get many rapes, burglaries, stuff like that in Northern Ireland. In England, kids going missing, women disappearing, blokes getting stabbed outside pubs are taken as read, but because a man's shot by a terrorist in Northern Ireland it's big news. So my personal view is that the terrorist is virtually finished in Northern Ireland apart from the occasional spectacular thing, like the Basques in Spain – you'll never beat that.

Sergeant, 45 Commando

The only way to solve the problem, I believe, is to take away the justification for armed struggle, and that will have to come by political action, because as long as they've got an excuse for using arms they will use them. The hardened terrorist now has been at it for a long time. He doesn't know any different: it's a way of life, and it's also big money. Some of the high-up members of the IRA and, for example, the UVF, are living comfortably on the troubles in Northern Ireland, and as long as those people are in charge then they're quite happy. The reality of the violence doesn't concern them. They've reached a level in the hierarchy of their organisations where they don't have the dirty jobs any more, so for them it's big money, basically. You look at the funds from NORAID, for example: where do they all go? There is not one member of the hierarchy of illegal organisations on both sides of the fence who isn't well-heeled. That's what we're up against: money.

Major, 1 Para

Both sides are locked into the conflict. The British Army, we can go on for ever. It's built into the system, has been for years now: people are programmed to go there, and the casualties we suffer per annum are no more than soldiers killed each year in road accidents.

Major, 1 King's Own Scottish Borderers

The military campaign will end because politically the Catholics will see that there is light at the end of the tunnel, and the Protestants will have to come to terms with the fact that they could survive pretty well when that light comes. Somebody said that in about 2030 there will be more Catholic voters than Protestant, and they will be able to vote themselves out of the United Kingdom.

Corporal, 42 Commando

Obviously it has got to end one day. It must. It cannot go on indefinitely. One day something will happen and those soldiers are gonna be needed elsewhere.

Appendix I
ARMY FORCE LEVELS
1969–May 1987

These figures are an average of the monthly strength returns for each year. The only wide variations were in 1969 when the force level rose from 2,693 to 7,952 during the month of August and in 1972 when Operation Motorman temporarily raised the Army strength to 21,766 (excluding UDR).

The figures for the Ulster Defence Regiment until 1977 represent an almost entirely part-time force. After 1977 an increasing proportion of the UDR were full-time soldiers, the equivalent of infantrymen of any other Army regiment in Northern Ireland. The 1987 figure represents 3,662 part-time soldiers and 2,798 'Permanent Cadre' or full-time soldiers. The UDR figures also include, in any year, the Regiment's women soldiers who are known as Greenfinches. More than 600 are currently serving.

The number of regular Army soldiers attached to UDR Headquarters and UDR battalions are not included. In 1970 this figure was 34 and is now 111.

The figures for the regular Army include Royal Marine units.

YEAR	REGULAR ARMY	UDR
1969	6,107	0
1970	7,537	3,441
1971	11,322	4,563
1972	16,867	8,728
1973	16,814	8,124
1974	15,911	7,775
1975	14,701	7,716
1976	14,906	7,690
1977	14,286	7,721
1978	13,452	7,502
1979	12,984	7,322
1980	12,141	7,037
1981	11,098	7,165
1982	10,538	6,943
1983	9,882	6,701

1984	9,032	6,686
1985	9,000	6,600
1986	10,103	6,558
1987	10,170	6,460
(to 31 May)		

Appendix II
Deaths, Wounded/Injured, Bombs, Shootings
1969 – May 1987

	1969	1970	1971	1972	1973	1974	1975	1976	1977	1978	1979	1980	1981
DEATHS													
Army	0	0	43	103	58	28	14	14	15	14	38	8	10
UDR	0	0	5	26	8	7	6	15	14	7	10	9	13
RUC	1	2	11	17	13	15	11	23	14	10	14	9	21
Civ	12	23	115	321	171	166	216	245*	69*	50*	51*	50*	67*
Total	13	25	174	467	250	216	247	297	112	81	113	76	111
WOUNDED/INJURED													
Army	24	620	381	542	525	453	151	242	172	127	132	53	112
UDR	NA	0	9	36	23	30	16	22	15	8	21	24	28
RUC	8	47	105	94	94	59	79	74	51	174	117	136	219
Civ (wounded only)	139	60	1,880	3,902	1,765	1,394	1,213	1,087	406	253	305	266	433
Total	147	727	2,375	4,574	2,407	1,936	1,459	1,425	644	562	575	479	792
IED (bombs) made safe by the Army	1	17	493	471	542	428	236	426	169	178	142	120	131
EXPLOSIONS	9	153	1,022	1,382	978	685	399	766	366	455	422	280	398
SHOOTINGS*	73	213	1,756	10,630	5,018	3,206	1,803	1,908	1,081	755	728	642	1,142

Includes incidents that did not involve the security forces or result in injury

*Incl 3 prison officers *Incl 3 prison officers *Incl 2 prison officers *Incl 9 prison officers *Incl 2 prison officers *Incl 10 hunger strikers*

	1982	1983	1984	1985	1986	1987 (to 11 May)	Running Total
DEATHS							
Army	21	5	9	2	4	1	387
UDR	7	10	10	4	8	3	162
RUC	12	18	8	23	12	9	244
Civ	57	44	37	24	38	29	1,784
Total	97	77	64	53	62	42	2,577
WOUNDED/ INJURED							
Army	80	66	64	18	45	39	3,848
UDR	18	22	22	13	10	5	322
RUC	81	110	189	305	417	39	2,399
Civ (wounded only)	256	202*	252*	245*	322	137	14,522
Total	435	400	527	580	794	220	21,091
IED (bombs) made safe by the Army	113	101	55	65	82	54	3,825
EXPLOSIONS	220	266	193	136	173	120	8,433
SHOOTINGS*	547	424	334	226	385	218	31,107

*Includes incidents that did not involve the security forces or result in injury		**Incl 1 prison officer*	**Incl 1 prison officer*	**Incl 1 prison officer*			

Glossary

ARF – Airborne Reaction Force.

Armalite – lightweight automatic rifle of American design.

ASU – Active Service Unit.

ATO – Ammunition Technical Officer.

bullworker – muscle-building apparatus.

B Special – Ulster Special Constabulary predominantly part-time and exclusively Protestant, disbanded in March 1970.

BAOR – British Army of the Rhine.

brick – four-man unit.

Carl Gustav – 84mm anti-tank weapon.

CATO – Chief Ammunition Technical Officer.

civ. pop. – civilian population.

CO – Commanding Officer.

CP – checkpoint.

CS gas – choking smoke gas.

CSM – company sergeant major.

dixies – metal food containers.

Fenian – nationalist Catholic. The name derives from a nineteenth-century Irish revolutionary organisation founded in the US.

flak jacket – armoured jacket.

four-tonner – four-ton truck.

FRG – federal riot gun; a baton gun, firing rubber or PVC bullets.

Gardai – Irish police.

GOC – General Officer Commanding.

Greenfinch – female member of Ulster Defence Regiment.

heads –	naval term for toilet.
hiring –	accommodation rented by the Army.
Hotspur –	RUC Land Rover.
helipad –	helicopter landing site.
ICP –	incident control point.
IED –	identified explosive device.
INLA –	Irish National Liberation Army.
Int. –	Intelligence.
IS –	internal security.
IRA –	Irish Republican Army.
JCB –	mechanical shovel.
Long Kesh –	former name of HM Prison, Maze.
Kosbie –	King's Own Scottish Borderer.
LSL –	landing ship logistics.
LMG –	light machine gun.
Macralon –	armoured plastic.
MOD –	Ministry of Defence.
Murph (the) –	Ballymurphy.
NAAFI –	Navy, Army and Air Force Institute.
NCO –	non-commissioned officer.
ND –	negligent discharge.
net –	radio network.
NITAT –	Northern Ireland Training and Advisory Team.
NORAID –	Northern Irish Aid Committee, US based.
OIRA –	Official Irish Republican Army, largely inactive since it declared a ceasefire in May 1972.
OP –	observation post.
Ops –	operations.
own goal –	self-inflicted wound or death.
P Check –	personnel check.

Pig –	GKN Sankey AT-104 vehicle – an armoured personnel carrier.
PIRA –	Provisional Irish Republican Army, also known as Provos. Formed in December 1969 when the IRA Council voted in favour of token recognition of the Westminster, Dublin and Stormont Parliaments, thus splitting the Republican movement.
PR –	public relations.
Provos –	Provisional IRA.
PVCP –	permanent vehicle checkpoint.
QM –	Quartermaster.
QRF –	Quick Reaction Force.
RAOC –	Royal Army Ordnance Corps.
RCIED –	radio-controlled improvised explosive device.
recce –	reconnaissance.
RNAD –	Royal Navy Armament Depot.
RPG 7 –	Russian armour-piercing rocket.
RSM –	Regimental Sergeant Major.
RUC –	Royal Ulster Constabulary.
soak time –	the period of time before a manual approach is made on a suspect explosive device.
R and R –	rest and recuperation.
sangar –	stone or sandbag protective wall.
Saracen –	armoured six-wheel carrier.
SAS –	Special Air Service.
scoff –	food, a meal.
Scout –	Westland-built army helicopter.
SF –	security forces.
Shank (the) –	Shankill.
SIB –	Special Investigations Branch.
SLR –	self-loading rifle.

squaddie –	soldier, below corporal in rank.
stag –	a duty.
tabbing –	long, hard walk.
TAC HQ –	tactical headquarters.
TAOR –	tactical area of responsibility.
Thompson –	Thompson submachine gun.
UDA –	Ulster Defence Association: the largest Protestant paramilitary organisation, established September 1971.
UDR –	Ulster Defence Regiment.
UVF –	Ulster Volunteer Force, loyalist paramilitary organisation.
VCP –	vehicle checkpoint.
WO1/2 –	Warrant Officer, Class One/Two.
WRAC –	Women's Royal Army Corps.
wheelbarrow –	remote-controlled robot vehicle used in bomb disposal.
Yellow Card –	instructions carried by every soldier in Northern Ireland advising on the circumstances appropriate for the use of firearms.

Index

Index

Aden, 4, 10, 20, 36, 52
Africa, 12
Albert Street, *see* Belfast
Aldergrove Airport, 4
Aldershot, 116, 242
America, 5, 163
Andersonstown, *see* Belfast
Anglo-Irish Agreement, xxvi, 251
Anguilla, 18
Arbuckle, Constable (RUC), xvi, 11
Ardoyne, *see* Belfast
Armagh City, xxv, 197, 234, 239
Army Air Corps, vi, xxvii, 98, 99,
    104, 112–13, 135, 141, 161,
    196–7, 219, 240
Atkins, Sir Humphrey, Secretary
    of State for Northern Ireland
    1979–81, xviii

Balkan Street, *see* Belfast
Ballykelly, Co. Londonderry,
    xxiv, 44, 66, 155, 224
Ballykinler, Co. Down, 4, 133,
    136
Ballymacarrett, *see* Belfast
Ballymurphy, *see* Belfast
Bangor, Co. Down, 38, 43, 183
Basques, 253
BBC, 41, 89, 117, 216
Beechmount, *see* Belfast
Beirut, 159
Belfast, vii, viii, ix, x, xii, xvi,
    xxiii, xxiv, xxv, 1, 2, 3, 20, 78,
    83, 98, 99, 112, 165, 196, 204,
    205, 248, 252; comparison with
    Glasgow, 4; comparison with
    Liverpool, 18, 145–6;
    comparison with South
    Armagh, 173–4
    Albert Street, 19, 31

Belfast — *cont.*
    Andersonstown, 81, 104–5, 115,
        129, 144, 251
    Ardoyne, xvii, 22–3, 25, 41–2,
        53, 58, 60–1, 81, 93
    Balkan Street, xvii
    Ballymacarrett, 38, 114
    Ballymurphy, xvii, 51, 52, 53,
        58–9, 60, 81, 89, 103, 118,
        123, 147, 148, 152, 158, 164,
        260; attack on Henry Taggert
        School, 61–3; riots in, 40–1,
        46–7, 121
    Beechmount, 158
    Butler Street, xvii, 22, 60, 92
    Clonard, xvii, 50, 53, 59, 128–9,
        136, 155, 158, 214
    Crocus Street, xxiv, ambush in,
        151–2
    Crumlin Road, 23, 41, 59
    Crumlin Road Jail, 26, 106–7
    Cupar Street, 9–10
    Cyprus Street, 53, 154
    Distillery, 150
    Divis Flats, 15, 24, 88, 107, 121,
        153, 158, 166–7, 249–50;
        social conditions, 130–2
    Europa Hotel, 105
    Falls Road and district, xvi, xvii,
        5, 6–11, 14–15, 19, 36, 41,
        50–1, 107, 113, 115, 117, 120,
        122, 129, 139, 144, 145, 146,
        153, 157, 158, 246; curfew of,
        24–6, 65; social conditions, 3,
        90–1
    Flax Street, 23–4, 35, 95–6
    Girdwood Park, 6, 29, 210
    Glassmullan Camp, 115, 140–1
    Grosvenor Road, 10, 115
    Hastings Street, 19

Belfast – *cont.*
  Highfield, 101
  Leeson Street, 10–11, 56
  Lenadoon, xix, 161
  Mackies factory, 5, 79, 113
  MacRory Park, 129
  Mater Infirmorum Hospital, 31
  Milltown Cemetery, 110, 251
  Musgrave Park Hospital, 231
  New Lodge, xvii, 41, 81, 85, 89,
    91, 97, 100, 108, 161; riots in,
    28–31; social conditions, 94–5
  North Howard Street, 47, 61,
    146
  Palace Barracks, 33, 53, 106, 111
  Percy Street, 5, 37
  Rathcoole, 99–100, 105
  Royal Victoria Hospital, 5, 155
  Shankill Road and district, xvi,
    xvii, 1–2, 5, 6, 9, 14–16, 19,
    21, 24, 26, 33–4, 35, 38, 43,
    59, 63, 126, 128, 261; riots in,
    11–13, 33–5, 91–2; social
    conditions, 3
  Short Strand, 107, 109
  Springfield Road, 9–10, 53, 54,
    57, 59, 62, 63, 88, 115, 153,
    214
  Springfield Road RUC Station,
    139, 151–2, 171; bomb attack
    on, 49–50
  Tennent Street, 16, 24, 90, 110
  Tiger Bay, 85, 108, 161
  Turf Lodge, 25, 81, 121, 123,
    147, 156, 162, 238, 251; riots
    in, 67–9
  Unity Flats, 24, 25, 26, 32–3, 87
  Whiterock, 89, 118, 120
Belleek, Co. Fermanagh, 219
Berlin, 189
Bessbrook, Co. Armagh, 104,
  135, 178–80, 182, 186, 188, 192,
  195, 197, 218
Bickleigh, 245
Birmingham, 41, 238

Black Mountain, Co. Antrim, 4,
  58, 60
'Bloody Friday', xix, 87–8
'Bloody Sunday', xviii, 70–7, 87,
  91; descriptions of, 70–4;
  reactions to, 74–7
Bogside, *see* Londonderry
Borneo, 20, 36
Brecon, 175
Brighton, bombing of Grand
  Hotel, xxv
Bristol, 69
B Specials (Ulster Special
  Constabulary), xvi, 2–3, 5, 14,
  19, 44, 224, 232, 234, 259
Butler Street, *see* Belfast

Cahill, Joe, OC of PIRA Belfast
  Brigade, 58
Carlingford Lough, 198
Carrickmore, Co. Tyrone, xxvi
Castlewellan, Co. Down, xxiii
Catholic Ex-Servicemen's
  Association (CESA), 68
Chichester-Clark, James, Prime
  Minister of Northern Ireland
  1969–71, xvi, xvii
Civil rights movement, 2, 3, 5, 70,
  71; *see also* Northern Ireland
  Civil Rights Association
Clonard, *see* Belfast
Coldstream Guards, The, vi
  1st Battalion, 39, 43–4, 66–7,
    69, 74, 129–30, 159, 175, 183,
    190–1, 242, 244
  2nd Battalion, 116–17, 149, 151,
    243–4
Collins, Michael, 14
Corrigan, Mairead, founder of
  Peace Movement, xxii
County Fermanagh, 9, 153, 228
Creggan, *see* Londonderry
Crocus Street, *see* Belfast
Cromwell, Oliver, 248
Crossmaglen, South Armagh, xxv,

174, 178, 197, 198, 243–4;
description of, 175–7; bomb
explosion in square, 191–3;
mortar attack on base, 199–202
Crumlin Road, *see* Belfast
Crumlin Road Jail, *see* Belfast
Cupar Street, *see* Belfast
Curtis, Gunner, 94 Locating
Regiment, Royal Artillery, first
serving soldier killed, xvii;
reactions to death, 41–2
Cyprus Street, *see* Belfast

De Valera, Eamonn, 14
Devlin, Bernadette, 5, 8
Distillery, *see* Belfast
Divis Flats, *see* Belfast
Downpatrick, Co. Down, xxvi
Droppin' Well public house,
Ballykelly, xxiv; bombing of,
155–6
Drunahoe, Co. Londonderry, 74
Dublin, xxiii, 5, 14, 75, 229, 248,
261
Dundalk, Republic of Ireland, 104
Dungannon, Co. Tyrone, xxv, 229
Dunluce Castle, Co. Antrim, 156

East Tyrone, 228
Ebrington Barracks, Co.
Londonderry, 156
EEC, 185, 186
Enniskillen, Co. Fermanagh, 170
Europa Hotel, *see* Belfast

Falklands Campaign, 153, 162;
comparison with Northern
Ireland, 250
Falls curfew, 24–6, 65
Falls Road and district, *see* Belfast
Farrah-Hockley, General
Anthony, 34
Faulkner, Brian, Prime Minister
of Northern Ireland, 1971–72,
xvii, xviii, xix

Feakle, Republic of Ireland, xx
Fianna na h-Eireann, youth wing
of IRA, 94
Flax Street, *see* Belfast
Forkill, Co. Armagh, 104, 137,
188
Fort George, *see* Londonderry

Garrison, Co. Fermanagh, 215,
225
Germany, vii, 20, 39, 46, 83, 141,
147
Giant's Causeway, Co. Antrim, 4,
156
Gibson, Sir Maurice, xxvi
Girdwood Park, *see* Belfast
Glasgow, 4
Glassmullan Camp, *see* Belfast
Gobnascale, *see* Londonderry
Green Howards, The, 80
Grosvenor Road, *see* Belfast

Harland and Wolff, 8
Harrods, bombing of, xxv; bomb
scare at, 154
Hastings Street, *see* Belfast
Helen's Bay, Co. Down, 54
Hermes, HMS, 153
Highfield, *see* Belfast
Hong Kong, 203
Household Cavalry, The, bomb
attack on, xxiv, 154
Hunger Strike, 141–5, 151
Hunt Report, on B Specials, xvi
Hurson, Martin, PIRA
hunger-striker, 145

Internment, xiii, xvii, xxiii, 56–63,
70, 108, 115; events leading to,
53–5; effects of, 63–5
Irish Guards, 226
Irish Republican Army (IRA), ix,
x, xvii, 2, 9, 15, 26, 34, 40–1, 44,
51, 58, 60, 61–2, 65, 71, 75, 76,
84, 87, 88, 89, 93, 96–7, 98, 103,

Irish Republican Army – *cont.*
104, 106, 109, 110, 116, 120,
122, 125, 140, 142, 143, 145,
150, 154, 158, 168, 170, 174,
187, 188, 190, 191, 208, 215,
217, 225, 228, 229, 232, 233,
239, 254, 260; appraisals of,
250–1; attitudes to, 90–1, 230,
246–8; *see also* Official Irish
Republican Army (OIRA) *and*
Provisional Irish Republican
Army (PIRA)
Irish National Liberation Army
(INLA), xxii, xxiv, xxv, xxvi,
142, 188, 208, 216–17, 260
Irish Northern Aid Committee,
see NORAID
Irish Republican Socialist Party
(IRSP), 112
ITV, 41, 61, 89

Jonesborough, Co. Armagh, 174

Keady, Co. Armagh, 183, 184
Kenya, 12
King, Tom, xviii
King's Own Royal Border
Regiment, The, 115
King's Own Scottish Borderers,
The, vi;
1st Battalion, 3–4, 20–1, 23–6,
26–8, 29–33, 49, 52, 53, 65,
67–9, 79, 81, 99, 106–7,
108–11, 114, 115–16, 126–7,
128–9, 130, 131–2, 136–7,
156, 157, 161, 169, 170, 175,
176–7, 180–1, 181–2, 182–3,
184, 187–9, 199–202, 213–14,
224, 241, 246, 251, 253, 254,
260
Korea, 6, 87

La Mon Restaurant, Co. Down,
bombing of, x, xii
Lancashire, 69

Leeson Street, *see* Belfast
Lenadoon, *see* Belfast
Light Infantry, The, 80, 120–1
Limavady, Co. Londonderry, 155
Lisburn, Co. Antrim, ix, xxiii, 82,
196
Little Diamond, *see* Londonderry
Liverpool, 18, 116, 145–6, 148
London, 36, 146, 154
Londonderry, viii, x, xvi, xviii,
xxiii, 46, 66–7, 70–1, 84, 104,
128, 139–40, 142, 159, 208, 229,
234, 253; riots in, 44–6, 141–4
Bogside, xvi, 39, 43–4, 81, 88, 143
'Bloody Sunday', 71–6
Creggan, 69, 71, 72, 75, 81, 88,
98, 143
Fort George, 141, 143
Gobnascale, 116, 124–5, 127
Little Diamond, 76
Masonic Camp, 143
Rosemount, 143
Rossville Flats, 72–3
Long Kesh, 37, 64–5; *see also*
Maze Prison
Loughgall, Co. Armagh, ambush
at, xxvi
Lurgan, Co. Down, 141

Mackies factory, *see* Belfast
MacRory Park, *see* Belfast
Magilligan Point, protest march
to, 70–1
Maguire, children of family killed
by gunmen's car, xxi, 115
Manchester, 14, 216, 238
Mason, Roy, Secretary of State
for Northern Ireland 1976–79,
xviii
Masonic Camp, *see* Londonderry
Mater Infirmorum Hospital, *see*
Belfast
Maze Prison, xx, xxii, xxiv, 141,
142, 228, 260; *see also* Long
Kesh

McDonnell, Joe, PIRA
hunger-striker, 144
McGurk's Bar, North Belfast,
bombing of, xviii
Milltown Cemetery, *see* Belfast
Monaghan, Republic of Ireland,
197
Mountains of Mourne, 4
Mountbatten, Earl, and family,
xxii; reactions to deaths of,
136–7
Musgrave Park Hospital, *see*
Belfast

Narrow Water, Co. Down, 134,
135
NATO, vii, 20–1
New Lodge, *see* Belfast
Newry Canal, 198
Newry, Co. Down, xxv, 97, 125,
133, 134, 146–7, 153, 198, 226,
247
NORAID (Northern Irish Aid
Committee), 167, 254, 260
North Howard Street, *see* Belfast
Northern Ireland Civil Rights
Association (NICRA), xvi,
xviii, xxi
Northern Ireland Training and
Advisory Team (NITAT), 159,
217, 260

Official Irish Republican Army
(OIRA), xviii, xxii, 68, 85, 137,
188, 260; feud with PIRA, 123;
see also Irish Republican Army
(IRA) and Provisional Irish
Republican Army (PIRA)
O'Hara, Patrick, INLA
hunger-striker, 143
O'Neill, Captain Terence, Prime
Minister of Northern Ireland
1963–9, xvi
Operation Motorman, xix, 88–91,
100, 255

Orange Order, xvi, 21, 98

Palace Barracks, *see* Belfast
Parachute Regiment, The, vi,
78–9
1st Battalion (1 Para), xxviii, 5,
12–17, 26, 33–5, 36, 37, 38–9,
40, 41–2, 46–7, 48, 49, 51–2,
53–4, 54–5, 70–1, 72–3, 74,
75–6, 76–7, 87, 90, 91–2, 137,
153, 173–4, 175–6, 179, 180,
191–6, 207, 217–18, 254
2nd Battalion (2 Para), 2–3,
18–19, 35, 37–8, 39, 42–3, 47,
49, 50–1, 54, 56–8, 89, 97,
101, 102, 103–4, 105–6, 108,
116, 117–20, 133–5, 135–6,
137–8, 149, 178–9, 182,
184–6, 189–90, 191, 198,
212–13, 216, 241, 242, 247
3rd Battalion (3 Para), 48, 95–6,
123–4, 242, 250
Peace People, xxi, 115
Percy Street, *see* Belfast
Portadown, Co. Armagh, 141
Portrush, Co. Antrim, xxi, 155
Portstewart, 155
Prince of Wales's Own Regiment
of Yorkshire, The, vi, 4–5,
201
Prior, James, Secretary of State
for Northern Ireland 1981–85,
xviii
Provisional Irish Republican
Army (PIRA), xvii, xviii, xix,
xx, xxi, xxii, xxiii, xxiv, xxv,
xxvi, 58, 68, 120, 122, 128, 151,
154, 163, 176, 188, 199–200;
1972 truce with British Army,
85–6; 1974–75 truce with British
Army, 102–3, 104–5, 108; feud
with Official IRA, 123; *see also*
Irish Republican Army (IRA)
and Official Irish Republican
Army (OIRA)

Pym, Francis, Secretary of State
for Northern Ireland 1973–74,
xviii

Queen's Own Highlanders, The,
135, 136

Rame Head, HMS, 104
Rathcoole, *see* Belfast
Rathlin Island, 4
Redgrave, Vanessa, 5
Rees, Merlyn, Secretary of State
for Northern Ireland 1974–76,
xviii
Republic of Ireland, xxii, xxv, 5,
14, 46, 65, 104, 134, 135, 173,
174, 185, 186, 187, 191, 196–7,
199, 215–16
Rosemount, *see* Londonderry
Rossville, *see* Londonderry
Royal Air Force, 234
Royal Anglian Regiment, The, vi
2nd Battalion, xxviii–xxix,
40–1, 1–82, 83, 88, 98, 121–2,
131, 136, 139–40, 141–2,
143–4, 154, 155–6, 167, 170,
187, 243, 252
Royal Army Medical Corps, vi,
140, 218–19
Royal Army Ordnance Corps, vi,
28–9, 83, 92–3, 112, 203–7,
207–9, 209–12, 214, 215–16,
216–17, 219–21, 247, 261
Royal Green Jackets, The, vi
1st Battalion, 10–11, 56, 87, 90
2nd Battalion, 44–6, 50, 52, 56,
66, 67, 70, 72, 73–4, 76, 83–4,
85–6, 88–9, 93, 101, 102–3,
122–3, 125, 145–6, 147–8,
150, 151–2, 157–8, 168, 181,
241, 242, 245–6, 249–50,
252–3
Royal Hampshires, The, 153
Royal Horse Artillery, vi
2nd Field Regiment, 64–5

3rd Field Regiment, 91
Royal Marines, vi, viii, 134, 255
40 Commando, 81, 85, 86, 87–8,
94, 95, 96–7, 104–5, 126,
244–5, 247, 248–9, 250–1
42 Commando, 80–1, 89,
99–100, 140–1, 248, 250,
251–2, 254
45 Commando, xxix, 21–2, 49,
94, 122, 123, 142–3, 144–5,
158–9, 160–1, 162, 163–4,
165–6, 168–9, 171–2, 198–9,
243, 244, 245, 248, 249, 252,
253–4
Royal Military Police, vi, 1–2,
78–9, 82, 87, 111–12, 113–14,
120–1, 124–5, 125–6, 127, 128,
146–7, 153, 209, 252
Royal Navy, 104, 179
Royal Regiment of Fusiliers, 139,
155
Royal Regiment of Wales, vi
1st Battalion, 5, 6–10, 35,
36–7, 80
Royal Ulster Constabulary
(RUC), vii, viii, ix, x, xi, xvi,
xvii, xviii, xix, xx, xxi, xxii, xxiii,
xxiv, xxv, xxvi, xxvii, 78, 82,
105, 116, 122, 124, 127, 128,
129, 132, 137, 139, 152, 157–8,
168, 169, 170, 187, 204, 228,
232, 233, 257–8, 259–60, 261;
Special Branch, ix, 233
Royal Victoria Hospital, *see*
Belfast

Sandhurst, 214
Sands, Robert (Bobby), PIRA
hunger-striker, MP for
Fermanagh and South Tyrone,
142
SAS, *see* Special Air Service
Saudi Arabia, 12
Saunders, James, staff officer,
PIRA Belfast Brigade, xvii

Scots Guards, vi
  1st Battalion, 84, 140, 243
  2nd Battalion, 139, 214
Shankill Defence Association, 16
Shankill Road and district, *see* Belfast
Short Strand, *see* Belfast
Sinn Fein, xx, 157
South Armagh, viii, ix, xii, xxi, 104, 153, 167, 173–202, 226, 250, 251–2; comparison with Belfast, 173–4
Spain, 253
Special Air Service (SAS), xxi, xxvi, 109, 181, 189, 233, 261
Spence, Augustus 'Gusty', leading figure in UVF, 1
Sperrin Mountains, 4
Springfield Road, *see* Belfast
Springfield Road RUC Station, *see* Belfast
Stormont, xviii, 53, 54, 261
Strabane, Co. Tyrone, 66, 214, 215

Tennent Street, *see* Belfast
Thiepval Barracks, ix
Tiger Bay, *see* Belfast
Tone, Wolfe, 97, 248
Turf Lodge, *see* Belfast

Ulster Defence Association (UDA), xviii, xix, 84, 91–2, 101, 106, 238, 262
Ulster Defence Regiment (UDR), vi, ix, xi, xii, xvii, xviii, xix, xx, xxi, xxii, xxiii, xxiv, xxv, xxvi, xxvii, 1, 19–20, 99, 100–1, 113, 174, 186, 215, 222–3, 224–40, 251, 255, 257–8, 259, 262

'Greenfinches', 225–8, 229–30, 230–1, 235–6
Ulster Special Constabulary, *see* B Specials
Ulster Volunteer Force (UVF), xvi, xx, xxi, xxiv, 1–2, 15, 63, 78–9, 91, 101, 102, 109, 254, 262
Ulster Workers' Council (UWC) Strike, xx, 99–101
Unity Flats, *see* Belfast

Vinegar Hill, Battle of, 248

Wales, 175, 246
Warcop, Cumberland, 237
Warrenpoint, Co. Down, xiii, xxii, xxiii, 119, 199; PIRA ambush at, 133–5; reactions to, 136–8
Welsh Guards, vi
  1st Battalion, 160, 162–3, 164–5, 167, 168, 171, 241, 246–7
Westminster, 86, 261
Whitelaw, William, first Secretary of State for Northern Ireland 1972–73, xviii, 80, 81
White Park Sands, Co. Antrim, 156
Whiterock, *see* Belfast
Widgery Report, on 'Bloody Sunday', xviii, 76–7
Willets, Sergeant Michael, 2 Para, killed in bomb attack on Springfield Road RUC Station, 49–50
Williams, Betty, founder of Peace People, xxii
Women's Royal Army Corps, 118, 126, 150, 159
Women's Royal Army Corps Provost, vi, 159, 169, 215